To Mine

With esteem and much
appreciation for many years
of friendship and admiration
for all you have done for
The Univ. of Utah!

Rocco
April 5, 2005

WALKING ON SAND

Rocco C. Siciliano

with **Drew M. Ross**

WALKING ON SAND

The Story of an Immigrant Son and
the Forgotten Art of Public Service

Foreword by Vartan Gregorian

The University of Utah Press
Salt Lake City

The Defiance House Man colophon is a registered trademark of the
University of Utah Press. It is based upon a four-foot-tall, Ancient
Puebloan pictograph (late PIII) near Glen Canyon, Utah.

LIBRARY OF CONGRESS CATALOGING-IN-PUBLICATION DATA

Siciliano, Rocco C.
    Walking on sand : the story of an immigrant son and the forgotten art of public
service / Rocco C. Siciliano with Drew M. Ross.
        p. cm.
    Includes index.
    ISBN 0-87480-805-7 (alk. paper)
    1. Siciliano, Rocco C. 2. Political consultants—United States—Biography.
3. Italian Americans—Biography. 4. Eisenhower, Dwight D. (Dwight David),
1890–1969—Friends and associates. 5. Businessmen—California—Biography.
6. Siciliano, Rocco C.—Philosophy. 7. Common good—Philosophy.
8. Social service—United States. I. Ross, Drew M. II. Title.
    E840.8.S537A3 2004
    338.0973'092—dc22

                                                                    2004014583

09 08 07 06 05 04
5 4 3 2 1

To my wife,

Marion Stiebel Siciliano

German Jewish refugee, whose aggressive intellect has been a constant reminder to me for more than half a century that mankind exists on this earth for an express purpose: to serve, to support, and to love all living things.

CONTENTS

FOREWORD

FOR MANY YEARS, I have been urging my colleague and friend Rocco C. Siciliano to write his memoirs, not for the benefit of his children alone but also for the sake of history. I am glad that he has done it.

Walking on Sand is a riveting personal history of a boy born of Italian immigrant parents from Calabria. His journey from Mormon Utah through the Depression, World War II infantry combat, and all the way to Washington, D.C., to become the first Italian-American presidential appointee at the White House is an invaluable chapter in the history of American immigrants, a great American success story, thanks to effort, hard work, motivation, inspiration, drive, and character.

This book provides compelling insights into the social history of Utah and California, as well as the domestic public policies of the Eisenhower and Nixon administrations. Above all else, however, it is the narrative of the life of a great American citizen who combines dedicated public service with exemplary and outstanding roles in the corporate and nonprofit sectors of our society.

The enduring theme of Rocco Siciliano's career is leadership framed by an utter devotion to the United States and the fundamental values that undergird its promise and its legacy. His story—a testament to the prevailing power of generosity, hope, service to others, and ideals—will resonate with all who believe in the resilience of humanity to overcome the challenges of living in an increasingly complex and interconnected world.

Rocco's legacy reinforces the assertion that one individual, by sheer determination, courage, and a sincere heart, may have an indelible impact on the lives of many and, in that struggle, receive meaning and a lasting hope in the opportunities of the future and in our collective spirit.

Vartan Gregorian,
President of the Carnegie Corporation of New York

PREFACE

THIS MEMOIR STARTED for a traditional reason: I intended it for my family. And just as traditionally, it soon took on a life of its own. Recollections progressed from youthful pursuit of undefined goals through challenges, frustrations, and successes. Memory flowed from schools in Utah through war to Washington, D.C., and the Eisenhower White House to law practice and the Nixon administration to the corporate boardrooms and then to public entities of California and the nation.

When I was about twelve years old in Hawthorne elementary public school in Salt Lake City, I wrote "government man" in response to a school district questionnaire regarding my ambition. As years passed, it took on a more modern term: public servant. But first I had to emerge from my circumstances. I was an impatient American boy of reasonable intelligence, born of Italian immigrant parents from Calabria, Italy, who, with minimal education, were struggling in typical Depression-era fashion in the desert and mountain beauty of Utah, amidst the dominant Mormon populace.

The story becomes deeper. It begins with the acceptance of someone with a name like mine living in an atypical American community, followed by my first love, then army infantry combat in Italy, my fifteen minutes of fame in Washington, D.C., permanent love and family growth, the business world, and always the incessant calls for service in both governmental and private causes.

My memoir change of plan came about one evening because of a sunset, which I was watching over the Great Salt Lake, some ten miles away from the city and university where my life had its start. Another oral history session with Greg Thompson of the University of Utah was over. Perhaps the natural setting prompted me to accept the notion that my story could be of interest beyond family and friends. As the following pages attest, changes in my work life have made it difficult for even my family to understand the story of the life I have lived. Helping me to assess and put order into this book has been the charge of my close ally, Drew Ross.

This memoir was largely completed before September 11, 2001. The reasons for the young and old to appreciate public service in its varied forms have been long evident. The tragedy of that bright September day has only magnified those reasons. The need for trust in government is ever more apparent.

Public service, like walking on sand, can be a strenuous undertaking. The winds blow and the sands shift, and the results of public service may be transient. But the work is absolutely essential.

Just as a faith can draw those who want to serve humanity on behalf of God, public service has a unique appeal for those who want to help their neighbors live a better life on Earth. I hope I have made this kinship clear to the reader.

PART I

Confronting Invisible Barriers,
1922-1948

The story of my boyhood and that of my brothers is important only because it could happen in any American family. It did, and will again.

—Earl Eisenhower, on growing up with Dwight and his other brothers, *American Weekly*, April 1954

ONE

TO BE LIKE THEM YET NOT OF THEM

IN LATE NOVEMBER 1936 I boarded the Western Pacific train departing San Francisco and bound for Salt Lake City. I traveled alone, without my family, and, at age fourteen, I performed my first big-man act. I wore a suit, I remember that, because you traveled that way; it made me feel like an adult. I sat up in my seat, the cheapest ticket, throughout the overnight seventeen-hour ride.

My parents had already returned to Salt Lake City in the family car, leaving me behind for a big event in my life at that time. Before San Francisco, we had lived in Salt Lake City, where my dad, after trying his hand at a number of things, including a restaurant, had been out of work for two years—no restaurant, no saloon, no job of any sort. The nation's economy was deep in the Great Depression. The drastic decline was continuing. After my brother Sam's graduation from South High School in June 1936, our parents leased our house and we left Salt Lake—the place where my brothers and I were born and had grown up. We moved to San Francisco, "for good," we all had agreed. Another Italian American family, the Sam Granieris, joined us on our westward migration. My father and Sam Granieri had worked closely together for several years, and they hoped to find an opportunity together.

The drive on Highway 40 across the parched alkaline Utah desert to the cool maritime air of San Francisco was a metamorphosis for us. My dad searched for a business opportunity, but the other family members each had their own reasons. My mother loved San Francisco. The move reunited her with her two brothers, Carmie and Phil, both well-established businessmen. That alone made things easier for us because we immediately connected with a family. For my two brothers and me, it was a whole new world, a starting over, you might say. We took instantly to the environment and the joie de vivre for which the city is known. Of course, it had a huge Italian American colony. My name was not different; I did not feel different. That August, I enrolled in the eighth grade in Jefferson School, on Nineteenth Avenue, near the Golden Gate Park. I liked the school. It was quite different from Salt Lake. It was harder.

We had arrived, but my father could not get established. He wanted to open a saloon, a restaurant, or some combination of the two. Sam Granieri, his partner-to-be, went to work as a bartender. My dad did not want to take a job; he did not want to work for anybody. After just a brief time, in two to three months, he grew restless and very unhappy. He missed Salt Lake City where he had been established and knew everybody. So, late in the fall, he and my mother decided to move back to Salt Lake City. My mother was not particularly happy about it, but she went along.

Just before the move, my school's dramatic club offered me the role of the infamous Aaron Burr in the school play, *The Man without a Country*. I was eager to do that, but the play was scheduled for November 19. If I moved with my family back to Salt Lake City, I would miss the play by two weeks. With my family ready to leave, I insisted that I couldn't go back with them: I had to do this play for the school. For complex reasons, I had earlier decided that I had to be a good student, and the play was a part of that ambition. My parents relented, and I stayed in San Francisco with my uncle Carmie.

The evening of the play began with a "Salute to the Flag" put on by the ROTC, followed by the Pledge of Allegiance and *The Star Spangled Banner*. The music throughout the evening was Bloch's *America* and *March Americana*. The play, based on the short story written by Edward Everett Hale, was popularly used for ingraining patriotism, especially in young men. Hale was popular when I was young, and his quotes were used as patriotic mottos, such as "Look up, not down, out, not in, and lend a hand."

I played the villain, in a sense, because Aaron Burr got young Lieutenant Philip Nolan in trouble with the United States. In the play, Nolan has been seduced by Burr's grandiose ideas of a new country. The play is set in 1807, the year Burr was tried for treason and acquitted for scheming to carve an independent nation out of the American Southwest and Mexico. However, in the play, Nolan had become a disciple of Burr, and upon being questioned by the court about the scheme, he renounced his country, wishing he would never again hear the words *the United States of America*. His wish became his sentence; he was imprisoned on a ship and put out to sea. He very much grew to regret his insolence. "Poor Nolan," as the narrator in Hale's story called him, never saw nor heard of his country again.

The story of the play had no great meaning to me at that time, though it probably did influence me as was intended, that is, it cultivated my patriotism. At the time, I couldn't comprehend the Americanism issues my parents faced as Italian Americans; all I knew was that I was an American. Perhaps more than anything else, at that time, I simply needed the experience of playing a part in a play. In retrospect, the whole series of events—my part in the play, my parents' decision to allow me to stay, and the train ride—approached an epochal moment for me: it meant a great deal to me to be regarded by my parents as someone important enough to stay behind for school purposes. They were honestly not that interested in the play. Already at fourteen I had been reading for several years everything I could put my hands on: some novels, but mostly historical and political books. Even at that age I was fascinated by the idea of government, that such an entity existed. The play enhanced that. I used to wonder if my parents understood what it meant to me. They obviously respected it. My father had not worked for two years, yet they allowed me to stay behind and bought me a train ticket.

When I arrived on the train in Salt Lake, my family was not in our home. The man to whom they had leased it for two years refused to vacate until expiration of the lease in June 1938. They had to rent another house, at 155 Lincoln Street, a quiet side street closer to downtown. Though an unimpressive home, it was adequate and everything worked. I remember my parents paid the same amount for rent, fifty dollars per month, as they were receiving for the other house. My mother never hid anything from the children. These numbers were talked about at the family table to impress upon us the tight situation of the Depression era. I knew the cost of everything, from a loaf of bread to what we were paying for rent.

Salt Lake City sits halfway between the sea and the sky—on the edge of the briny Great Salt Lake and at the foot of the lofty peaks of the Wasatch mountains. The climate is dry and mild, with severe winters a rarity and summers ranging from a moderate simmer to a suffocating broil. Geographically, the city is centrally located in the American West, and from the beginning it was the commercial, industrial, and social center of the Intermountain West—parts of Idaho, Wyoming, Colorado, Nevada, and all of Utah—comprising several hundred thousand square miles. In serving this area, Salt Lake's retail business exceeded the normal volume for a city of 120,000, yet it retained a small-town feel. Also, the mining industry of Utah made Salt Lake one of the greatest smelter cities in the Western Hemisphere; the smelters alone produced 20 percent of the nation's mineral wealth. The state held large deposits of coal, copper, iron, silver, and other metals and materials to keep the industry going into the twenty-first century.

At the time I was born, in 1922, Salt Lake City was seventy-five years old, and growing strong as the headquarters of the Church of Jesus Christ of Latter-day Saints, the Mormons. It was the human hive, the heart of Mormon country. The beehive is the state symbol—*Industry* is its watchword. The Mormon story is well known. Their founder, Joseph Smith, organized the church relating divine inspiration from God. The faithful were persecuted and chased out of state after state, from New York to Missouri to Illinois. They reached the Salt Lake Valley in 1847, which at the time was a part of Mexico and inhabited by Native Americans. The Mormons were outcasts, and they purposely left the United States, led by Brigham Young, who intended to establish a self-sufficient state called Deseret. As Salt Lake City grew, it was obvious that the Mormons would dominate the city and the region. Non-Mormons—or Gentiles (which included Jewish people)—were conscious of their minority status. When young, I felt that Mormons were intolerant. In later years, I felt they were as tolerant as anyone; they just wanted you to be one of them. It was a subliminal form of their proselytizing.

And the non-Mormons were not necessarily *anti*-Mormon. By 1920, the leadership in Utah was established and easy to understand. Surprisingly, the governing group in the 1920s was multifaith, made up of Mormons and Gentiles. Several non-Mormons had become the wealthiest Utahns. Samuel Newhouse, a Jewish mining magnate and land developer, was very prominent. Thomas Kearns, a Catholic and a

Confronting Invisible Barriers, 1922–1948

millionaire at thirty-eight, was publisher of the *Salt Lake Tribune* and was elected U.S. senator in 1901, one of Utah's first two senators. The division between the two groups was seen in the pragmatic manner in which the Utah legislature would fill the two Senate seats prior to the enactment of popular elections: one seat was Mormon and the other was non-Mormon. A good description of the difference between non-Mormon and *anti*-Mormon was written by the noted nineteenth-century traveler Sir Richard Francis Burton, who related that every event had three consistent explanations: "that of the Mormons, which is invariably one-sided; that of the Gentiles, which is sometimes fair and just; and that of the anti-Mormons which is always prejudiced and violent." I did not know it at the time, but while I grew up, I was making a deliberate choice among these three views of the community.

I find it difficult to describe growing up in Salt Lake City. I clearly felt different. In school I was quite aware that the most common name was Jensen. My grade school class was lower- and middle-class Caucasians, and they were all Mormon. At least it seemed to me they were all Mormon. As in every community, the Utah society had its hierarchy and its pecking order. Scandinavians and Anglo-Saxons were in control. As Italians, we felt that we were at the very bottom of that pecking order, along with the Greeks, Yugoslavs, Japanese, American Indians, and a handful of Hispanics. The local mores were matter-of-factly controlled by "the Church" and were dominant in every aspect of living. To be a non-Mormon was a matter of keeping your own counsel.

The house that my parents rented in 1936 (after the sojourn to San Francisco) was in a totally different section of the city from where we had grown up. The new neighborhood was a significant social change for me. Italian families have a reputation for being large with deep integration of extended relatives. Sociologists have observed that most southern Italians cannot live in isolation. This pattern originates in their homeland lifestyle, where they live in close-knit villages made up of homogeneous groups. Because of the emigration patterns, the Italians gathered in the larger cities, and they were able to surround themselves with fellow countrymen. Salt Lake City did not have that kind of support system. In Salt Lake, as in the Italian American communities in Montana, Colorado, and California (with San Francisco being the exception), you could not find an identifiable "Little Italy" ghetto. The thousand Italian immigrant families were widely dispersed throughout the large Salt Lake Valley with the greatest congregation of Italians in the boardinghouses on the west side of the city, by the railroads where most of them worked.

Nonetheless, we had a circle of Italian immigrant friends. For example, we would buy cheese from an Italian man who had goats in Magna, on the west side of the valley. We would never talk about this outside the house. To tell any of my friends that we had cheeses called ricotta or mozzarella would have sounded seditious. We almost felt a little ashamed to be a "spaghetti bender," as they called it. I am amazed that we used to hide the foods we ate, which today are popular foods. The network of Italian Americans was very loose because everybody was too busy making their living, trying to survive the hard times of the Depression. We were not neighbors, so these encounters with other Italian Americans did not just happen when you walked out the door of your home. Our extended family, beyond our nuclear family, was relatively small for that reason.

When I say I felt "different," I use that word carefully. I don't mean to imply discrimination. I couldn't do much about my last name, though there were times when I wanted a simpler name. The catch was my first name. With a name like Robert or John, it may have made a little difference. But Rocco, in itself, back in the 1930s, in Salt Lake City, was very different. Back then we pronounced it the Italian way, Ro-ko, rather than today's Rock-o. Ironically, while the first name used to bother me, society accepts it today. The name Rocco has captured the imagination of the American people. In my day, growing up, I had to explain it. People always asked, what kind of name is that? Though it was originally the name of a French Italian saint, I was named after my grandfather.

Not being Mormon was very much a handicap in my mind, yet I had no desire to be one. I knew I was Italian American and that I had been baptized a Catholic. My parents were nominal Catholics, but they did not go to church and neither did I. Actually, I found that not going to church was a great convenience. If I went to the Catholic church it would have made me feel even more different from all the kids I played with, who were, by and large, good churchgoing Mormons. I kept that quiet and never said a word about my own private beliefs, or about being Italian. My name said it all.

When I returned to Salt Lake and discovered our new home, I didn't expect the folks to be living on Lincoln Street. Though the rented house wasn't too far from the home in which we had grown up, it was in a very different neighborhood. It was nearer to where the wealthy, successful people lived. I immediately enrolled at Bryant Junior High School, though I was about six weeks behind because school had already begun. Even though the Depression was still most evident in 1936–1938, there was not much evidence of it in this student body. My mother was quite conscious that we were living in a better area. The kids came from fairly prominent families—furriers, jewelers, and other merchant and professional families. In those days, the boys wore ties and jackets and the girls wore makeup. Not all of them, and not many, necessarily, but I still remember a couple of them. They were very pretty and very well dressed. I felt very awkward because of the clothes. My folks allowed me to improve that a bit. Otherwise, Bryant was different because many of my fellow students were non-Mormon. At Bryant, my whole attitude of being from a minority and being from a less-than-the-best background was ignored. The teachers were not conscious of anything different about me. Though I was no longer singled out, I felt inadequate in the smooth society of those upper-crust teenagers. They had wealth and stature in society; they were polished, articulate, and to be envied. I felt in a secondary role. I was there, by accident, in this middle/upper-class junior high school. All my friends—Hope Adams, Kathryn Snow, Fern Clark, Kay Ritchins, Jack Winder, Keith Engar, and Bill Ryberg—were from affluent families (at least I thought so); they were self-assured and confident. They seemed older than I was. I emulated them. I wanted to associate with the leaders.

But I was unsure and still sensitive to my position with those around me. I remember my first date to an afternoon dance in the gym. She was a Jewish girl, the daughter of a local wealthy furrier. She even wore a fur coat. I was so awkward. I could not dance and was embarrassed throughout the encounter! I hardly ever spoke to her again. It mortified me, and my embarrassment just multiplied. I was a social dinosaur at Bryant.

At that point I was a decent student but still felt handicapped—insecure, feeling not as bright as the other students. I now realize the missing element—home educational support. My parents were behind me, of course, but they were not able to assist me with my home studies. They never asked me about my homework. I was on my own. One day, Miss Jessie Harroun, the principal at Bryant, quietly asked me into her office and asked me if I knew the meaning of a double negative. I looked pretty blank and said no. She explained it to me and said that I was using double negatives in my speech. I was horrified. I grew up hearing and using double negatives. Miss Harroun was very much aware of my home environment. She saw something in me; I guess, that

I was striving for something. That is why I look back at my part in the San Francisco play and see it as an initial moment in establishing confidence. It gave me a toehold on ambition. I thought I could achieve certain goals. The play gave me a taste of the recognition I was looking for. I needed it. I wasn't going to get it from my parents, so I needed it from other sources. It made me believe I could go into Bryant and succeed.

At some early point in my life I had to make a decision about my place in the Mormon community. I did not make a conscious decision at the time, but I knew I had to choose one. Obviously, I wouldn't join them. My choice then was either to reject them and become negative in that rejection or to become accepted by the majority. I was extremely careful with all of my friendships that I was trying to develop and maintain during those years. I was envious of my friends who had this enlarged family of social intercourse, which was an intimate part of their religion. But I could not accept the fundamentals of the Mormon Church, even though I became quite familiar with them.

I had a choice. I could stay with the old heritage of devotion to the family and avoid all American institutions, as did some of those second-generation Italian American kids who grew up in a Little Italy. They were left with a meager future stuck in a low-paying job, with little security. If we had grown up in a major city with a significant Italian American community, a place where there was more isolation from the majority, it might have been easier to take this path of least resistance. In Salt Lake City we were a tiny minority mixed in with an overwhelming majority. Our family remained very close, and we adhered to some simple Italian traditions, especially in the habits of food and drink. Yet I often felt I was being watched. In today's reality, the conflict between being American or being true to the traditions of the Italian community is minimal, if it exists at all. I did not suffer from any chronic identity crisis, but I was unwilling to exist on the sidelines, as neither fish nor flesh.

I now believe this feeling of striving for something started back in Hawthorne grade school. Before I went to San Francisco, played Aaron Burr, and rode the train back to Salt Lake, I had several episodes in elementary school that made me aware of the difference I felt, emphasized the insecurity, and, ultimately, helped develop my ambition. I began to make my choice at a very early age. It may have started with gaining the acceptance of my Mormon friends, but it went much further, much deeper into my psyche, than that.

I did not go to kindergarten but instead went right into the first grade, in 1928, at age six. The elementary school was not too far away from where we lived, though the blocks seemed many for a little boy to walk (Brigham Young designed very long blocks and wide streets). At that time, I do not recall being much of a student. In fact, it must have been so because, for some mysterious reason, I was asked to repeat the second grade. A number of others were held back too, including a Swiss immigrant girl who lived in the next block. Nobody seemed to think much of it. I do not ever recall any explanation, but my parents were pretty obliging when it came to the system. They took it for granted that the educators knew best. I discovered later that this was a common treatment for immigrant children simply due to our poor English. In the larger populations of Italian Americans, up to one-third of the students were held back, which was the highest percentage among ethnic groups.

I began to believe at that early age that perhaps I was not quite adequate mentally. The teachers liked me very much. I was the only Italian American in my grade. Of course, I looked it because of my olive skin, which I heard about all the time. Miss Brown and Miss Blackett were two teachers who always talked about my big brown eyes. They were very friendly with me, though they were the teachers who kept me behind! So I repeated the second grade. I really was quite bothered by it as time passed. It made me a year older than most of my classmates.

Then I thought I had the chance to catch up. Everything had gone fine from the second through the fifth grades. When I reached the sixth grade at Hawthorne, something called the Articulating Unit was created. I can still remember that phrase because it was a big word for me in those days. In our class of thirty students in one room, on one side of the room were us sixth graders and on the other side of the room the seventh graders (the kids that I had started out with, such as Dick Wetzel, who became my closest lifelong friend). I never understood the arrangement, but I thought: Maybe now is the chance for me to catch up with my former classmates. I suddenly became a more conscientious student. I paid attention. But they did not move me into that other half of the room. I stayed one grade behind. Today, I realize that this doubling up of classes was a Depression-era economy move, necessitated by a reduction of the twelve-year elementary school system to eleven years.

In any case, in fifth grade, I had a teacher who loved me, and I loved her, Miss Bernice Whitaker. She was very fond of me and singled me out for special art projects. I enjoyed drawing and entered a city contest, submitting a "poster child" for an American Red Cross program. I didn't win anything, but I got a certain amount of satisfaction and some recognition. A "special" assignment was to hang up art drawings and paintings. She claimed that my eye could substitute for a yardstick, and I was very proud of this odd talent.

One day in class, she did something she never should have done, something that we know today is absolutely terrible. She went through the SI scores (SI being the scholastic intelligence test), one by one, reading down the list to the whole class so everybody could hear. I remember Bill Zwick was 132. Everybody scored higher than 100, 110, and so on. Then she got to my name, and she said, "And poor Rocco has 88," which was probably the lowest in the class. Well, that convinced me that I was not as smart as the rest of the kids in my class. It hurt, and in many ways you could say it almost crushed me.

That same year I had scarlet fever. I missed thirty days of school, a major sensation in those days. Those events in fifth grade—scarlet fever and a poor SI score—made me realize that I would have to work harder to keep up with my classmates. I became obsessive with my schoolwork.

I have tried to analyze what happened, and why and when. To me, my focus in life, my ambition to achieve something, began about this time, when I was around twelve years old. Everything about me was converging: my name, my ancestry, my response to Mormonism, my insecurity. One thing that clearly emerged: I wanted to be accepted. That was a choice. I became determined to make it at least appear that I was a part of their group. I wanted to show them that I thought like them, and that I, in every respect, wanted to be like them, except that I did not go to their church services. By assimilating with the majority I gained friends. I found that academics were another way to become accepted—to excel. I made my choice in the fifth grade, though it wasn't conscious, and I stayed with that decision, through my years at Bryant, until I finished high school.

I wanted to be like my Mormon friends, or at the very least I wanted their recognition and acceptance. I had no idea at the time that the odds were very much against me. I had no knowledge of immigrant assimilation in the United States generally. I only knew something about myself. In retrospect, maybe it's better that I didn't know. Otherwise, I might not have tried.

TWO

FROM *FAMIGLIA* TO FAMILY

My DAD CAME back to Salt Lake City with one thing on his mind: he gambled on opening a restaurant again. He found a partner, and they bought some furnishings, which in those days were just common tables, chairs, and a lunch counter. The location was not the best, because they weren't on Main Street, but they wanted to try it. The Capri Italian Restaurant at 121 South West Temple was opened on New Year's Eve, December 31, 1936. It was an auspicious beginning during a low point in the Depression. "Where Cooking Is an Art" was their proud slogan. The food was so good that customers, often European-born and from nearby Wyoming, Idaho, and Nevada, would come, dying to taste some real Italian food. Italian food in Utah's capital had arrived.

Everyone who came to the restaurant knew my dad affectionately as "Papa Joe." His quick smile, easy humor, and natural warmth made him someone that the restaurant customers would seek out. At the restaurant Papa Joe was in his found element; he loved to serve people. He wanted to satisfy them. He was extremely generous. Whether it was extra butter (during the World War II shortages) or an anchovy on the side of the salad, he would personalize the customer's visit to his eating place. More often, he would personally bring a plate of unordered spaghetti to the delighted customer.

Papa Joe loved people. He was most conversational and spoke well but also had a quiet side. He never revealed, even to his family, what he was thinking or what his dreams were. Never. It was, as they say in Italian, *fatti suoi*, his business. I don't think it was a philosophical bent. He was pragmatic and a good judge of human character. He concerned himself with getting more customers to come in, serving them well, and educating them on the fine aspects of Italian food. In that sense he was a natural marketeer.

He had a certain polish about himself. He was very proud and quite vain, in a normal male way, always clean shaven and well dressed. I do not recall him ever in casual clothes. My grandfather, his father-in-law, I was told, was the same way. Both men always wore suits, including vests, a gold watch, and a formal hat. My father always looked like a prosperous merchant. From Pop's point of view, if you were to succeed, you had to have a suit. You had to dress.

He was outgoing in many ways, but he felt limited. He knew his limitations, even if he could not articulate them. My dad was not going to try to crack the class difference. He had done what he could to rise out of the unskilled labor field. Yet he was not foolish. He knew that he had no education. His English was basically without an accent with a limited vocabulary and not always grammatical. He never learned to write, except for a few words, like his name. I remember I sat down at the breakfast table with him and helped him fill out the application for intention of citizenship. The reason I did it this way was that the application stated it had "to be filled out by the applicant." To me, being very literal at sixteen years old, that meant my dad had to personally write it. I know better today. Anyone could have filled it out, and he just needed to sign it. Well, he could hardly write. So he and I sat at the breakfast room table, and I filled it out with my pencil and he would copy it on the form in his halting penmanship. It took us a couple of days to do it. I remember that he had murmured something about his early "troubles" but did not ever follow up on the comment. *Troubles* was the word that remained undefined for nearly thirty-five years.

That's when I realized with some degree of concern that he was limited. I never understood how he could speak as well as he could. His appearance and speech didn't translate into his writing. We always took the local newspaper. My dad liked to look the headlines over, understanding enough to comment on national and state news. I imagine that's why he loved the radio, and later, of course, the TV, because he could *hear* the news. He gave the impression of being a much better-educated and more well-rounded man than he really was. He loved learning, but he never felt comfortable in an all-American educated group, because they would sense that though foreign-born, he was also uneducated. That is why he was anxious that his three sons be educated.

My older brother, Sam, has said, "I have always wondered what he could have done if he had been educated. He had a knack. He was on a first-name basis with all the local politicians and officials. He just had the guts to do things. There's a big black-and-white picture of the Columbus Day parade on Salt Lake's Main Street. In it, there's this open touring car for the Utah governor, George Dern. And in the seat behind the governor is my father with a derby hat on. He is riding down Main Street with the governor. How he did it, I don't know. That's the way he was." (Governor Dern became President Franklin D. Roosevelt's first secretary of war—today called defense.)

Papa Joe instinctively understood power and influence. He had a respect for "position" in the Salt Lake community, whether it was professional (medical doctors were probably on the top of his list), business (success in life was ultimately based on money or your worth—this was my mother's belief also), political, or church. He observed that the Mormons often combined all these elements. He was very familiar with local politics. He knew who was running and what positions were there. In his business life, from his barbershop to his restaurants, he was around professionals every day. He knew so many people because they were his customers. He had a very realistic view and an instinctive understanding of politicians. His knowledge was not built on theory. His pragmatic approach influenced me greatly.

At home, we would have visitors; they would be *paesani,* meaning old-country native Italians. Most of them were not educated, and they had very limited English. The visitor was sometimes the father of one of the many children my parents had served as godparents. These visitors would come to ask my dad what to do about a situation that might involve a license or a permit. It might involve a ticket. They really did not know and understand the political processes. He would explain where they should go, what office they should go to, and what he thought they would have to pay. It amazed me. My dad just explained it simply. He was a man of information. He understood the art of doing;

ideas were something he could not really express, but how to get a business license or a ticket taken care of was something he could accomplish.

In a way, he was doing a service that Mr. Anselmo, the Italian vice consul, might also do. *Cavaliere* Fortunato Anselmo, himself an immigrant, was an educated Italian who held an honorific title of recognition from the home country. He was a food importer and American citizen who also served as Utah vice consul for Italy for some forty years. As the official Mr. Italy in Utah, he was the respected spokesman for Utah's Italian ethnic group in all matters until his death in the late 1960s. He spoke proper Italian, and he wore a vest and a tie all of his life. My mother would always call him *Mr.* Anselmo and always spoke English to him. He appeared to understand her reasoning; he also liked to be addressed as Mister! (Even years later, when Italian-speaking Mormon missionaries called periodically at our house, my mother would never speak the dialect to any educated Italian, only English. How incomprehensible it would have been if she had spoken Calabrese to them! She was embarrassed, she said, because they would know of her hillbilly roots. The Italians called a person from Calabria *capoduro,* "hard head." Many years later, Governor Mario Cuomo of New York used that term for me when he learned my parents were from Calabria.)

The *paesani* were a little afraid of Mr. Anselmo because he was so formal. My dad was speaking this Calabrese dialect, so they felt more comfortable with him. My father's sympathy showed to those people looking for assistance. Most of them were at best semiliterate, and they had no understanding of a democratic society, of a government responsive to the wishes of its electorate. Most had never voted. Many of them never became U.S. citizens because they could not read, write, or speak English. They were Americans, however, and most proud of their children's Americanization. My dad felt good helping them. He got nothing for it, though later might come a homemade pastry or some fresh produce. To the people it was understood as a facilitation; it was the way the system was supposed to work. He loved people, so it did reward his ego. In his own way, during the late 1920s to the early 1940s, he became an unofficial but recognized leader in the Utah Italian immigrant community.

Before opening the Capri Restaurant, my father had tried many other things. After a brief stint as a barber, he had worked for his father-in-law, Rocco Arnone, prior to 1923. They sold wine and worked in the soda-pop bars in the twenties. People were looking for wine, and bootlegging was the way to get it. As very young boys, Sam and I helped make some wine at our home, which was legal for home consumption, but my mother soon ended it; she could not tolerate how it smelled up the house. Then in 1928, my father began a string of business ventures. For a few years, he ran the West Side Imported Grocery. In 1933, he opened a restaurant called the New Italian Café. Prohibition had been repealed, and he immediately began to serve wine and beer at his restaurant. He was doing well, but then Utah quickly created their state liquor-law system, which outlawed the sale of hard liquor and wine in public meeting places and restaurants. Profit from food alone became too difficult, and he closed the café. In 1934, he opened the Joe & Rocco Buffet, which struggled for about one year. My father said it simply: No wine with spaghetti, no business. Pop tried anxiously to build up the notion that Italian food alone was worth a visit. Until World War II, Italian food had a true social stigma, at least in the mountain West. Only Chinese and Mexican food had even less status. How times have changed!

Salt Lake's fashionable restaurant of standing and status was over on Main Street. The Rotisserie Inn was owned by two northern Italians, though they did not call it an Italian restaurant. On the contrary, it was a "continental restaurant," or a French restaurant, which was easily accepted by the people of those times and in that city. The northern Italians, like the French, use more butter and cream, which is different from southern Italian cooking: spaghetti, meatballs, ravioli, and lots of tomato sauce!—what most people think of as Italian food. The owners, Francesco Capitolo and Ceasare Rinetti, were very polished figures who comported themselves very nicely in the community. For that reason, they were very prominent and respected, and their restaurant functioned beautifully for many years.

In those days, Main Street was the heart of downtown. For example, near the Rotisserie, the Boston Building was the professional center where the people went to see their doctors and lawyers. Along with the main post office, Main Street had the nice stores—Arthur Franks (the men's dress store) and Mullett and Kelly (another famous upper-class men's store). The doctors and lawyers went to Lettieri's cigar store, just two doors down from the Rotisserie Inn, for lunch—a sandwich and a beer—along with a smoke and a game of pool. Main Street was *the* street. The Capri was on West Temple, only one block over, but it did not have the same prestige. Even State Street, which was sort of second echelon, had more prominence than West Temple.

When they opened the Capri, my dad and his partner, Tom Campanaro, didn't try to compete with the Rotisserie Inn. They knew they couldn't, especially because of their location. But they did want to run a real Italian restaurant, which they thought might be an attraction in Salt Lake. I think the Capri was, arguably, the first true Italian restaurant in Salt Lake.

The atmosphere of the Capri was very informal, as was my father. He wanted everybody to enjoy their time there, so much so that if a waitress would spill something on a table or a piece of crockery would fall on the floor, he would inevitably yell out, "Did somebody call me?" Everybody would laugh.

His partner took things more seriously. Tom was not at ease with the diners and had little ability for small talk. Tom was tougher, even cantankerous, but he was a very efficient buyer of produce and vegetables. He was not a cook nor did he understand the cooking process, of which my father was a master. So my father ran the kitchen and Tom bought the food. Nearly every morning, Tom would run around the Salt Lake farmers' market looking for the best fresh foodstuffs. In one instance, just before the war began, Tom went to a cannery outside of Salt Lake and bought eight hundred cases of tomato paste in gallon-size cans—an enormous purchase for a small restaurant. Fortunately, they had a basement and stored the paste there. You can imagine what this meant when the war rationing started—they had the one basic ingredient essential for the cooking of pasta. Tom was forever gloating about the fact that he had gotten the item that helped the restaurant survive the tough early years of rationing during World War II.

They named the restaurant after the Mediterranean island of Capri. The idea came from the lyrics of a popular mid-1930s song, "'Twas on the isle of Capri that I found her." They had a very simple menu that featured American and Italian dinners, with seafood specialties and choice steaks. During the week, there were two classes of full-course dinners: a six-course dinner for sixty-five cents and a seven-course dinner for eighty-five cents. On Saturday and Sunday, the cost was eighty-five cents or one dollar. There also was a four-courses-for-forty-cents lunch: soup, salad, an entree, a drink, and dessert. You could also get a nice big cut of homemade pie and coffee for a quarter.

The Capri was modest in size, being narrow and deep with high ceilings. It had an eating counter in the front, with four open booths and some tables on the open tile floor. In back, it had booths with curtains that you could pull closed for some privacy. Now and then, men would bring their lady friends to the restaurant. That person could be a prominent businessman, city or state official, or a church person. We would hear about it at home. Dad would mention it when one of these men came in with his mistress. They wanted to go somewhere where their privacy was respected. We were, in a way, sort of sophisticated, if you want to use that word to describe this kind of knowledge. I learned fairly young about some of the human frailties of the leaders in the state of Utah.

As the years went on, the Capri became quite a successful restaurant, particularly when the war started. It became a madhouse to get in. The war brought in young GIs who were in training in the camps between Salt Lake and Ogden. That first year, the Salt Lake area saw some thirteen thousand new jobs in the burgeoning defense industries, including establishment of a U.S. Army Air Force training center. I can still remember these crowds of young men, often from cities like New York and Chicago, coming in "dying for an Italian meal," they themselves often being of Italian or Mediterranean background. The restaurant was just overloaded with GIs—and Italian food was becoming nationally accepted.

Trade and businessmen were the core supporters of the Capri. J. Bracken Lee, mayor of Price, Utah, was an early patron and remained one through the later years when he was Utah's governor and later Salt Lake City's mayor. I first came to know Senator Wallace F. Bennett when he was president of Bennett Glass and Paint, which was right around the corner. He would go out the back door of his building, into the back door of the Capri, and through the kitchen. He was a very faithful customer and liked my father. He came to know me more personally after I became a close friend of young Wally, his son, at the University of Utah. I never dreamed he would become my political mentor.

I enjoyed watching my father's success. He worked very hard at all hours. He was good at it, and he had finally reached some financial security. That took a good bit of fortune and good timing. Upon his arrival in the United States, he did not meet the most favorable conditions for survival. He came as part of a wave of new immigrants from southern and eastern European countries, a group that was different, from their dress to their impoverished state. The swelling numbers of Italian immigrants raised the prejudice against them. They were scornfully viewed as the most degraded of the newcomers. Papa Joe was part of this large force, yet he managed to stand out.

My father grew up in the southern toe of Italy. He was born on December 14, 1889, in a small mountain village called Cotronei, in the Catanzaro Province of Calabria, the last regional state in the Italian "boot"—across from the island of Sicily. (Our name means "from Sicily," but my father did not want to hear that he was a Sicilian!) Cotronei probably had four hundred people at the time he was born, and I doubt if it had many more in recent years when I have visited it. Italians call the entire southern region the Mezzogiorno, while others have referred to it as backward, "the land that time forgot." The terrain is beautiful but harsh. Agriculture is the backbone of a meager economy, but the land seems opposed to life itself. The land is barren from centuries of deforestation, and the winter rains have eroded the topsoil. The stony clay soil makes it difficult to grow wheat crops. Some of Italy's best vineyards and olive groves can be found in these provinces, but most of these small mountains roast in the dry, hot semitropical sun. The rains fall mostly in autumn and winter when they do little good for the crops, though it is perfect for malaria. The greatest insult comes when the crops need rain, and instead the hot, dry winds off the African desert, known as siroccos, blow the life out of the crops.

For centuries, the people have clustered in small, isolated towns perched on the hills. Hardened by the conditions, they depended on their family and their village. Everyone was poor, which limited any ambition. Northern Italy changed with the Industrial Revolution, along with northern Europe, which broke down feudal class barriers and created a large, forward-looking middle class. Southern Italy repeated their same timeless cycle of life.

My father grew up in a very stratified society, cast in an age-old medieval feudal system. At the bottom were the rural peasants who lived in small villages and worked the fields; then the artisan class, though not much better off financially, consisted of an urban group of literate, skilled laborers; and at the top were the landowners and professionals—doctors, lawyers, pharmacists, and teachers. Nearly everyone was in the peasant class and could be identified by their speech and dress. Very few of them owned any land, and those who did could hardly make a living from their small parcels. Changing your social status was impossible. The circumstances you were born into determined your future.

This oppression had been ongoing for centuries. In order to survive, the people adhered to a system known as *la famiglia,* which included all of one's blood relatives, even distant cousins, aunts, and uncles. Like a clan, established through paternity, it had an unwritten, complex set of rules for behavior and responsibilities, parts of which have become well known, such as the important relationship of the godparent. The traditions evolved over the centuries and became known as *la via vecchia,* the old way. For most, what they learned from their father or mother was their only education, and an important one. A good education in Calabria was not about going to school, but learning to honor the old way. Survival depends on these means in southern Italy and in America's Little Italys.

In this harsh setting, the people of the late nineteenth century were exposed to unbearable conditions. Beginning in the 1880s, the recently established national government (located in northern Italy) increased the tax on grain and the price on salt. This indebted the peasants, and forced most of them into the humiliating status of day laborer. Things only got worse. Before the turn of the century, the average income dropped while the cost of living doubled. Unemployment grew and the army occupied the country to repress the people. In an odd twist of numbers, food became scarcer and Italy's population doubled—despite wars, famine, huge volcanoes, killer earthquakes, and the exodus of millions in the seventy years between 1860 and 1930. The population increase, due to the improvements in medicine and sanitation, put more pressure on the land.

While the people of the Mezzogiorno of this period seemed to be driven to incomprehensible despair, the world economy was in transition. Transportation improvements allowed American grain to enter the European market and reduced the demand for the Mezzogiorno's hard, durable wheat. The U.S. citrus industry in Florida and California began producing enough to reduce Italian exports. And a Franco-Italian tariff war, along with the emerging California vineyards, reduced the exportation of Italian wine. The people were forced to change their economy by moving away from their feudal traditions and customary rights and enter the world of contracts, which was based on rent. Cash had been of little use to them, ever. But the changing economy required it. Many landowners went insolvent and lost what little land they owned. They had to pay high rents and interest rates on loans. The debt they encountered was complicated by the high taxes.

The need for money put them in situations of second jobs, day labor, and, ultimately, emigration. They heard stories that they could find work and bread in the strange land America. Though none of these events alone were of catastrophic proportion, together they created the same mass exodus as Ireland's potato blight.

My father left that Italy and came to the United States—alone—in 1903, at the age of thirteen, while the tide of Italian immigrants was still rising. In that first decade alone, the United States received more than eight million Europeans, nearly two million of them Italians, second only to the Germans. The wave crested in 1907 at three hundred thousand Italian immigrants in one year. Most of the Italian immigrants to the United States, 85 percent, were from the oppressed and depleted Mezzogiorno. Most of these immigrants (more than 80 percent) were men who came over to work. At age thirteen, my father was just coming into his working years. Like three-quarters of the men, he was an unskilled laborer who was in high demand in America's expanding industrial sector. Most Italians sent their earnings back to their families in Italy. They worked for cash and initially did not seek work that required investment of money. They wanted to make enough money here so that they might return and buy their own land in their home country.

My dad came to join an older half brother, Earl B. Ringo, who had left years earlier and lived in a Montana railroad town. Immigrants often followed the path established by those who had come before them. About that time, steerage from Naples to the United States would have cost about twenty-eight dollars. He landed in Boston, where he was told by the Italian interpreter (who had probably gotten off the boat just a few months earlier) to exchange his money, perhaps thirteen dollars. He later discovered that he had received a pittance in return for it. Most likely, he had been taken advantage of, but he knew that there was nothing he could do about it.

Wearing a tag around his neck, he took the train to New York City. He walked down the bustling streets looking for a half sister he didn't know. Most of the Italian immigrants clustered in Little Italys. New York had three: on Union Street, Mulberry Street, and Arthur Avenue, in Brooklyn, Manhattan, and the Bronx, respectively. Even by the time he arrived, the Little Italy sections were ghettoes, crowded with people living in dilapidated housing with poor sanitation and diseases. He was probably able to find the right neighborhood just by asking people on the street where to find people from Calabria, and then Catanzaro, and maybe even the town of Cotronei. The immigrants tended to coalesce in neighborhoods with people from their own province and village for support and familiarity in the New World. These Little Sicilys or Little Calabrias made it possible for him to travel in this strange city. As he told the story, his half sister had been waiting for him and saw him from her window as he walked down the street.

She, in turn, put him on another train with the tag (which he couldn't read anyway) still around his neck, and sent him all the way out to the small Far West railroad-tough town of Livingston, Montana, some two thousand miles away! His trip, especially at the age of thirteen, was rare for an Italian immigrant. Nearly all of the southern Italian immigrants settled in the North Atlantic area. Only 1 percent went west, and most of them were headed to California, or maybe Colorado. The number was limited to a few thousand, except for California. To travel west was fortuitous, though it took a special person to leave behind all these people who spoke the same language. It took a strong, confident individual, and a bit more money. But an Italian who crossed the Mississippi would find more opportunities and a better chance of rising socially and economically. The expanding railroads and mines needed unskilled laborers. My father was, of course, unaware of this, but it was to shape his life and mine.

He arrived in Livingston, which sits on the banks of the Yellowstone River as it leaves the Absaroka Mountains and strikes out onto the broad, open plains. The preeminent railroad town in the Yellowstone Valley, Livingston was an important repair and maintenance center on the Northern Pacific main line and the gateway to Yellowstone National Park. In 1901–1902, the railroad added to its passenger services and maintenance and repair operations. For this expansion, the Northern Pacific added hundreds of people to its workforce, an obvious draw for my father and his family. My grandparents Salvatore and Anastasia Garubo Siciliano joined my dad in Livingston, about a year or two later, as did three other sons: Louis and the very young twins, Frank and James. Upon their arrival in Livingston, they all got jobs with the railroad. They lived in the east-side residential district, adjacent to the machine shops, an area that was built mostly for railroad workers. A small community of Italian immigrants lived in these houses that were practically new, much better than the homes they had left in Italy.

As my dad told the story, after his arrival in Livingston, he went to school. He was thirteen and they put him in the first grade. This giant of a kid was put in the first grade, and he didn't even know the language. They ridiculed him. The teacher greeted him with such epithets as "dago" and "wop." He didn't stay long, maybe six weeks. He quit, and he never went to school again. He went to work as a water boy on the railroad, a laborer like the rest of his family.

After some time in Livingston, Papa Joe moved south to the railroad town of Pocatello, Idaho. With his energetic personality and his ambition to succeed, he had moved out of day labor and was working for the railroad as an armed security officer. The significance of this job and its responsibilities cannot be overstated. His promotion would have come amidst intense prejudices against his people. The great influx of southern and eastern European immigrants, of which he had been a part, was met with a hostile movement known as "nativism," a reaction to the massive immigration of those times. Their behavior was ridiculed, and they were stereotyped as inferior and undesirable. It's true that throughout America's history, most mass immigrants have been welcomed this way. In their case, the swarthy Italians of Calabria and Sicily were put down; they had a different look, with dark skin, strange habits of dress, and "foreign" manners. They were at the bottom in the ranks of labor, without exception the "last hired, first fired." In contrast to the depiction of American norms by which all were judged—hardworking, independence loving, and devoted to family— the southern Italian peasants were portrayed as lazy, irresponsible, and violent. The strongest critics deemed them incapable of adopting American ideals and assimilating to American life; they were called a failure in the United States. This xenophobic atmosphere was perfect for gossiping about the criminal societies, namely, the Black Hand, the Omerta, and the Mafia. While these attitudes originated on the East

Coast, they traveled quickly across the nation. So for Papa Joe to have the responsibility of an armed guard speaks of his character.

In this bigoted atmosphere, an event of life-changing proportions enveloped my father. In December 1912, Papa Joe was out celebrating his twenty-third birthday with a friend by the name of Arnold. They went to the American Restaurant on Pocatello's East Clark Street for dinner. What happened follows, according to the report in the *Pocatello Tribune* of December 16:

> Exactly what started the row which ended in the killing of Vaughn is not definitely known. Bell Hill, a waitress employed by Vaughn, is the woman in the case. Miss Hill became ill a few days ago and was placed under the care of Dr. H. Townsend Low.
>
> Arnold and Ceciliono [my father's name was consistently misspelled] entered the restaurant Saturday evening and ordered supper. While it was being prepared Arnold asked Vaughn, who was behind the lunch counter, when Bell was coming back to work. Vaughn responded by linking the girl's name with that of Ceciliono in an insulting manner, and demanding why Arnold was butting in. One word led to another, Ceciliono taking no part in the argument, until Vaughn reached over the counter and slapped Arnold. The latter picked up a sugar bowl cover and hurled it at Vaughn. Vaughn took off his coat, came from behind the counter and attempted to eject Arnold. While the two men were wrestling near the front door, Cecilono is said to have ordered them to stop, drawing a gun and exhibiting a policeman's star. No attention was paid to him, and while Vaughn was reaching for Arnold's collar to drag him out of the place, his back being turned to Ceciliono, the latter fired one shot, which missed its mark and passed through the walls of a private box. A second shot entered Vaughn's back near the left shoulder blade. Vaughn released his grip on Arnold, turned and walked to the door of a private box, said in a surprised sort of way, "Well, what do you think of that?"—entered the box and fell forward on his face, dead.

What really happened that night is difficult, if not impossible, to piece together. What really caused the shooting? What were the insults that Vaughn slung at my father? Was there jealousy over Miss Hill? Since my father was a peace officer, and he followed the protocol of showing his badge and issuing verbal commands, what was the aggressive Vaughn doing to Arnold that caused him to shoot? Did Vaughn have a gun?

Panic followed the inexplicable action, and my father fled. He ran down the street and into a deputy, who shot my father at least two times. He was arrested and taken to the hospital in serious condition. The judge held the preliminary hearing in the hospital and charged my father with first-degree murder. In a plea bargain, the newspaper stated on January 3, "the Italian was prevailed upon to save the expense of a trial and avoid the chance of paying the penalty of his crime on the gallows and plead guilty to second degree murder." It's difficult to determine the degree to which nativism influenced the justice system in Pocatello, but its presence was very apparent. The newspaper accounts were inflammatory and very anti-Italian, most often referring to my father not by name, but as "the Italian," such as "the Italian arraigned today," or "the Italian has a court hearing," and so on. When they used his name, it was consistently misspelled as "Ceciliono," among other variations. Another newspaper reported Vaughn "had hosts of friends" who made "many threats . . . of summary vengeance against his alleged slayer." This nativism, or hatred, was the same across the nation. Between 1874 and 1915, thirty-nine Italians were lynched or shot by vigilantes in the United States, including five Italian laborers lynched in nearby Colorado. This racial prejudice, entangled with class prejudice, was aimed at the southern Italians who were mostly illiterate and poor. Even worse, they were viewed as criminal in nature. In this light, a jury trial seems daunting, perhaps even an ensured death sentence.

Five days later, on January 8, my father "employed Attorney Carl Barnard to take care of his case," according to the newspaper. The attorney requested the judge postpone the imminent sentencing while he looked "into the merits of the case." They weighed the possibility of withdrawing the guilty plea and standing trial on the original charge of first-degree murder. The judge, "in consideration of the fact that life imprisonment [was] involved," agreed to wait for the attorney and gave him "all the time needed to prepare a defense." In a short five days, the attorney decided the plea bargain was better than putting Papa Joe in front of a jury for such a serious charge. On January 13, a month after the incident, the judge handed him a thirty-five-years-to-life sentence for second-degree murder. Still suffering from his injuries, including a badly wounded foot, he was carried to the depot for transport to prison. Whatever her role was in the case, Miss Hill, "the handsome American girl who caused the tragedy," according to the newspaper, was at the depot to say good-bye.

Growing up, my brothers and I knew nothing about this incident in our father's past. We heard stories and oblique references, usually on a hush-hush basis from relatives, to what was euphemistically called "Pop's troubles." But he never elaborated. Mom never uttered any comment at any time. My first knowledge came, I believe, in 1938 when I assisted him with his citizenship application and he made reference to his early "troubles." In February 1971, he was in his last months when I hesitantly asked him about "his troubles." We were alone in his room at the nursing home. His mind was still sharp at eighty-one, and he was alert and willing to talk. After I left his room, I made a note of our brief conversation consisting mainly of the names of the people he recollected. He died in May 1971. He said nothing about why he was in prison or the length of his stay there or the length of his sentence. The "incident" was December 15, 1912, and they were celebrating my father's twenty-third birthday. He spoke primarily of the people who helped him—naming names. I gave this information to my younger brother, Joe, some twenty years later. I learned the following facts only after Joe went to Idaho and made his own private investigation and uncovered the newspaper reports and archive documents.

Pop told me the warden of the prison, John Snook, and the former attorney general of Idaho, D. C. McDougall, believed that he had had an unfair trial and that his guilty plea was actually a trick. They felt he had been grossly mistreated, and, over several years, they helped him appeal his case. While serving his sentence, he worked in the warden's house, and he learned how to cook, how to read and write a little, and how to speak fluent English. After fifteen months in prison, the Board of Pardons took up his petition for pardon. McDougall represented my father. Also present on my father's behalf was the coroner of Pocatello, who had handled Vaughn's dead body. According to the records, the board decided, upon review of his case and after "examining the numerous petitions by prominent citizens and officers, and affidavits as to the previous good character" of my father, "that the ends of justice would be served by a diminution of the sentence." They reduced the charge to manslaughter with a ten-year sentence. Yet Snook and McDougall were not satisfied. Within a year, they applied for a full pardon, which was denied. They remained diligent and persistent. In their next attempt, in April 1916, they were successful in getting the sentence commuted to eight years. Then, in December 1916, after he had served four years in the Idaho State Penitentiary, my father was granted "a full and unconditional pardon," with his full civil rights restored. Amazingly, as I listened to him fifty-five years after the fact, he could talk only about the names and positions of the people who had helped him. Along with Snook and McDougall, there was Joe Jones (chief special agent for the Union Pacific Railroad), John Allot (Pocatello chief of police), and Joe Peterson (attorney general and on the Board of Pardons).

Finally, a dark family secret, kept even from his three sons, had come out into the open. I can only wonder what impact the incident had on my father, his life, and how he raised our family. The questions are endless: What would my own life have been like if I had known this while in high school and college? How would my ambition for public service have been affected? If I had known, I feel certain I would have been quite bothered by it. I grew up reading and hearing countless accusations and charges of the Mafia being in the background of every aspiring Italian American seeking public office—elected or appointed. This was not the Mafia, but it could have been twisted by publicity, or even worse, when I was given any of my four presidential appointments or the two times I required Senate confirmation.

My brother Joe's research led him to this poignant conclusion in a 1991 letter to me:

> I have come to realize many wonderful things about [our father]. He truly was an amazing father and provider. Considering the many obstacles that he faced, he showed much strength, intelligence, and wisdom particularly in his later life. We certainly were cheated in not knowing the details of his early years. I wish I could have shared them with him when he was alive. He was a tremendous person and I have the highest regard and admiration for him. I wish he was around for me to tell him so. Our Italian heritage was made much better because of him.

THREE

FUEL OF MY AMBITION

AT THE END of 1916, Papa Joe moved to Salt Lake City and immediately went to the Salt Lake Barber College. They issued him a certificate upon his graduation, and he joked that this was his college degree. He had crossed an important threshold. The profession of a barber was a skilled job, and he was no longer working for the railroad, which was all his family knew in America. The new status meant that he had moved up in the world, something that would never have happened in the stratified society of Calabria. During those years, he still lived on the west side near the railroad tracks. He had left Pocatello for obvious reasons, and he was now twenty-seven years old; it was time to get on with his life. Papa Joe had quick, skilled hands, and he was a good barber. The barbershop gave him a point of movement, visibility, where he could look for a wife.

One of Papa Joe's customers, Rocco Arnone, was a big man in Salt Lake Italian circles. Arnone was also big physically, with a stout lower jaw and a large brow. He dressed like the founder of Bank of America, A. P. Giannini, always with a suit and gold watch. Arnone would often fall asleep on the barber chair. My dad, who had an incessant corny sense of humor, would play pranks on Arnone. While Arnone was asleep, my dad would put the lather all around his face and put shaving cream about his nose. Everybody in the shop would roar with silent laughter. Then Arnone would wake up and very gruffly shake himself, once he discovered that he was the subject of a prank.

Rocco Arnone had a daughter, Mary, who had come over from Italy a few years earlier. Mary had been born in a tiny hill town, Celico, in the province of Cosenza, the center of the toe of Italy, on January 15, 1900. Though she and my dad were born in places one hour from each other (on today's roads), they would never have met in Calabria. The people of the Mezzogiorno rarely traveled far from their small towns. In those tight clusters of stone houses perched in the arid hills, the social boundary of each town was defined by the sound of the church bell, *il campanile.* This attitude, known as *campanilismo,* meant the people held their strongest loyalty for those who lived within hearing range of their village's church bell. My mother was the most powerful influence on my growing years. She was a matriarch. She always wanted me to stay within the range of the church bell, and all I could see was beyond it.

Mary came to America in 1912. For the first time in her life, at age twelve, she met her parents and siblings—two brothers and two sisters, of which she was the second oldest. Mary had been born during the time that her father was visiting Celico after spending some of the 1890s working in the Utah coal mines. Shortly after her birth, her parents left for Utah, taking with them their ten-year-old first-born son, Carmie. They left Mary behind as an infant, too small to travel. Her aunt, Rosaria Mastroianni (her mother's sister), raised her in Calabria. In the meantime, two younger sisters (Rose and Lena) and a brother, Philip, had been born and raised in America. They were completely American. They all spoke English in the house, though they spoke the Calabrese dialect to their mother, Carmela. Mary had come from the most primitive Italian hill town with an outdoor privy and fireplace cooking to the clean and prim society of Salt Lake City. She moved from the eighteenth century into the early twentieth century. For that and other reasons, Mary never felt completely at home with this large family she met. She never felt that she belonged.

Her older brother, Carmie, was her favorite. He, in a way, gave her the ability to survive in this new country, with this new family. Though born in Italy, he was ten when he arrived in Utah and so spoke flawless English as well as good Italian (both proper Italian and the dialect). Through his insistence, she went to school. Even though she was twelve, she had to start in first grade. She was heavyset and the kids were five years younger. She learned quickly, but was unhappy socially in school, partly because of being the biggest in her classes. When Carmie left home, married an American woman, and moved to San Francisco, Mary quit school, having achieved a fifth-grade level, able to read, write, and speak English. Even though her two sisters and a younger brother went on to be high school graduates, no one else encouraged her, and she did not have the motivation.

When she left school, she was physically mature and marriage was what she wanted. Her father obliged and began looking for likely candidates. He brought the would-be suitors into his home while she hid behind the curtains so that she could reserve the right of rejection. She was very strong-minded and knew what she wanted. "No shrimp," she said (influenced by her father and brothers who were all six feet tall). Then he brought home his bright-eyed barber who let nothing pass him by. Love won out over height when she met Papa Joe—who, at a normal five foot eight, was dashing, laughing, and unpolished. Joe, of course, spoke the same dialect as Mary, which made it easier in terms of her family, her father and mother in particular. They were married in a Catholic church on September 22, 1917. She was seventeen, which, being from the Mezzogiorno, was the right age to get married. She became pregnant quickly. The first-born, a boy, was born and died on July 10, 1918. Though we were never told what happened, I know that was a big blow to her. A year later, she had my brother Sam, on June 16, 1919. I was born nearly three years later, on March 4, 1922. Joe Jr. was born on April 11, 1928.

Our mother stood a stout five foot three inches, weighing two hundred pounds. Her physical strength matched her tough resolve. She ran an immaculate home, so we were always very clean and we never wore any torn clothing. The portrayal of family well-being was very important to her. A well-kept home was the symbol of a sound family— the site and the source of all that gave meaning to life. She also knew the physical sides of home maintenance, be it painting or repairs. She had worked hard with her hands, and she was almost ambidextrous. I couldn't get over the fact that she could one minute be using a carving knife with her left hand and the next minute she would be using it with her right hand. She shifted back and forth, without thinking. She was also the disciplinarian. She had a strong mind and a very strong tongue.

Most of all, she had a clear, strong voice. When we were younger, my brother Sam and I would get into fights, but when she stepped into the room we broke it up immediately. She looked at you squarely. She did not cower. She was not subservient. She had a very attractive face with level and even-set eyes. Her gaze made you feel like you wanted to move after a bit. You didn't want to argue with her, but I did challenge her orally, constantly, for years. Of the three sons, I was the only one who entered into these very lively, controversial talks with her. I was always trying to explain the American point of view, lifestyle, and what you should do.

The other symbol of well-being was plentiful food. Uppermost in my parents' minds was to make sure that we ate well. They remembered life in Italy, where they had so little. Dad would bring food home from the restaurant kitchen, and that gave us a sense of surplus that made us feel better off than others, especially during the hard survival days of the Depression. Food was the major issue. Of course, they were always concerned about our health and our well-being, but other than that, they were single track! They liked to think about food and the future with food. I can still remember this from having our usual fairly substantial Sunday dinner at which time we would have a pasta dish, as well as a meat dish like roast beef. The meal, which was relaxed and full of conversation, took some time. Once, when we were talking around the table, they were discussing quite animatedly what to have for the following Sunday. That was a little too much that particular day, and I finally said, "Why don't we just eat this meal and not worry about next Sunday?"

Without my mother, my parents would have had nothing to show for my dad's years of work. His humane nature was to give it all away. My dad had a fairly good cash flow in those Depression days. I remember sitting in the backseat of the car when he had the New Italian Café. I was about twelve years old. Pop would get into the front seat of the car, and he would hand the money to my mother. Initially, she would put it in a bag, and then she would take it to the bank. She ran the finances and he was happy to have her do it. He never questioned it. He knew very well that she could do it better than he. My parents were not putting the money under the mattress or in the socks somewhere, which a lot of Italians did. Though my mother believed in cash-only transactions, they did use the banking system. They accepted the banks, even though they did not understand the financial system. This is what Americans did. Then, in early March 1933, President Roosevelt, having just taken office, proclaimed a national bank holiday. One result: the Deseret Bank in Salt Lake did not reopen. I remember all of the consternation: "How could this happen?" My folks had two thousand dollars in that bank, as I recall. They were absolutely distraught because that was an enormous amount of money. Eventually, they did get quite a bit of it back—but it took a few years.

We did not speak Italian at home because of our mother. Growing up in an American household, she learned English to the point that she spoke without an accent. My parents mainly fraternized with the people from Celico, my mother's hometown. Without advance call, we would get in the car and drive to someone's house for a visit. As a youngster, starting at the age of ten, I can remember bringing a book and reading in the corner while they had cake and coffee and talked in the dialect. I never spoke the dialect, and neither did my brothers. My parents would speak the dialect with their Italian friends because the Italian-born women spoke no or very little English. With the men it was different. They, at least, had learned enough English to do their work (though some of them really murdered the English language). They had not been educated here. They had no opportunity to go to school. So as a result, their children, who were our friends, all spoke the dialect and English.

Today, I wish I had learned the Italian language by speaking it. But I didn't want to when I was growing up. We wanted to be Americans. Our parents wanted us to be Americans. They chose how they would live their lives by blending the old into the new way. Some Italians held tenaciously to the old way. It became a great issue for those living in a Little Italy where they could live in a self-perpetuating system. But in Salt Lake City, the small number of Italian Americans was more exposed to new ways of life. For some Italian Americans, the Americanization effort might have made them feel that they were either "a man without a country" or one with two countries. But my parents were different. Or, at least, I felt so, and I was proud of those differences. They had become Americans, I felt. I wanted them to be Americans.

Nonetheless, my mother was always conscious of her foreign birth. Her father, Rocco Arnone, was a part of the mining group of immigrants that came to the state to work down in the Carbon County coal mines, as well as in the copper mines at Bingham and up in Park City's silver mines. When he came over in 1900, he headed back to Carbon County, where he had worked in the 1890s and it seemed the whole village of Celico had immigrated. He went to work in Sunnyside, a remote coal mining town about 120 miles south of Salt Lake City. The railroad had a monopoly on the coal mining industry and owned all the coal camps in the surrounding area. The landscape, an arid, rocky, and rough terrain, made the living conditions just as poor as Calabria. Many of the Italian immigrants put up tents in an area known as "Rag Town." Even the company-owned houses were shabbily constructed units. The conditions were bad enough that in 1903 the local United Mine Workers of America went on strike (they coordinated it with another coal mine in Colorado). Nearly half of the workers were Italian, as was the strike leader, so the Italians were held responsible for the strike. They protested a variety of things, from poor pay to the horrible conditions under which they lived and worked. The mine operators received strong support from the Utah state leaders, which resulted in the Utah National Guard being ordered to evict the striking miners. It was Utah's baptism in labor violence. The newspapers gave readers a stereotyped image of the Italian immigrant as a lawless creature having a violent, criminal nature. Over the next twenty years, there were more strikes throughout the state that embedded the antiforeign sentiment in Utah.

Many of the blacklisted miners accepted the railroad's offer of a free return trip to Italy, while others settled nearby. In 1904 (after the birth of Aunt Lena), my grandparents took off on a circuitous journey: they fled to Arizona, then Missouri (where my uncle Philip was born in 1906), and found the mining conditions there just as bad. Shortly thereafter, my grandfather moved everyone back to Utah and opened a saloon near the railroad depots in Salt Lake City. He had become a U.S. citizen and made good money, this big, impressive man, proudly dressed in his suit. He never went back to the mines.

My mother didn't improve her American status by marrying my dad. She was a citizen when she came to America, because of her parents' naturalization. Her three younger siblings were U.S. born. According to the law at that time, she lost her citizenship by marrying my father, a foreigner. Today, I can easily understand the reason he had delayed his application for years because of the Idaho prison experience. He learned only years later that his civil rights had been restored.

He applied for citizenship in the fall of 1938 and received his citizenship in 1939. Mom applied for it in San Francisco and regained it in 1938. A fortunate benefit—but not foreseen—was that as legal citizens, they were not subjected to the U.S. government's World War II roundup of about 12,000 West Coast alien Italians who were placed in a large camp near Missoula, Montana. These were uneducated people, primarily men, who, though they may have lived here up to forty years, were not citizens. Their confinement received scant publicity and was overshadowed by the 110,000 Japanese Americans who were interned in camps throughout the American West.

My parents became citizens, not because war was imminent, but because their children were growing up and they wanted to be like them. Both parents told me that they wanted to vote. During the 1920s and 1930s in Utah, the nativism movement still viewed the Italian and Greek immigrants (they were hardly differentiated in Salt Lake) as an economic threat. All those stereotypes—the lack of desire for education, the lack of a fighting and persevering spirit, sending money out of the country to Italy, no concept of the principal values of the Protestant work ethic, and (ironically) not planning for the future—were still evident. A hyphenated name, such as Italian-American, suggested a divided loyalty. Nonetheless, many Utahns felt an unease and wanted to do something to eliminate this "internal threat" to America.

Thus came a public effort to Americanize the immigrants with the creation of the Utah State Committee on Americanization. Their goal was to provide "an opportunity to know American ideals, American institutions, and what is in store for them as citizens of this great republic." Bills were written in the Utah legislature to Americanize the immigrants, requiring that anyone between sixteen and forty-five years of age be able to speak, read, or write English as required by fifth-grade standards. They were to attend evening classes. Other bills proposed a tax on each unnaturalized alien. This nativism movement culminated on the national level with the Immigration Act of 1921 and then the National Origins Act of 1924, which drastically restricted the incoming number of southern and eastern Europeans. Utah, without a Little Italy, allowed Salt Lake residents to get to know Italians, and the tension became somewhat relaxed. As the Mormon paper, the *Deseret News*, wrote in an editorial: "[I]t should be remembered that many of these foreigners are American citizens with American ideals."

Because of our name and my dad's restaurant, it was quite obvious who we were. To blend in meant to speak English without an accent. My parents bought a house in 1928—a significant long-term investment and goal for immigrants—in the middle-class section of town. It was the immigrant's American dream because it was inconceivable for them to own land in Italy. It also reflected the position that my dad had attained in the Salt Lake City community. They owned a car and later had two cars. They did all this but did not deny their Italian heritage and so did not go as far as my father's older half brother, Erminio Siciliano, who changed his name to Earl B. Ringo, never spoke Italian or the dialect, was a U.S. veteran of the Spanish-American War, and married a well-educated American woman. He even changed his birthplace to Chicago. He became totally American.

I tried to persuade my mother that in every way she was an American, but it was not easy. She was a very proud and private person, and very Calabrese—a mountain person, taciturn, with an infrequent use of "thank you" and other civilities. Often, she revealed a private resentment for what life had done for her. Yet she was devoid of envy or spite. She was very self-reliant. She was one of the few immigrant women who could drive a car and one of the first women in Utah to get a driver's license (when she was about twenty-six). She drove all her life and was a good, solid driver. Her problem: she was not comfortable "out there" in society. She didn't view herself very high up on the social ladder. On a ten-rung ladder, she probably put herself about the third rung. She was not going to try to move in circles where she thought she did not belong. When I was at the university, we had a mother's club for the fraternity. She came to one, perhaps two, of these social meetings, but she was uncomfortable. She would not say so to me but stopped coming. She felt the class difference very much. I tried to boost her ego: she was speaking decent English, yet she was feeling inferior. I did not succeed and it was frustrating. I even boasted of my own ambitions to achieve. She would listen but said little—with no sign of belief or support. She thought, I'm sure, that I had pretensions, that I was too ambitious, that I wanted too much.

My personal outlet was my best friend—Dick Wetzel—from grade school, through high school and college, through today. Wetzel had an extremely irreverent sense of humor. He was very funny; all of his one hundred pounds pushing me around while cracking jokes. I would throw it back at him in some real horseplay. He decided early on he wanted to be a doctor. I had decided at age twelve that I was going to be a lawyer. We never changed. It was fixed in his mind and it was fixed in mine, and we both realized our dreams. Our main concerns, and the reason we were so close, began when we thought we were social dinosaurs. In high school we didn't think we fit in. His one hundred pounds were on a small five-foot-five frame. That was always a handicap for him. I was the Italian American with the long crazy name in a school where everyone was Scandinavian, German, or English. I couldn't dance. He couldn't get any girl to look at him. We were not shy. We were part of a fairly large social group of at least thirty students, both female and male, all Mormon but me. It's just that we felt different when it came time for school dances. We were always intellectually together in wondering where the human race was going.

Our friendship was cemented by the fact that I accepted him for what he was, a very good Mormon, and he accepted me as I was. His judgments were carefully made, and his tolerance of human difference was refreshing—then and now. He was not only innately kind, but very generous in his opinions of people. For that reason, we could talk by the hour, and we did. No subject was immune from discussion, including religion; no pressure about me becoming a Mormon. On the other hand, I never questioned his being a tithe-paying Mormon. We long ago decided that we had covered that subject, and we rarely, if ever, have talked about it. To have this friendship with Wetzel relieved the pressures I felt everywhere around me.

For example, when my good friend Owen Hansen received his "call" for a Mormon Church mission, Owen invited me to speak at his church farewell. I said in my talk at the time, "It may seem a bit unusual that a fellow with a name like mine should speak in behalf of a young man named Hansen," but it was "indicative of the kind of fellow he is." It seemed inevitable that I would find myself in this kind of circumstance because so many of my friends were Mormon. When I finished that speech, several mothers asked me, "Why are you here? Why are you saying good luck and you're not a member of the church? Obviously, it must be on your mind. When are you joining?" It was a natural question for them. I had been baptized as a Roman Catholic, but, like so many Italian Americans in Utah, I had never been a churchgoer. I was completely ignorant of Catholic theology and practice, but comfortable with the simple fact of baptism. I had no feeling for institutional religion. God was always a universal presence for me, and private. I have never tried to set it down in writing. I don't know if I ever could. It seems it would be subject to constant editing. Moments like this, in those mothers' eyes, made it seem that I would join their church. It was a contradiction of behavior on my part; why would I wish this man good luck and not join the church? What could I say? That it is the last thing in the world I would want to do? I could not say it aloud at the time: I like you and what you are and would like your acceptance, but I have my own beliefs.

Through high school, I worked during the summers and on weekends. Beginning at the age of seventeen, I worked for the Salt Lake Parks Department in Liberty Park, across the street from our house. I did all of the things you do as a laborer: mow the grass, wash pots, weed the flowers, even stomp knee-deep manure into the flower beds. They were hard and long days. I took several other jobs of menial labor. Nothing ever lasted very long. One particular job, which I really failed at totally, was during a Christmas holiday when I was at the university. My uncle Earl, who was the division road master at Union Pacific, got me a job with the section gang, which paid fifty cents an hour, a lot for laboring work. Most of my friends were getting twenty-five cents an hour. The first task: a coal car had accidentally spilled many tons of coal on the tracks, and our gang was to shovel the coal off the tracks. Even though I was head-and-shoulders taller than any of the crew, which was mainly Greek and Yugoslav, I could not keep up with them. I came in with a lot of enthusiasm and quickly found after a couple of hours that I was dead. My muscles were gone. The foreman knew that I was not keeping up with the others. They were pacing themselves and doing it right. It made me realize my own limitations. Youth was not enough. The next morning I did not go to work. My dad understood and said okay. My mother thought I was a copout, that I had failed.

At home, among her family or close Italian American friends, my mother was not at all shy. She was very free with her opinions and very strong in expressing them. Whenever she was with the Americans, she would not say a great deal. She always reminded me that she had only a fifth-grade education. In 1936, when we were in San Francisco, she announced her decision to finish high school. I was fourteen and I was very excited about it. I urged her to do it. That's when I saw that she felt so inferior. She didn't do it. When we moved back to Salt Lake City, she was burdened with the task of raising three sons and worrying about the Depression with my dad out of work. She never went back to school. She would remind me of it during our incessant discussions. She was sometimes explosive and expressive—"You want to be like your uncle Louie and work as a section hand on the railroad for three dollars a day? Get an education!" Along with gaining the acceptance of my classmates, excelling in my studies became my way out of the "low class," as my mother called it.

I had an insatiable desire to learn more and more from my junior and senior high school teachers. I tried to do everything right. I was never going to be late. When I graduated from high school, I had not missed a day of school since the seventh grade and had never been tardy. I started a string of straight As in every marking period, which I maintained for the two years at Bryant Junior High School and the two years at South High School. Exception: I did get one B—horrors!—in metal shop at Bryant, a nonacademic subject. I consoled myself with an A in carpentry shop. I was obsessed with getting all As. This obsession—for that is what it was—became obvious to the faculty. One incident involving a homework assignment still sticks in my mind: a geometry teacher at South High told me, "Don't you worry, you will get your A." His calming tone actually embarrassed me—as if I had exposed myself.

I remember some excellent teachers. Because they saw that I was striving for something, I had a lot of attentive care. One of the best was the Bryant Junior High principal, Jessie Harroun. She was the one who kindly informed me about my use of double negatives. Beyond that, she encouraged and nurtured me in the development of my interests. One day in my first year she announced that the school was going to inaugurate a junior high yearbook, the *Brytonian,* and she asked me to be its editor. Of course, I was very pleased. We worked hard for several months and produced a paperback book, with the usual classroom pictures. As I mentioned, these students were more affluent, they were part of that group that had means, and I admired their advanced social graces, which I lacked. I learned from them while working with them on the *Brytonian.* Many of the writers and associate editors of that publication became lifelong friends. Thinking back, my role as Aaron Burr in the play had given me some indication of the attention I was striving for, but the Bryant yearbook experience gave me my first real ego boost.

About that same time, when I was fifteen, I got to know Fred Tedesco, the coach at Bryant Junior High School. His family was of the old *paesano* group of Italian immigrants that had settled in Salt Lake City (they were from the same area of Calabria as my mother). He himself was a famous football quarterback, and later became a well-known public figure in Utah, serving as an elected city commissioner. He also knew my parents well and so we became friends. His advice to me, hearing of my ambition to attend law school, was that I should think in terms of leaving the state. His was one of the first voices I can remember urging this course of action. Though he was a generation older, I never thought of him as being born in Italy. He did not have the reservations of my mother. He had huge ambitions. Because of our shared background, his advice had a special meaning for me.

After I finished at Bryant, our home on Thirteenth South opened up and we moved back. The house was old territory. Both Sam and I were "park bums." We spent our summer days across the street in Liberty Park, which was eight large city blocks and featured a zoo, a lake, a free swimming pool, and handball courts. The courts were free, so we would play handball. I was good, but I was never Sam's equal. He used to bring me to the championships, which he would often win. The one sport I did like was ice skating. In the winter, the lake, which was right across the street, would freeze over, and the ice would be crowded with kids. My father bought us the box-toe shoe skates, and we were among the first to actually wear shoe skates (instead of the popular clamp-on type), which were basically hockey skates with a hard box toe. We enjoyed our exalted status.

I was never the physical or athletic type. I felt I could do it, but did not have time for it. I loved to read. I bought used books at a bookstore near my dad's restaurant. I used to go in and buy books for five or ten cents. (Later I was told not to go into it because it sold communist books.) My father had a customer whom he had told about my reading. This man would bring magazines and books for me. One was the *Illustrated London News,* which I found to be an incredible magazine. I didn't know that it was a famous publication. As the name indicates, it had a lot of big black-and-white photos, but it also had a lot of copy. I was totally fascinated. In a Bryant class on contemporary history, we had a "do-your-own" project. This was in 1936–1937, when General Franco was winning out over the Loyalists in the Spanish civil war. I used clippings from the *Illustrated London News* to illustrate the battles and created a good-sized portfolio. It was a big success. The teacher was pretty astonished that a boy in her class would come in with this. She showed it to the class and used it to help her description of the tragic happenings in Spain. I began to see the big world out there.

My mother and I spent hours and hours discussing the subjects of life. You know, what were we going to do? Where was I going? She would have been perfectly content if I had set my sights on something that was a full-time job that would last the rest of my life with one employer in Salt Lake City. She was very satisfied that my brother Sam was working for my father in the restaurant. My dad's twin brothers, Frank and James, portrayed a typical Italian American trait in that they both went to work for the railroad as machinist apprentices at seventeen years of age, and happily remained as journeyman machinists for the rest of their lives. She expected that of me. Get a good job with a regular pay-roll and work at it and that's that. Back in the 1930s, fifty dollars a week was big money, and if you could achieve that you had arrived. She would have understood that. She could not quite grasp the idea that I wanted to leave the state to make a career somewhere else. She and I would discuss and, yes, argue often about why this was a perfectly appropriate thing to do. At the time, I would get exasperated with her saying, "No, I don't understand," and we would just go back and forth. She had no imagination and could not see the big picture. She didn't encourage my "big ambitions." I was out to prove to her that I could advance, against her own judgment.

The South High experience was a challenging one, socially. I entered South High School in 1938, a few years after it had opened. A two-year senior high school, it accommodated the southern part of the city, thus relieving the crowded classrooms at West and East High Schools. It immediately became the largest high school with some two thousand students. At South High School you were either in sports or in the Reserve Officers' Training Corps (ROTC). I didn't go out for foot-ball or basketball, which attracted the more athletic students. The top athletes were, of course, the "big men" on campus. You had little chance of becoming a celebrity when you were a "rookie," the name given the ROTC cadets.

I applied my usual self, and in that first year I was made a corporal, the only "first-year" student to reach that level. That same year we were given a special test—the Army Citizenship Test. Of the 275 cadets who took it, I was the only one to get 100 percent. During a parade in drill formation on the school campus, the battalion stood at attention and watched as I received the Citizenship Medal. The *Salt Lake Tribune* ran a picture of me, which was my first picture in a newspaper. My dad was very proud. He had given me a lot of contacts through his circles. In the restaurant, he would introduce me to important people, not just politicians but also doctors and lawyers. He wanted me to meet these customers, who in his mind were the professional, successful people of Salt Lake. As a result of my picture in the newspaper, a man who had been the state prison warden, a lawyer then near retirement, called and asked my dad about the award and asked to see me. Pop said this lawyer was a very prominent man in town and encouraged the visit. I went to the lawyer's office in the Boston Building on Main Street. He was very kind and interested and asked what I thought about my future, and so on. I told him that I wanted to be a lawyer. He liked that and said if I ever needed help, or wanted advice, to visit him. He was just curious, I guess, to see what this Italian American boy was all about. I never saw him again, but it made me think that maybe I could achieve something.

The Cadet Hop was the big dance of the year for ROTC students. This—my junior year—was my excruciating challenge: my first big date with a white gardenia (what else?!). Once again, when I picked my date up, I felt the close scrutiny and comments of her parents, perhaps a normal thing but not for a nervous non-Mormon boy. The program included a rifle drill team of twelve cadets, and I was its leader. I used both a whistle and my voice. The maneuvers on the dance floor were fancy and intricate—while moving we changed our rifles from right shoulder to left shoulder, then presented arms, saluted, and crisscrossed lines. It appeared very involved, but was more tricky than complicated. Though I was a bit clumsy with my date and dancing—the rage was the jitterbug, not real intricate but still I had trouble—the rifle team's performance was a big hit.

The success in these events gave me momentum, which I tried to communicate to my mother. As far as senior high school was concerned, everything began to flow for those two final years. I had a lot of friends. I became prominent as editor of the high school newspaper, was an ROTC leader, and maintained my "all As" reputation. The all-girls' edition of the *South High Scribe* labeled me as "most brains," though I envied those selected who were "best looking" or "best personality." "Best dancer" was out of my bounds. I was active in and liked the debate club, which was my first endeavor in public speaking. I took every chance to be involved with programs and all kinds of organizations, from the Willing Workers Club to the nationwide radio broadcast called *American School of the Air,* from the Board of Control (a governing student-body organization) to a summer state National Guard program, "Boys State," where I was elected to the state supreme court.

The newspaper, of course, gave me easy access to the pulse of the school. One of the more formative efforts was my junior-year column, "As I See It." I used an anonymous byline, "By a Bystander," because the column paraphrased items from current-affairs magazines and newspapers. I usually selected subjects on domestic and international matters. I was fascinated by what was happening in Nazi Germany. On September 1, 1939, the German army rolled swiftly across Poland, and the war was on. I followed it closely and included the attitudes and news in Europe in my column. One column dealt with the speculation that Hitler would create a puppet Ukraine republic in order to assume control of the food basket of Russia. In another piece, I reported on the Nazi storm-trooper newspaper denouncing the Lambeth Walk as "Jewish mischief and animalistic hopping." (The Lambeth Walk was at that time one of the most popular dances in the United States.) And there was, of course, Hitler's rejection of President Roosevelt's peace plan. The comments I wrote had some editorial judgment. For example, one piece read: "$400,000,000! What a colossal sum the oppressed Jews in Greater Germany must pay because they are JEWS! It is said that God created all people to be equal but apparently that isn't believed by some individuals."

In my senior year, I was editor of the paper. Crowning achievement came when the managing editors of the four Salt Lake City dailies selected the *South High Scribe* as the "best high school paper" in the state and ROTC Company C, of which I was cadet captain, won the Kiwanis Honor Company Cup as the Outstanding Company of the Year. The real capstone to my high school career was being named school valedictorian of the graduating class of nearly one thousand, the state's largest. The salutatorian was Ruby Tashima, a good friend and first-generation Japanese American.

I gave my valedictory speech at the South High auditorium. I wrote the speech without any help. I had memorized most of it because I wanted to do a Winston Churchill, but I finally realized I had better stay with the paper in front of me. At the time I thought it was really good. Though I have much less regard for it now, it does show what I was thinking at that time. The pressures I had been living with in Salt Lake had allowed me some insights on human nature. In 1940, world war seemed imminent. Throughout the year, we had digested war news as part of our breakfasts, lunches, and dinners. We listened to reports of naval engagements while tackling geometry problems. At all hours of the day, radios were blaring news of death, destruction, and heartbreak. All of us wondered, "Where is the world headed?"

I titled the speech "The World Is Ours." I professed about our future, where we would be going. "The Industrial Revolution has really just begun," I said. Proof of this could be found in every house, in such everyday things as the "talking picture, electric refrigerator, and radio," which were all relatively new. Somebody, now forgotten, had ignorantly quipped that with those inventions, "there was very little more to invent." My remarks centered on people and their needs within this bigger picture, their needs for a sense of change and challenge. I talked about the individual's "four primary wishes"—security, response, adventure, and recognition—in obtaining a happy life. By this time, I was already aware of the need for recognition in everybody's life.

Only my mother attended my graduation ceremony. Group family occasions were for weddings or funerals. Graduations did not qualify. This was a by-product of the Calabrese mentality of those days. But this occasion fueled my ambition for the rest of my life. The two years at South were the breakthrough: I became socially acceptable. I had experienced success as a student and stretched my intellectual abilities. Being valedictorian was a big boost for college expectations.

At the end of senior high school, I was offered a complete four-year scholarship to Stanford University by Miss Winifred H. Dyer, South's vice principal. I turned it down, much to her surprise. It was even contrary to feelings I had expressed at the time. I was looking for this way out, I had chosen academics as my means, and here was a very positive result. And yet—why? I did not want to go to Stanford because I was not ready to leave Salt Lake City. Today, I realize that I did not then have the total confidence—the inner security—needed to leave hearth and home. I did not explain it that way to my friends. I sloughed the real reason and explained it simply as not wanting to leave my Utah friends. I wanted to go to the University of Utah and excel in every way—academically, obviously, but also in the extracurricular sense. If I had gone to Stanford, I suspect the same aspects of my personality would have emerged. Stanford was "big time." I would have been a total stranger in a class filled with strangers. Only in my senior high school year had I emerged with what today is called "leadership potential." I felt confident—with today's hindsight—that I could understand the student body composition of the freshman class at the University of Utah. I knew many of the students and understood what I might encounter. At Stanford, I don't think my ambition would have changed, but the challenges would have been greater.

In the years that have passed, I now think of my ambition from my mother's viewpoint. I realize that her experience—coming from Italy at the age of twelve, meeting her real mother and family for the first time, then marrying at a very young age—limited her vision of my future. (By the way, she later criticized that tradition: she felt that to be married at seventeen was too young, and that she had never enjoyed a childhood.) Of course, now, at this point in my life, I realize that she knew of my father's prison record. She never once mentioned it, yet she had that hanging over her head. My dad never mentioned it, while at the same time he was dreaming with me. He thought that maybe I could achieve something. When I found out the full story about my father's prison record, I was nearly seventy. It amazed me, and it also told me even more about my mother.

Americans, in general, live with a sense of time that is progressive. These economically based thoughts anticipate that each year will be different, better. In Salt Lake City, where the state motto is Industry, these thoughts are pronounced. Where my parents grew up, there was no guarantee that anything would be different in the future. It could even be worse. Southern Italians view time in terms of cycles, based on the agricultural seasons, with little sense of progress. You didn't grow toward something. You persisted. If something happened in the past, it could happen today, and it would happen tomorrow. Nothing ever changes. At any time, an act of God—anything from sickness to a sirocco—could destroy your health or your livelihood. There was no escaping it. That bred pessimism and had an outward appearance of resignation, *la miseria*, fatalism, and little ambition. In so many ways, my mother had changed to learn a new life different from her upbringing. But she could change only so much. Laughter was a relatively infrequent expression. Praise from her was a rare thing. Now I can see how she felt. She figured she knew her class, she knew her status in society, and she didn't want me to step out and be hurt. I might strive for too much and then lose and find that it was not achievable. She felt that I should be content with life as it is because it is a tough, hard society out there, outside the *campanilismo.*

My parents lived in that brick bungalow house in suburban Salt Lake City for the rest of their lives. For a Calabrese, life in one place was natural. I remember we could sit out on the front porch and look at the park across the street. My mother loved to sit out there and watch the lake. Some nights, friends would ring our doorbell, and most times the visit would take place out on our porch. They would sit on the porch and talk for an hour or more, with coffee, sweets, and occasionally a bit of wine—for the men. And that would be it. At another time, there would be big eating somewhere, usually at our house.

Born in January 1900 and left behind in Italy as an infant, my mother arrived in Salt Lake City at age twelve and met her parents, two brothers, and two sisters for the first time. Here with her family, *from the left,* brother Philip, Uncle Mike, father Rocco Arnone, my mother, mother Carmela, sister Rose, and sister Lena (brother Carmine not pictured).

My father and his father-in-law, Rocco Arnone, about 1920, in Salt Lake City. Despite my father's easygoing style, he was heavily influenced by the nativism movement, from the day he landed in America at age thirteen, through his jobs in Montana, Idaho, and Utah. It wasn't until his final days that I learned some of the facts of his "troubles." We didn't learn the full facts until 1991.

A traveling photographer finds two young customers—in Rocco and Sam—1926.

In the yard of the home on the west side of Salt Lake City, before my father had reached the middle class. This house was near the railroad tracks before we moved to a new home across the street from Liberty Park.

My older brother, Sam, and I with our father, at our great-aunt's farm in Ogden, north of Salt Lake City.

In the early 1920s, my mother was one of the first of the Italian immigrant women to get her driver's license. Despite her strength (pre–power steering) and her accentless English, she did not feel comfortable outside her own social circle. She and I struggled with our different ideas of what America offered.

In Salt Lake City of the 1920s an Italian immigrant felt "different." We were a close family (with Joe Jr. coming along six years after me). We stayed in touch with the small community of immigrants, but the community was dispersed and with no Little Italy we assimilated in our own way.

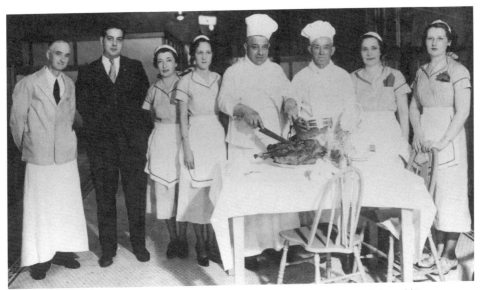

"Papa Joe," as the customers knew him, acting as the chef, loved hosting and would bring out extra butter or a side of spaghetti during the ration days of World War II. Brother Sam, in the suit, was the manager.

The first-ever attempt by a Salt Lake junior high school to have a yearbook, 1938. Even though I (center, rear) was the editor of the Bryant Junior High yearbook, I admired the style of Hope Adams (second from left, bottom row) and Bill Ryberg (far right).

Governor's Day 1939. I am seated to the left of Utah governor Henry Blood. I was elected justice of the Utah Supreme Court at the first Boys State, sponsored by the American Legion.

In June 1939, I visited my mother's family in San Francisco and took in the World's Fair. I really thought I had it all figured out at that time! I loved San Francisco, but when I received a scholarship from Stanford I found myself rejecting it.

My first years at college were an explosive experience. I was quite involved—the pins on my jacket show some of my campus affiliations. With the world increasingly unstable, I found my first love, which painfully ended because of my inability to join in her devout Mormon belief.

From grade school through college—and thereafter—lifelong closest friends, Dick and Betty Wetzel.

On rest leave, March 15, 1945, in Florence, Italy, I penned one of my many letters to my best friend, Dick Wetzel: "What used to be accepted seems like splendid nobility now. . . . I've been sleeping between sheets with even hot water easily available (in morning only)."

My closest army buddy, Don Fox, and I at Camp Swift, Texas, 1944, just before we shipped out to Italy. The combat experience brought us as close as any human relationship could be. Don went from deep concern about himself and emerged as an outstanding combat infantry leader—winning the Purple Heart and Silver Star.

We graduated from the grueling pace at Officer Candidate Infantry School at Fort Benning, Georgia, October 3, 1944. The password was leadership, which we were glad to know we had. Six of us from Salt Lake City were assigned to the 10th Mountain Division. *Left to right:* Gordon A. Anderson, me, Don Fox, Veldon Larson, and F. Ray Slight (Bill Ryberg took the photo). Bill Ryberg and Ray Slight were killed in action in the Apennines Mountains of northern Italy.

The "Old Homestead Place" in Pietra Colora, Italy (a village in the Apennines), probably around April 1, 1945. The war was nearly over, though the enemy did not seem to think so. Some very close calls were yet to come—in particular, a dud artillery shell that landed three feet away from me.

Ten months after the war's end, I was granted emergency leave because of surgery on my father. Upon arrival in Utah, I was discharged immediately. This family picture was taken the next day, April 17, 1946. *Left to right:* Joe Jr., Papa Joe, Sam, Mom, and me.

On April 4, 1947, I met Marion Stiebel at the International Student House near Washington, D.C. We fell in love that first night and saw each other every night thereafter. Law school was the realization of a lifelong dream, but Marion was more than I could ask for.

Marion, when she was nine
years old, in the countryside
of Germany, 1933.

Marion's mother, Eva Kohn,
and her stepfather, Fred
Oppen. I found a family with
amazing inner strength and
the deepest of intelligence—
and no affectations. The best
in-laws one could imagine.

FOUR

LOVE AND WAR AT THE UNIVERSITY

THE UNIVERSITY OF UTAH sits at the base of the majestic Wasatch mountains, perched on the benches overlooking the city and valley of Salt Lake. The small campus in 1940 was focused around the Presidential Circle, a U-shaped drive lined with five large classroom buildings. The four thousand students made up a thriving community that was small enough for you to know the majority of people, especially those involved in student activities. In a lot of ways, the university then was sort of a "super" high school. It was dominated by Salt Lake City high schools: East High, the middle- to upper-class students, furnished the largest number of freshmen and the leadership in our freshman class, and South High and West High students were from the middle and lower classes. Trying to make yourself known among the couple thousand students who are also trying to make themselves known meant staying active. I jumped right in. I ran for freshman treasurer, my first try at elected politics, and I won by quite a large majority.

For a freshman trying to make an impact on the student body, the best place was in the sororities and fraternities. The Pi Kappa Alpha fraternity caught my eye because it was organized as a political machine. Many of its members were political science majors, and they ran and supported people for student body offices. They had the record: most class officers and most student body presidents. They were interested in me because I had already won a student body position. I joined them at the beginning of my second quarter in early 1941. I did not move into the fraternity house and remained at home. Joining a fraternity was not an easy decision at my home. My mother did not know why I wanted to spend all this money to join an organization. I tried to explain: it would give me an identity in the school. My dad was a well-networked businessman and had a lot of involvement with politicians. He understood and supported my decision. He liked it that I had entered into a political career at college. I didn't have to justify anything to him.

At the end of my freshman year, I ran for office again, this time for vice president of the sophomore class, and I was elected. The president-elect of the sophomore class was a Sigma Chi. At that time, Pi Kappa Alpha and Sigma Chi were the two rival fraternities that dominated campus politics and fought for student body–officer positions. That fall their member, the president, failed to make a passing average, and I replaced him as class president. At the end of my sophomore year, I ran for second vice president of the student body, the highest office that was possible for a junior to hold and often the prelude to being student body president of the University of Utah, my ultimate ambition. I was quite easily elected. The other officers were Bob Barker, Betty Hinckley, Shirley Bangerter, Mary Skidmore, and Jim Hawkins. These were and are all very prominent Utah names. Perhaps surprisingly, we were a very close, cohesive group that had fun while working well together.

In all, I ran successfully for student body office five times. I learned the organization and management of a campaign, with all the diversity and differences with supporting groups and contrary individuals, including fraternities and sororities (the "Greek" vote) and the "door-to-door" vote. I became, in hindsight, a campus politician—never to be repeated in the real world.

The rumblings in Europe escalated in our first year of college. Germany invaded Poland on September 1, 1939, the beginning of World War II. Then, in 1940, as I entered my freshman year, the German blitzkrieg overran Denmark, Norway, Belgium, the Netherlands, and France. Life seemed to be normal and orderly, yet interrupted by the chaotic, turbulent times—this omnivorous war erupted and crept closer, pulling us into it. We faced big unanswered questions: Where do you go? What do you do? How do you plan a career when you know the war will interrupt it?

My friends and I figured we were going to war. It seemed inevitable. The draft became legal with the Selective Service Act in 1940 (it passed Congress by one vote!). Some guys got married and some had kids to defer their call to duty. Everybody thought about it, but I don't think anybody could plan a course of action. I tried to get some education and experience, and I hoped for any assignment but the infantry. Many of us joined the college ROTC, a four-year field artillery course that led to your officer's commission. Maybe by that time the war would be over. Our field artillery unit trained on a field south of campus using World War I horse-drawn 75mm artillery equipment. Tanks were fighting World War II, and we were training with caissons pulled by live horses!

Even with all the worldly concerns, we lived a very easy social, free-wheeling kind of lifestyle on campus. Big bands were *the* thing and everybody danced. A group of thirty or forty people would get together each Wednesday night at a sorority or fraternity for a "swing session." On weekends, we danced at Jerry Jones's Rainbow Rendezvous. Late at night, after the dances, a small group of close friends went to my dad's restaurant after hours. (He was pleased to give me the door key.) We devoured roasted chicken, turkey, or roast beef, and I introduced several friends to pasta and ravioli. Wetzel called me "Casanova," but that was more about the trying than the killing. I slowly built my social abilities until I dated very heavily. Many of my Bryant Junior High classmates were now close social friends, and the old envy had disappeared.

After becoming the South High School valedictorian, I assumed I could conquer any subject and take home only As. I learned a needed lesson in the required physics course that taught me more than the facts about matter and energy; it was my comeuppance. It felt like a foreign language to me, and I barely squeezed a C, my first ever. I realized my intellectual limitations. I found mathematics acceptable, but physics— forget it.

In those few years, our campus underwent a pivotal change. It began to lose its small-town serene atmosphere. While I focused on academics and my future, with possible military service always of great concern, a good deal of my energy went into special activities. Besides taking lecture notes, attending dances, and losing sleep over term papers, I developed my abilities as a student body officer. I served on the prom committees, worked on publications, and handled relations between fraternities and nonfraternity students (who were in the majority). I made no effort to work on the school newspaper; simply put, Sigma Chi controlled it. The Intercollegiate Knights, a service organization that worked with other campus groups, reported to me as second vice president. Other parts of that job were to meet with the student council, to conduct the elections, and all of the assignments that pertained to the fraternities and sororities. For the most part, the weight of these duties was more play than seriousness. But during my junior year, we began to shift gears. We started to bring in special events, such as assemblies related to the war effort, every Friday. I organized the blood drives. People sold war bonds and rolled bandages. The war crept into our isolated town of Salt Lake. The weight of individual responsibility began to reach us as students.

On December 7, 1941, Japan bombed Pearl Harbor and immersed America in World War II. The attack—an intensely unifying force—hit this country and crystallized public opinion. Millions of people immediately wanted to help their country. All the ROTC students were soon sworn into the Army Reserve. From that point on, we waited for the call to active duty. You felt like you were sitting on top of a volcano and the world was going to pieces. You were no longer in control, and no one could predict what would happen to you or your friends. Little did I know that graduation from the university itself was at stake.

Then, there she was—beautiful, of course, with a formidable intellect. I met her on the steps of the Park Building, which was then the center of campus. She was looking at her grades for the fall quarter, 1941, her first quarter of school. I jokingly asked if she got a four-point. She surprised me when she said yes. My curiosity was piqued, and I asked her out to learn how a country girl like her could pull all As. Her name was Norma Broadbent, from the nearby small, rural mountain town of Heber City, Utah. She was a year younger, a freshman. We began an intense romance.

Norma and I had a very public campus romance. Her interest in school activities matched mine: she was an actress in school plays; a play manager; on the debate council; a pledge at Alpha Chi Omega; a member of Spurs, the pep club; in Cwean, the freshman Honor Society; and on the editorial staff of the yearbook. We shared many of the same interests, and we were very compatible intellectually. Because of my position with the student government, I had an office in the Union building, and I often met her there. Though governed by Utah's strict morals, we were involved and passionate. It was the first love affair for each of us, and we lived it to the fullest. One of the highlights of my life: we were full flush in love and walking among the blooming flowers in Salt Lake's Memory Grove park. I was walking on air I was so taken with her. We were dreamers, and nothing could interfere with our lives. We talked for hours about the future—our joint future, when the war would be over. Nothing could stand in our way.

But it was not to be. The excitement, the serenity, and the conviction were interrupted. A returned Mormon missionary helped remind Norma of the life promised during her first eighteen years of growth by her church. I was intensely jealous—he had something I did not; first of all, he was Mormon. He had a presence I couldn't reach. He seemed older and wiser. All this was occurring as our ROTC class was told that we would be called to active duty on April 5, 1943. In spite of repeated affirmations of our feelings, it was becoming clear that my world—our world—was falling apart. Today, the answer to what and why it happened is easy to explain: my emotions were fighting my intellect, and the intellect would prevail.

We were in the car in front of Norma's sorority house. I thought we had to end it.

She said, "If that's the way you want it."

I said, "It isn't the way I want it; it's the way it has to be."

The memory of a first love can be disturbing, and though the impact is not always definable, it is real and memories remain. We broke up on the evening of April 4, 1943. An easy rationale was not then apparent, and it bothered me for a long time. The next morning, my ROTC class met at the university's Park Building where—in an emotional setting—army trucks carried us to nearby Fort Douglas for active-duty induction. War and combat (in my case) were uncertain, but the turbulent times did not bode well for calm, rational thought. However painful, our decision turned on our differences in religious belief. I was not a Mormon, nor was I interested in converting to the faith. Neither of us wanted to break it off, even though I eventually came to realize that our love was a brief excursion into the forbidden for both of us.

The military is the great equalizer—your personality has no opportunity to peek out; the system ignores it, even steps on it. Our basic training took place in a fairly godforsaken part of California (Camp Roberts, near Paso Robles)—a lot of heat and stifling humidity. We marched, hiked, and sweated for hours. None of us would have willingly volunteered for this, but we had common enemies—Japan and Nazi Germany. The military experience, at any level—whether a private, a noncommissioned officer, or an officer—transformed my generation. Our whole way of life was changed. As privates, we lived in huge barracks that slept forty people on a floor. The common bathroom had no partitions between the rows of toilets and the showers. In front of everybody you were naked. Privacy did not exist, day or night. We had long, physically exhausting days of field maneuvers, which caused my legs to cramp in the middle of the night. The unbearable pain would wake me up. I would hit Bob Shriver in his bunk next to mine so he could massage my calves and straighten out the huge knots of muscles. That intimacy with what we called your "asshole buddies" is unequaled in any other part of society.

We went out in the desert, sitting in the backs of trucks, and dust storms rolled in and enveloped us. After two hours, dirt caked all over our faces and in our nostrils, we felt miserable and hot with a whole day of field maneuvers ahead of us. We set up the 105mm howitzers and practiced firing them with about eight men on a gun—one man set the sights, another loaded, another pulled the trigger, and so on, then we changed places. Of course, some places were more favorable than others. As the day wore on, the little things became overblown. People got petty and whined about when they would be the gunner. After a few months of that, I dreamt of escaping to officer candidate school (OCS), where I hoped for an easier life.

The "U" group from Salt Lake—Don Fox, Bill Zwick, Dale Barton, Warren and Art Anderson (brothers), Bill Ryberg, Vernon Zinik, and many others—stayed close together. Ryberg and I, with our last names so close alphabetically, spent a year and a half together in daily association, particularly in the barracks. We had a lot of fun, but I was in a very different state of mind. They received long letters from their girlfriends and spent hours writing their replies. The news of Norma's engagement, just a few weeks after our breakup, sent me into a trough. I stumbled through those memory tumbleweeds . . . all those plans of marriage, then family, career, future, and all those other poignant bits of nonsense that were as permanent as the tides. I read of her wedding and saw her picture in the newspaper and realized how much plans and people can change in six short months. In that sense, during this tumultuous period of trying to understand the loss of Norma, Wetzel served as my confidant. I had no one else. I sent him a barrage of letters (and luckily, he saved them for me). We had a total abiding faith in each other. To this day, after many months of no communication, we can call each other and talk as if only an hour had passed since our last conversation.

The heartbreak became a driving force for me, and I resolved to maintain my independence. I even felt particularly superior to the "poor bastards"—"if their girls didn't write them pages nightly they would be valueless," I wrote Wetzel. I wanted to be dependent upon *no one*. I even wrote letters to myself. Instead of hanging out with the people writing love letters, where they said very little, I found fellows who knew of the war. I always sought intellectual contact with people. I shared some invigorating talks with a few guys in the barracks, and at times we had lively philosophical discussions about world events. Then, too, the whole barracks would reach despondent lows, and we would discuss our reasons for fighting. The deadening grind of army life also deadened our minds—an indescribable feeling.

At the same time, we managed to keep our spirits up, and everybody had fun despite all of the stressful work. In the army, as at the fraternity, I often organized the group activities. My father used to playact. We have many photos of him posed in comic situations, like milking a horse. I discovered that I had inherited some of that comic behavior and inflicted it on my army buddies. Those crazy photos make me realize how an environment can change your behavior.

Those weeks of basic training were the most eye-opening, satisfying, enjoyable, hellish time in my life up to that point. I experienced so many different views and challenging people. Meeting people, more than anything else, relieved me of homesickness and dark wartime thoughts. One day, a friend called me "the father of the whole goddamn barracks." I didn't devote my whole time to this pious mien, but I constantly took at least a cursory interest in other people's thoughts. It helped me maintain a spirit of kindled enthusiasm for that life. Personally, I discovered that people want *others* to be interested in only *their* problems—they are interested little in anyone else's. When you show interest in them, everything is fine. While on leave, I walked around the town of Paso Robles and enjoyed the people immensely. I saw such variety—I felt vibrant, "as if ice picks were probing my mind and spine. Really, Wetz, that further convinces me that this sort of moving, challenging life is what I want. The women were fascinating."

One morning, one of the boys received the University of Utah yearbook. We looked at it—bragging frats, women, and so on—and afterward I thought about how different we looked and felt. By that time, we were all so "damned GI" that we could only dream of days that used to be. Of course, in the army, all we could do was bitch about it—and we naturally did plenty of that. Without reservation, our cuss words shocked no one. Expressions that four months previously I would not have tolerated seemed the only way to fully explain what you felt. Indignation over anything ran rampant—especially in the last concluding weeks.

"Oh yes, we bitch but if we couldn't do that there would be no morale," I wrote. "That's as necessary for the maintenance of morale as its removal would mean the collapse of that very thing. Though all of us assert that our minds are sinking because of disuse—which is true, yet give us the chance and we will amaze even ourselves at the way a new matured mind sprouts." Though our training was routine, it was an unbending grind that grates a person's nerves and intellect. All of us desired the opportunity to get back into something where we could use a pen and our heads instead of a carbine and our hands.

During those summer nights the boys sometimes felt extremely homesick and disgusted. At times it seemed so unfair. Everything was utterly beyond our powers. Night and day, our future flew about on the varied rumors, wishes, and hopes. The rumors had us going in every possible direction—stay there, or return to Utah to await call, or be sent to another camp to await call, or maybe go to Fort Sill for OCS. Tempers and tongues flew fast and furious. We had no idea what was going to happen: I heard that lamenting refrain so often I sometimes walked away with fatigue from hearing it. Our morale fascinated me. I saw how seriously our morale affected us, not just the bitching, but the degree to which morale influenced our efficiency. At that moment, morale meant more to me than just a nice-sounding word. Morale, I realized, determines everything in life. If a person can develop inexhaustible reserves of morale, he can own a bit of power over his life. Those who don't assume some level of sustainable morale continually curse their luck and "the breaks."

On August 2, I again summed up our mood to Wetz:

The boys are very, very restless and dissatisfied with what we're doing. Even though actual work is little it's just the uncertainty that is distressing. . . . Frankly it's only *one* thing that makes them desperately long for return to Salt Lake: They are wrapped in a cocoon of love from which the only escape is to once again make contact with her. Oh they admit it—it keeps them going and their thoughts channeled. Gather the effect on me. I personally would like to be in Salt Lake about one week, but then—yep you're right. Wetz—I feel that I have left Salt Lake cleanly and sharply. . . . I often wondered if once I was away from Salt Lake would I still have you know—the old ambitions—they are even stronger than I thought.

In late August 1943, we returned to Salt Lake City, which made us happy since it wasn't like going abroad. We returned to college under the Army Specialized Training Program (ASTP), and, unfortunately, you could not choose your curriculum; you *had* to enroll in engineering classes. I found myself repeating physics. I had to take advanced math. I was stuck in the one area that I have absolutely no aptitude for and had fled with enthusiasm. Meanwhile, the army was telling us we would be lucky to finish the quarter. They anticipated recalling us to active duty before the year was out.

Upon my return, I met a young freshman from Salt Lake, already a well-known skier and later an Olympic skier. I liked him and I put his name up for fraternity membership. We had an alumni fraternity adviser, a very prominent lawyer in Salt Lake whom I liked a great deal, who came to our weekly fraternity meetings. One night as we were discussing his admission, this man stood and emphatically said we could not let him join because he was a Jew. I was absolutely horrified. He went on about when you let one in, before you know it you'll have to let them all in. I had never heard that kind of language before. I was especially shocked that this was coming from an educated man, a church leader, and a beloved adviser. Despite my position in the fraternity and on campus, I couldn't persuade enough people to stop this. My friend was blackballed. For the first time I really saw the operation of prejudice in action. I felt that if someone was anti-Semitic, they were probably anti–Italian American. My valued fraternity experience ended on this sad note. I never put it on my résumé.

During this interim, I lived at home and usually studied at home, though once in a great while I would study at the university library. One night at the library, in uniform like so many others, I took off my jacket and loosened my tie. Later, an army captain came in and told us we had to button our shirts, tighten our ties, and put on our jackets. Those "offenders" who had rolled up their sleeves or were wearing their "soldier's aid" sweaters as an outer garment were reprimanded and given citations. All in all, the interruption upset everyone concerned. Though not cited, I thought it callous overkill to punish a person for removing his jacket. The injustice of it made me quite indignant. I went over to the student body offices and typed out a letter. The editor of the newspaper, the *Chronicle,* a dear friend of mine, Margaret "Midge" Thomas, printed it. In part, it read:

> It seemed all that the captain succeeded in doing for some was the creation of an apple of discord. I mention this malcontent as being contrary to the normal surveillance which we all realize is necessary and needed. But certainly even the army doesn't want this type of enforcement with its resultant disunion. What inclination and urge does the soldier feel for study after he has just had his name taken for an alleged rupture of rule?
>
> It seems pathetic that most of the men must suffer from the silly consequentials that come with relaxation while studying. This, then, is a simple plea for a bit more moderation and tolerance toward these men while in the study halls. In the field, why go to it! Discipline and regulation are needed still in amounts there. Here, in the educational manors, relax somewhat. Have supervised study but temper it with a bit of understanding.

I signed it anonymously, "A Private."

The results were catastrophic. My letter infuriated the army's commanding colonel at the University of Utah, and he demanded the author's name. He promised to court-martial the author and "send him overseas." Several people knew my name, aside from Midge—in particular, Keith C. Brown, the graduate manager of student activities. We had a quick consultation, and obviously I was at their mercy. Midge refused to reveal my name. The colonel went directly to the university president, Dr. LeRoy Cowles, and insisted my name be disclosed. In an effort to pressure Midge, they suspended her as editor for two weeks. Fortunately, they did not expel her. The president convoked the Publication Committee, made up of faculty and students, to review and decide the matter of disclosure. The three faculty members voted yes, because this situation jeopardized the relations with the army authority, which represented a lot of students and therefore income. The three civilian students, joined by Keith Brown, said no. The president (who did know me) accepted their numerical majority, and my name was not revealed.

In terms of my lifework, that was one of my most perilous points. The whole issue shook me. Later, I rationalized that these events—the fallout due to my letter, the fraternity blackballing a Jewish student, my breakup with Norma—all were adding chinks in my emotional armor.

Soon enough, the time came when we knew we would leave for the "real army." Meanwhile, I had received my ASTP grades. They weren't my usual grades, but I was passing as an engineer. I went to my old friend Dr. John Ballif, dean of men, my French teacher, adviser, and confidant who had always helped me greatly. I explained my case: I was close to the hours required for graduation, and if I graduated I could go directly to law school after the war. Dean Ballif was amenable to the idea. He liked me, and at least my other grades were very good. He got departmental approval for me to receive a bachelor of arts, with honors, in political science. As it turned out, for those who did *not* finish, it meant two or three years of college after the war.

Our next assignment came in March 1944: go to OCS in field artillery at Fort Sill, Oklahoma. Within the first week there a horrible rumor swept camp—we were destined for infantry officer school at Fort Benning, Georgia. We didn't want to believe that. Infantry is a totally different animal. It turned out to be true: the army had too many field artillery officers. Some men tried to resign their OCS rights. The colonel in charge called us together—some four hundred college students—and announced that the next man who tried to resign his OCS rights would be court-martialed. We were all going to Fort Benning, Georgia.

Few wanted to be infantry officers. Even graduation from the tough seventeen-week course was not ensured. Of those who entered field artillery OCS—college types heavy with mathematics needed to know how to fire long-range artillery guns—95 percent graduated. The infantry school emphasized physical fitness and the magic word *leadership.* At Fort Benning, the graduation rate was 50 percent. Those who washed out went directly overseas to a combat unit—as corporals. I watched my Utah colleagues get picked off one by one. The valedictorian of my high school one year ahead of me, out. My OCS class finished October 3, 1944, and by that date some of the first washouts were already killed in combat. The system was brutal in the school, with washouts occurring until the day before graduation. You never knew if you would graduate until they pinned that gold bar on you. Seventeen weeks put me in great physical shape. I lost twenty pounds in the process.

We learned how to handle all kinds of different "pieces" or guns: an M1 rifle, .50-caliber machine gun, .30-caliber machine gun, pistol, the Browning automatic rifles, mortars, and so on. I nearly washed out at the rifle range during the marksmanship test. Nervous, I got angry at my adviser-buddy classmate. Fortunately, the gunnery sergeant substituted another man to "calm" me. "This past week was hell," I wrote Wetz. "I sweated blood just barely qualifying with the M-1 rifle. Had to shoot a 140 to stay in class—I squeaked out 150 after the most taut day yet. Never—never do I want to go thru another one like that." Never in my life had I realized so much was at stake. Failure to qualify was an automatic washout. You couldn't breathe optimism because you were too scared.

Even more than in basic training, our spirits dipped really low at times. "My hell—you almost felt like dying just looking at the poor bastards (boy I was low too)," I told Wetzel. "Yet, now, I really feel okay. . . . It's a damn good thing I don't have a woman to make things worse." I had become very determined. Nothing, as far as I was concerned, would interfere. "And if I don't make it why I will have tried regardless. Pessimistic, perhaps. But realistic, I know that," I stated resolutely.

The days were filled to exhaustion fussing around with live dynamite and TNT, making makeshift hand grenades, firing the Browning automatic rifle ("really a nice rifle," I thought at the time), tossing live grenades, crawling through swamps on night combat missions, firing on the machine gun range all day, going out on four-day bivouacs, and all-night problems that finished at five in the morning. It was the *real* army.

We came to the dreaded fifth week when we ran the obstacle course, fired a machine gun, and took the Platoon Leaders Computation test.

The fifth week washout board primarily eliminated the low academic boys. My work in the field was fine—but some grades were low. In the map-reading exam, which was the easiest test, they asked a series of interlinked questions. As I finished the test and rechecked it, I found a mistake at the very beginning. I worked quickly but did not have time to rectify the mistake. I got a D. The tactical officer (TO) could have flunked me right then and there. While I was losing sleep over this, a friend overheard my TO bragging to his fellow officers about my capabilities. Then the TO himself said to me that poor grades can happen to anybody. He wasn't looking at that; he was looking at our leadership qualities. Leadership has plenty of intangible qualities, and it was hard to know what made sense. The man with the highest grades in our section and best scores in weapons washed out because they said he lacked a commanding voice and looked poor. I don't know why I didn't wash out, except for the good impressions with the TO and the captain; they were the key. They eliminated persons who they felt had no "leadership." We heard this talk about "leadership, leadership"—that's all they wanted. We knew what they meant, but it was hell proving you had an innate ability. If I thought basic training was hellish, OCS was the most miserable existence.

We always eagerly read the newspaper from back home, sent to us by our families. That's where I read that a close friend, Kent Harmon, the *South High Scribe* editor before me, had died in battle. I went chilly. "God—death is coming quickly to those we know," I wrote. "There are so many things that I wished I had been able to talk to him [about]." We were informed of the terrific casualty rate among our rank, infantry second lieutenant, the initial rank as a commissioned officer. "If overseas assignment comes after 3 months as they've told us—boy then look for some of the familiar names. Naturally we're all anxious to do our duty. Ha!"

We kept one eye on the war and one eye on our graduation date and hoped that the German war would be over by the time we graduated (we assumed the demand for infantry would drop and we would not go into combat). My thoughts were free enough at one point to consider postwar plans, and I decided to work in government after the war, which for me meant Washington, D.C.

As the days rolled on toward the end of our course, we crossed our fingers ever more tightly. We had seen and heard of too many of the day-before washouts. Finally, we graduated from OCS on October 3,

1944. We reported to Camp Swift, Texas, and, in an unusual circumstance, five of my close college friends—Don Fox, Gordon Anderson, Veldon Larson, Ray Slight, and Bill Ryberg—and I were assigned to the 10th Mountain Infantry Division, the U.S. Army's only mountain-trained troops. Known as the Ski Troops, it consisted of volunteers who knew the mountains. Our last-minute assignment brought the numbers closer to a normal division, typically fifteen thousand men, but we—the late joiners—had no mountain training. We were issued mountain equipment, but not skis. Just as well, as I was not a skier. For practical purposes, we were like other artillery and infantry units.

Three of us were in the First Battalion of the Eighty-seventh Mountain Infantry Regiment, a unit of some nine hundred men. Each of us was given a platoon of forty men to lead—Don Fox in A Company, I in B, and Bill Ryberg in C. We trained with our men for two months. The division, because it was largely made up of volunteers, had the highest IQ-rating average of any army outfit. Most all the GIs were college men, and degrees floated all around the place. The replacements were not up to such high standards, much to the disgust of the old-timers. I worked hard to win the respect of my platoon—and most of all their support. This may sound dramatic, but at that time nothing else mattered. I knew I couldn't afford to be wrong very often.

We were officially "alerted," which meant that we would leave in January 1945, though we had no idea where we were going. Because we were mountain infantry, most assumed we were headed to the mountains of Italy. "Maybe then I'll have time to learn Italian," I joked to Wetz. We made out our wills and powers of attorney, and as personal affairs officer of my company I helped about twenty-five men to do likewise. Our morale was surprisingly good, and the men were cheery—all anxious to get going. I took on an extra job—assistant defense counsel for the Eighty-seventh Regiment, which meant working on special court-martial cases.

After a lot of work, I was told (indirectly and directly) that my platoon had "accepted" me. They gave me the nickname "Mike Kelly"—Irish, in line with my long-standing joke about my last name being Irish. This gave me a peculiar pride. We made a percentage score of 91 in the platoon proficiency test for the division, the highest in memory. We celebrated with a steak-and-beer party. "Twenty-six of us drank 13 cases of beer; gawd, they really swallowed that stuff."

We were just killing time, not knowing where we were going, waiting for our call. Bill Ryberg and I went into Austin and double-dated. His date, whom I will call Rebecca, came from Jackson Hole, Wyoming, and they knew each other in Salt Lake. She got me a date. However, I liked Rebecca, so I took her out the next night. After that, Rebecca and I went out enough times for her to profess affection. I heard that old sense of permanence knocking about in her thoughts. I couldn't seriously contemplate anything until she could change her way of thinking and living. "Boy, I've really gotten independent now; I can't see ever worrying and scraping my mind as before," I wrote to Wetz. Our farewell was emotional, but "Oh well—too bad it's wartime."

I was ready to go, I told Wetz: "As perhaps you can sense, I'm all set. I have an excited sense of expectancy. . . . It isn't a noble patriotic feeling, but, that old urge for change or excitement (which I once talked about at graduation) has hit me something fierce." The army training experience altogether took a year and a half. By the time you go overseas after so much training, you begin to think you know what to do, that you know how to handle men. Even so, I wrote to Wetz: "Isn't it funny, it has taken so long that very often you think that you'll never get to a fighting front. But now that it's here, you hardly know what to make of it. Because you are moving constantly and seeing something different the actual positioning of ourselves for fighting has an unusual attraction. We are undergoing that phase now. Ugly reality will, very likely, knock us on our derrieres."

FIVE

TEST OF FIRE
The Italian Front Line

AS WE PREPARED to embark for Italy, I was transferred from B Company to the special weapons platoon in the First Battalion Headquarters Company. Reason: my field artillery training. Typically an antitank unit, they changed into an artillery 75mm pack howitzer unit because we would be in the mountains. I was as close to the artillery as possible but remained in the infantry. I had twenty men (half the number of a rifle company platoon) under me. I worked only with Lieutenant Colonel Ross Wilson, the battalion commander, for direction, and he permitted me some independence as to what and where we would fight. I welcomed this looser arrangement because of the dispensable nature of second lieutenants. They died first. The second lieutenant who took over my platoon in B Company was killed very quickly; the second was hit. If a combat infantryman was not killed or wounded after one hundred days, celebrate—so said the wiseacre.

We shipped out from Newport News, Virginia, on January 3, 1945, on the USS *West Point*—originally named *The America,* the largest passenger ship ever built in the United States. Most of the trip I was seasick; I would make a terrible sailor. Within a week, we passed through the Straits of Gibraltar, and as we approached Italy, we slipped close by the island of Capri. I thought of my dad and his Capri Restaurant—

wouldn't he be surprised. We docked at Naples on January 13 as cold rain squalls pelted the harbor town. Most of the division debarked and boarded Italian freight cars for the long trip north. My battalion, except for D Company, waited nearly three days before sailing north to Leghorn, or Livorno, near Genoa. While waiting, we saw the ravages of the war everywhere on our "exercise marches."

By this time, the war had entered its fourth year, and the end was obviously near. The Germans' last-ditch effort, the enormous counter-offensive known as the Battle of the Bulge, had been raging in mid-December just before we shipped out. That winter, the Italian theater, known in the history books as "The War the World Forgot," had come to a standstill. It took the Allies nine months after invasion in September 1943 to reach Rome, from essentially the southern half of Italy. It took eleven more months to capture the Po River, the last viable enemy line of defense. When we arrived, the German front in the Apennines range, known as the Gothic Line, had been stationary throughout the winter. The Germans were dug in with well-fortified defenses and ample supplies. We would first fight for a foothold in the Apennines, with an ultimate destination of the Po River. The Germans would be as fierce as a cornered cat. It would take four months, and our division would suffer some of the war's highest casualties: one of every three men was killed or wounded (my regiment of 3,000 men had 303 killed and 1,250 wounded). We would never be able to go back, thinking as we had before, to the lives we had before combat.

With my new assignment, I found the "new" equipment awaiting us in Italy: three 75mm artillery pack howitzers of World War I vintage. My tiny platoon of 20 men had never seen the weapon before. First, before we could fire them, I needed more men. A regular artillery battery would have about a half-dozen officers and 150 men. My frantic request resulted in being assigned some 20 more men and another second lieutenant. My battalion commander also allowed my Salt Lake classmate Don Fox to help me. As for "training" my platoon, this section of Italy had no place for practice, and the order came down: try the guns out "against the Germans," unorthodox but deemed necessary. Thus, we fired the Eighty-seventh Mountain Infantry's first shots in anger against a living and present enemy on January 27, 1945, two weeks after our arrival in Italy. My platoon was the first recipient of the Combat Infantryman Badge in the Eighty-seventh.

The 75mm shells were good-sized and normally used at the one-half- to two-mile range. You shoot artillery in a trajectory, not typically as direct-fire weapons. My infantry-trained battalion commander knew nothing about these guns. The conquest of Mount Belvedere was our first major offensive. It was our most memorable battle and the one in the history books. Colonel Wilson ordered me to take the three guns up to a mountain and fire directly at the enemy. As he told me that, we saw heavy-duty army trucks being blown up on the narrow roads going up the mountainside. The roads were mined, and he quickly changed his order. Lucky for us. Otherwise, we would have been sitting ducks. After a month with those guns, a higher authority took them away. Someone realized, after a deadly disaster occurred to a sister special-weapons platoon in another battalion, that they were not meant for direct fire by infantry troops in mountain warfare—at least not without advance training.

After the 75mm, they gave us three 37mm guns. A modified World War I direct-fire gun mounted on a reinforced 50-caliber–machine gun tripod, it used a small, long, narrow shell. It broke down into loads for packs on your back—the "breech" was thirty-six pounds of metal right on the square of your back (my platoon sergeant, Jim Belcher, remembers carrying the "recoil section" at seventy-three pounds!). We didn't think too much of that gun either because it was ineffective. One day, a lieutenant colonel of ordnance came to get my opinion about this new gun. He carried a clipboard. I told him it could break windows and paint at two thousand yards. He got angry and said, "Don't be smart with me, lieutenant." Eventually, they assigned nine mules and ten Italian Alpine soldiers to us for portage. Much later, on the April 14 big attack, I lost *all* the mules and the ten Alpini disappeared. General George Hays, our division commander and recipient of the Congressional Medal of Honor from World War I, had seven horses shot out from under him. After the war's end, I heard people say, "Siciliano had nine mules shot out from behind him and only got a Bronze Star." Two of the guns disappeared with the wounded mules on the April 14 attack, but no one cared; we were trying to survive. We ended up with one 37mm gun, plus the ever faithful 50-caliber machine guns.

I had a jeep and a three-quarter-ton truck assigned to my platoon, which was unique for a rifle company. My platoon had three squads, and I usually assigned one squad with each of the three rifle companies.

Sometimes I would double them up. As a result, I moved constantly, at an exhausting pace. I painted a name on the jeep's front, "Change O' Plan," to match the frenzy. We installed, at the admonition of the battle-wise, a six-foot steel bar, welded vertically on the front bumper with a jagged V cut near its top. We often drove at night with no lights and with the windshield down, and the V would clear out wires that the enemy had run across the narrow roads and alleys at the driver's height. The jeep was a lifesaver. It allowed me to keep in touch with the course of action and find tactically sound places for the men. Often, I would personally attach myself to A Company (Don Fox's unit) and my platoon sergeant, Jim Belcher—an officer wearing sergeant's stripes—to another company.

The combat lifestyle was moment to moment. Even though I had more freedom than most second lieutenants in a rifle company, I still had to be with the companies of my battalion. You were just following orders: "We're pulling out—you're gonna go two hundred yards up—there's a creek and some houses," and you're part of the larger rifle company that's getting the same kind of instructions. You had maps, but unfortunately they were often inaccurate. Basically, you had no control as to what you were going to do. You're told where to go and what to look for, you hope. You have very little perspective on the larger points of view, say from the battalion, the regiment, and certainly not on the division level.

The combat infantryman was a lonely creature. Of the half-million American troops in Italy in 1945, about thirty thousand engaged in actual combat (artillery, engineers, tanks, and infantry). The rest provided essential administration and support, such as quartermaster, postal unit, transportation, and ordnance. Often forgotten is the army medic, the unheralded hero of infantry combat—without arms of fire but with arms of solace. Out on the front line, old-timers became fewer by the day. Most people knew that life on the front line was not healthy. We knew very well it was just a question of time and you would be wounded or dead. Of course, you hoped that you'd get hurt, something easy. The life expectancy of a platoon leader was computed as twenty-seven aggregate days of frontline duty; that of a rifle infantryman was not much more. You don't fight every day. You couldn't handle the physical and mental strain. After some heavy fighting, we would fall back to a bombed-out town (such as Castel D'Aiano) and relax for three or four days. Without that you would go out of your head. Then you would return to the battle zone.

In our second major offensive of early March we met with huge success. We took all objectives far ahead of schedule. The first day alone, we took more prisoners than ever taken before on a single day by any unit in the Italian theater. The travel could be slow, especially in heavily mined areas. At its most intense, the fighting went from bunker to bunker, hill to hill, objective to objective. We were fighting enemies in well-prepared positions. The towns were small clusters of buildings set in rough, rocky hills.

The Germans waited for us inside those buildings with their completely different attitude toward the war. Even though most everyone thought the war nearly over, some German soldiers had been told that German soldiers would be sterilized or enslaved at the war's end. Thus, German soldiers had only two ways out: to surrender or to die. If they deserted, they were liable to be shot by us, shot by a German officer or sergeant (all of whom were authorized to shoot on mere suspicion), or their families would be punished. So even a German without hope remained very deadly behind a weapon. They had heard we were mountain troops, and they believed we were handpicked, an elite corps made up of, as we found in enemy documents, "physically superior soldiers, sports personalities, and young men from wealthy or politically-significant American families."

In mid-March, after two months of being on the front line, I took leave in Florence. By that time, Roosevelt, Churchill, and Stalin had signed the Yalta Agreement, which planned for the defeat of Germany. The end was getting really close. I wrote to Wetzel:

> I'm writing from the Anglo-American Hotel in Florence which is now a 5th Army Officers Rest Hotel—it's really nice. What used to be accepted seems like splendid nobility now. For the first time since arrival in this country I've been sleeping between sheets with even hot water easily available (in morning only).
>
> Yep, I've seen my share (already) of action—and now feel that it was enough—wished the Jerries could say that. It is unusual the feeling I first had (and others too) when I went into the first action. My first feeling was—of all things—*curiosity.* The job I have naturally doesn't place me in the forefront of movement (in fact, I like

the rear echelon place I occupy initially). Anyway, after the initial attack the morning following I went up to the newly gained ground. There, I saw my first dead Jerries laid in a row of 5. And all that possessed me was a great curiosity. It wasn't until later in the day as I moved back that a faint nausea reached into me. Can't explain it anymore than that. Subsequent action has found me less curious and more alert. . . . I was hit as hard as anyone about the death of 2nd Lt. William S. Ryberg. I had talked to him the day of his death. Right now, I [am] sweating over the letter which I'm being allowed to write to his folks.

I had a hard time writing that letter. I had known Bill when we worked on the yearbook together at Bryant Junior High School, as fraternity brothers at the university, and throughout basic training and OCS. I always remember the date of his death: March 5, the day after my birthday. We, along with several others, had celebrated my twenty-third birthday two days early, on March 2, with a cherished bottle of scotch because we knew that on my birthday we would be on an attack. He had guts. He was leading his platoon during a night attack on Hill 813. They crossed the ridge and moved down a long open slope—about eight hundred yards—into a draw. Everything the enemy had opened up on them: light machine guns, burp guns, mortars, rifles, and rifle grenades. He and his men ran down the draw and flanked the positions, with a small ridge sticking out of the draw on their right. Out in front, he led them onto the ridge to flank the position on the hillside. Out in the open he became a silhouetted target, and the machine gun fire killed him instantly, as well as two privates.

I was just a few hundred yards away. One of his men came over to tell me that Lieutenant Ryberg had been killed. He pointed to a nearby tree where his body lay. I often regretted that I didn't go over. I just didn't want to. You're always fighting your emotions anyway when you're in combat, and you want not to crumble, you want not to get all charged up by the sight of a lifelong friend. I had seen a lot of dead people, but I didn't go over and look at him.

When I returned to the States, a year after his death, I went immediately to see Bill's parents. Bill was their only son, their hope to follow his prominent father in business. Bill's father criticized Roosevelt and blamed him for the war and for the death of his son. They were very bitter, particularly his mother. She left the room. I sat with Bill's father looking out over Salt Lake Valley from their lovely home on the upper east bench in the semidarkness. They never turned the lights on. It got darker and darker. It was very eerie. I was eager to get out of there.

Always on the soldiers' minds were home and sex, usually in tandem, of course. But my driving thought was *food*—that was supreme! Yes, food—we were *always* hungry. I was constantly on the lookout for food of any kind. Having a jeep made it easier in the Italian countryside. Sergeant Belcher remarks—to this day—"We never went hungry because your Italian was pretty good." I looked for bread and sausages, knowing that most of the Apennine mountain farmers had hidden supplies of these homemade products about their farms. Bread was rarely fresh, but the sausages and jars of peppers and preserves were dug out, literally, to give to the *Americanos,* whom they loved—at least to me. I still love bread and sausages. The compartments in my other vehicle, a three-quarter-ton truck, were amply stashed with food—occasionally even a bottle of vino. Our C rations (small cans, usually of Spam) were always available—easily portable and good for snack eating, but not much else. Today, I still look at Spam fondly on the market shelves, but not to buy. K rations—dried packages of food—were the last resort, which I was determined never to reach. On April 15—the day after our final attack began—two of my men found some large gallon tins in the side basement of a semidestroyed farmhouse. A smelly dead horse lay nearby, and smoke from explosions was all about. No matter. Food! Using a bayonet, I quickly sliced open the top of one of the tins. A gray pulp mixture looked up at me. I gingerly put a finger in it to taste. It was lard. Too bad . . . there were so many of them!

A few times a field kitchen would show up, and the word went out to nearby units to come quickly for a hot meal. One day the site of the army kitchen was right in the sanctuary of a recently bombed-out Catholic church. Why here? I heard some soldiers murmur. Why not a few yards away, one man said, pointing to a roofless building nearby. A passing major commanded—"Just eat!" We did, as Italian peasants came up to kneel and pray where the altar lay broken. I was uncomfortable. They too were hungry. We gave them food, which was a worldly supplement to their prayers.

About the fifth or sixth night of that final attack, the Germans started retreating in some mountain sections. Our orders were simple—

"Keep going." Easy to say, but we were still in the mountains longing for the descent down onto flat country. I received an order from battalion headquarters to rest the night. This we did by taking over a farmhouse occupied by two old Italian sisters in black. (Hindsight: They were about fifty-five years old—old to a twenty-three-year-old.) We were friendly and I apologized for us, eight or so American soldiers, for barging into their home. They had little food. One of my sergeants left, asking my permission to take the jeep. Before long, he came in carrying a twenty-pound tin of coffee, U.S. Army stock, plus a canned ham! I had never seen such a large can of coffee—even in my Capri Restaurant days! Coffee was made. One sister told me that was the first real coffee they had since Italy went into Ethiopia in 1936. We left the entire can with the sisters the next morning—with our compliments and their kisses.

Of the six University of Utah friends who went through basic training and OCS together and were assigned to the Tenth, two were killed: Bill Ryberg and Ray Slight. Ray Slight, a quiet, good-looking, and intelligent guy, was killed on April 14, 1945. That same day senator-to-be Robert Dole was gravely wounded. (Next to my unit was the famed 442nd Regiment of Japanese Americans, and it was only a few days later that senator-to-be Daniel Inouye was badly hit, losing his arm.) Don Fox and Gordy Anderson were wounded slightly. Veldon Larson and I were untouched. Nonetheless, April 14 was the day I should have been killed. That day we launched our final major battle that concluded with the end of the war in Italy.

Our role in finishing the war was to drive the Germans out of the Apennines and take the wide Po River valley, the breadbasket for their armies. We watched the magnitude of the task grow as more and more equipment arrived: tanks, tank destroyers, armored artillery, artillery field pieces, and heavy equipment of all types. While it gave us some reassurance, it presaged things to come. At the same time, we heard plenty of news from the other battlefields in Europe. From the radio we knew that the U.S. Army was moving rapidly in Germany, with just seventy-six miles to reach Berlin. All of us knew it was almost over.

April 14 was a bad day because the Germans were waiting for us. We aimed to hit the enemy forces at the center of their defense. To make it worse, the terrain was steeper and rougher than anything we had seen. Steep, lightly wooded mountains interspersed with bare, rocky cliffs and boulders. Our division spearheaded the offensive, and my First Battalion led the column of battalions.

Big attacks start with loud explosions. First, the planes drop bombs on the enemy positions. Then the artillery in the rear and the other ground weapons begin firing. Once you hear all this—the din of bombs, artillery, and supporting heavy machine guns—you feel the ground shake and watch in wonder as the dust and smoke settle over the hills, and you know your turn is drawing near. It seems impossible that anything could live through such a barrage, but as soon as it stopped and we approached, the Germans crawled out of their holes and opened fire.

We were in a ravine, trying to advance, when we heard the shell that was meant for us coming in. We all hit the ground simultaneously. I could feel a couple of men across my legs. I heard and *felt* a "whump." I looked up and the shell had landed within an arm's length, about half of it in the earth. I could see it. I could reach it. It didn't go off. I said, "My God," and I jumped up and ran down the gully. We all did. We were not waiting around to see if it exploded. Right away, I began to wonder what it meant. I've often thought about that. I've thought about it a thousand times. Is there a selection process here?

Combat is hard to describe. Too much has been written about it, and most of it is not understood, I'm afraid, unless you've actually been through that type of experience. The public is sometimes misled as to what a hero is. Survival is of course such an instinct in nature that, usually, no one really plans to be a hero. By and large most people are anxious to keep alive. So you try to figure out how you can do that. How do you stay alive? There is no answer. Yes, I felt luck was a factor. I also felt that you're going to survive if it's not your time to go. The shell that didn't go off—that gave me a certain confidence that maybe it wasn't my time yet. And you keep waiting and wondering, because people all around you are getting hurt or killed.

I thought of fear as much as dying. I agree with the veteran's quote in Stephen Ambrose's book *Citizen Soldiers*, "My worst fear was of screwing up or showing my fear to those around me." I remember now—as though it was this morning—leading part of my platoon the second day of the final attack, April 15. I carried a carbine (a small rifle of questionable strength), a small backpack, some hand grenades, and a pistol. I walked ahead of my men. My platoon sergeant, Jim Belcher, was about twenty to thirty feet behind. The other men, about six or eight of them, were scattered. It was cold in the early morning Apennines. We walked through a large open space, three to four hundred yards at most, toward the forested area ahead. Tall trees, all close together. My scalp started to throb and tingle, and the fear in my mind started to affect my body movements. I pushed myself, walking forward. We had to get an answer. Were the Jerries in those woods? Waiting? Waiting for us to get closer where we would become easy targets? I forced myself forward. I didn't want to be a sitting duck, but I was and I knew it.

I already had an experience with one man where fear overtook him. He had little pieces of shrapnel in the back of his jacket and his shirt, but no obvious deadly wounds. We couldn't see anything so we congratulated him and told him he was lucky. *He* was convinced he was going to die. He did not believe us. He did not hear us. He died of shock. Fear plus shock equaled death. We saw it happening, and we couldn't talk him out of it. It's an upsetting experience. He shouldn't have died. When you see it happening you wonder, when is it going to hit me?

As I crept toward the line of trees, I struggled to keep the fear under control. I was the platoon leader, for hell's sake. We walked slowly, crouching where possible. Listening, listening. Hearing nothing. Seeing nothing. Good signs, but were they? As we got closer to the woods, I began to feel better for some reason. The panic began to recede. The tingling in the scalp disappeared. I began to think they were not there. A few more yards . . . I was correct. The Jerries were still in retreat. We were safe, at least for the moment.

By the third day of the attack we traveled through the hills that led to the broad, flat Po River valley and penetrated the enemy's second line of defense. With the "breakthrough" the enemy retreated in confusion. Without any definite "front line" some Germans surrendered easily; some were stubborn and fanatical. In one situation a real battle erupted at the head of Lake Garda, where a German SS "retread" center was training selected noncommissioned SS men for last-minute combat. In an early morning attack, we captured "two to three hundred Super Nazis," as my colonel, Ross Wilson, called them. Those men had maniacal eyes staring off, and they stood rigid-straight in their fancy SS uniforms. We saw these absolutely unbelievable human beings. Fox and I talked about these people—how one spat in the face of the German-speaking A Company commander when questioned. These Nazis—the only ones we had personal contact with—were so dedicated, so twisted and indoctrinated philosophically, that their souls were owned by this omnipotent belief, this fanatic culture.

We reached the low banks of the wide Po River before daylight on April 23. We were exhausted, but our morale was high. Our success opened up the way through the mountains, and tanks and supplies followed with ease. In every village the *paesani* lifted our spirits with their cheers, wine, bread, cheese, onions, and embraces.

Crossing the Po would be an unknown because the Germans could be well fortified on the other side. The combat engineers brought up the boats with oars and motors for the crossing. As usual, I had to choose which company I would attach my unit to—do I stay on that south shore or go on those first boats going north? For some reason I felt I had to go on those boats. Don Fox was there with his Company A, and we went with them. We clambered down the bank, went across this big, wide river in the first wave of boats, not knowing what we were going to face. We expected that the Jerries would be on the other side. During the crossing we faced relatively light fire.

We reached the other side and found the whole situation had changed. The Germans had just left. Perhaps they knew the war was over because the Allies had crossed the Rhine River and taken Cologne. We had them on the run. Their stuff was scattered all over. Fox, several men, and I went into an empty underground bunker—slowly. The Germans had occupied it for months, comfortably entrenched. I saw a Luger pistol on the floor. We had been warned that these things would be booby-trapped, but still we were all inveterate collectors. I put a branch through the guard section of the pistol, walked some distance away, and pulled it carefully, waiting for it to explode. Nothing. I took the Luger as a souvenir (but I had to leave it in Vienna when I came back to the United States).

We came out on the bank and looked back across to the south side of the river. To our horror, we saw all the trees being shattered by anti-aircraft weaponry. The Germans, downriver a mile or so, had lowered their antiaircraft guns and were shooting into the trees to explode their shells. This debris poured down and caused great casualties on our troops. We looked at it and at each other.

From there on out everything moved fast. In no time we took over trucks and captured prisoners. Nobody wanted to walk anymore, and we looked for anything on wheels or hooves—enemy trucks, motorcycles, bicycles, and horses. We had our own vehicles but not enough. My men "acquired" a couple of trucks on the side of the road. As we went north, the Germans were coming south by the hundreds, even thousands. They didn't know where to go, and we didn't know where to send them except to motion them to the rear. When you see the enemy surrendering by the thousands you know the war is over.

That was the finale. Mussolini was killed on April 28. Berlin fell. Hitler committed suicide. The war ended in Italy on May 2. Germany surrendered on May 7, and the Allies declared victory in Europe. The surrender announcement found me eating a steak with Don Fox and other A Company officers—our first real American-style steak. In spite of expectation, the war's end surprised me. The celebrations were soft in noise but loud in spirit. As I wrote to another friend, "it seemed we took it in stride yet there was a difference I know in all. It was inside, in the mind and in the heart." We didn't really celebrate like the Italians. We weren't coldhearted; we just felt like saying, "Good." Like everyone else who came out alive and unwounded, I was thankful and felt only sorrow for the great many who didn't make it. The occasion of the war's end found me writing a letter to Wetzel:

> The two weeks of the drive? It's hard to remember days, but there are plenty of instances where terrific enemy artillery and mortar fire had me wondering *not whether I would get hurt,* but, rather, *how bad.* . . . I'm happy to say not one of my platoon was killed. . . . The days were fast—the hours slow. You can't describe battle of this sort. I've seen every type of wound and all shapes of dead men. And even now, those days are growing darker in memory. *That*—is the surprising thing. Simply, everything can seem to be normal again so quickly. Why even the "paisans" were moving back into their homes even as we just pushed the Jerries back.

We were all very aware that the Pacific war was still hot. I did not want to go with the division, which was going to go home to the States, get retrained, and fight Japan. I had done my bit in combat and in the field. I wanted to get into the military government of occupation. In so doing, I was able to get transferred into the Fifteenth Army Group, located in Verona, Italy. When I reported to the G-1 (personnel) office, the G-1 himself, Brigadier General William C. McMahon, happened to be there. He asked me a few questions (Did you play football, lieutenant?) and then told a major to assign me to that office! The major asked when I had been promoted to first lieutenant. A "field promotion," I answered. Soon we moved the headquarters to Austria, and the name was changed to "Headquarters U.S. Forces, Austria." We were supposed to go to Vienna, but it wasn't ready to receive the substantial organization, so instead we first moved to Salzburg. General Mark W. Clark, the four-star commanding general in charge of the Fifteenth Army Group in Italy and now commanding general of Headquarters U.S. Forces, Austria, put his offices in the Archbishop's Palace, historically the center of power for the whole province of Salzburg. We stayed there through the end of 1945 and in January 1946 moved to Vienna.

While still in Verona—in July 1945—I went to General McMahon and asked permission to visit my division, which was returning home. Mostly, I wanted to see Don Fox, and a few of the others with whom I had seen battle. He immediately said yes and told me how to get a flight to Naples, which was my first. We had a good visit. The night I left the division, Don and I got pretty emotional. We had become closer than any two brothers. They say that soldiers in training and combat develop closer friendships and ties than men in any other walk of life. By the time you come out of combat, you really feel you've seen a different side of life that you never want to see again. At the same time, you feel you've done it, you've shared it together. It is so unique that the only people who understand it are those who were there with you. It doesn't require conversation. For Don and me that is true. We met at the university in the fraternity and were close friends. The relationship intensified in the army. We went to OCS together and were both assigned to the 10th Mountain Infantry Division. We saw each other constantly in combat. We were Utah boys. We shared news of home, and I consistently saved all the *Salt Lake Tribune* newspapers sent by my dad until Don read them.

I saw Don's greatest change in dealing with men. As we were sailing to Italy he was so troubled with his self-confidence, especially in his ability to handle men, that it affected him almost noticeably. We knew platoon leaders didn't live very long, and he had great doubts about himself and his ability to be a platoon leader. He expressed it a lot to me, and I encouraged him not to think that way. I told him he could do it. That didn't mean that I didn't have doubts, too. Not only doubts, but fear.

During our months in battle, sometimes I would look for him and we would visit. One night we were standing by a haystack. The bottom of the haystack had been dug out, and the Germans had used it as their living quarters for two or three months. Some of our men were in the bottom of the haystack, and Don and I stood on the side of it. We suddenly became aware that Germans were shooting at us. In the growing dusk, we became visible targets. We quickly moved and Don got hurt slightly. We kidded him about his Purple Heart, because it was little more than a slight injury.

Don saw very intense fighting. In one particular fight, he led half of his Third Platoon down into a valley and assaulted the machine gunners. With cover from company fire, they advanced directly into the face of the machine gunners for about five hundred yards. A couple men were hit, but the rest kept going down into the grassy valley. Assaulting the positions, they killed six Nazis and took four prisoners, and the rest fled. As the regiment history says, "This was a brilliant maneuver." Don received the Silver Star for his action here.

As a rifle company officer, he was the driving force necessary to keep men going all the time—*that* is a job. After the second day of the last push, his platoon was down to seven men. They consolidated and he became executive officer (second ranking officer in a rifle company and far and away the biggest job in a rifle company in combat). He drove and led the boys wonderfully. His company suffered the heaviest losses in the division: 27 dead, 114 wounded. He ended up as acting company commander. He was moved from being a platoon leader of 40 men to executive officer, and then as acting captain of the company.

As we hugged good-bye, I could tell he was very satisfied. He had emerged. He had a strong inner confidence in place of the doubts of only a few months earlier. Always a religious man, he now exuded a quiet aura of peace. We had agreed that we were lucky to be alive, but more significantly, we had done well, much better than perhaps either one of us thought that we could do.

Don and the 10th Mountain Division left for the war against Japan. The guys in the division sailed into some luck: as they crossed the Atlantic, the A-bombs went off and Japan surrendered. World War II was over on August 15, 1945. Upon arrival in the States, they were immediately discharged from the army. From there, Don became the good solid American citizen that he is to this day: a devout Mormon, always discreet, with great ideals, a wonderfully soft and understanding person, but he's never forgotten his trial-and-test period. That's why when he sees me, he still hugs me. To this day he is one of my very closest of friends. (Don Fox died on January 14, 2001, after a long illness—but he never changed.)

And I wasn't unhappy for myself. My transfer initially kept me from heading for the Pacific, and now it kept me in the army. The army occupation duty would teach me a great deal, but my combat experience had taught me something about myself. I had proved to myself that I had either developed a sense of leadership or improved on that which I had. I became convinced that I was able to manage people in a way that made me acceptable to them as well as to the job that had to be done. Some of the lessons I had learned don't translate in postwar life—I am living in a different hierarchy of values. In the years of ordinary life that followed, I worried, felt anxiety, sometimes lost heart, but facing fear in the raw sense has never come up again.

SIX

MAKING THE GRADE

I WENT FROM being a foot soldier in combat commanding a small group of men with a limited future to suddenly finding
myself in the headquarters filled with some sixteen generals and dozens
of full colonels. From my desk in the general's outer office, I saw everything I wanted to know about structure—the hierarchy of what the U.S.
Army was all about. I found my first encounter with personnel management on such a large scale at Headquarters U.S. Forces, Austria, fascinating. I gave Wetzel my unedited view:

> When I think about home it seems to stop there—at home. Some-
> times, it's with a bit of effort that I remember the activities, people,
> and conditions peculiar to the "U" days. . . . For, like our military
> occupational government, there often exists confusion. Idealisti-
> cally, we know what we want but (as always) in practical execution
> there are so many factors working at cross purposes. I am still deter-
> mined to go back to school; how little we know is thrown before me
> every day. Academic knowledge has no real place here it seems—
> only so much as is necessary to help sell your personality. In a good
> many cases, neither of these (personality or knowledge) have con-
> tributed to the present position of the people of affluence in this

headquarters. Good old school and seniority! Wetz, you would be amazed and disgusted at this hierarchy of army brass-heads. We have here a structure whose architectural absurdity is like that of a whirling top built for permanence. Slowly, ever so slowly, the motion is slowing and sometime in the near future the whole edifice will begin toppling. Then, the scramble to get out and away to the safety of another like-built organization will be tragically comic to watch. . . . Mine is a first rate opportunity to watch the Army's post war attempt to tie in military government with the army reduction program. The result is a muddle of confusion filled with false starts and wrong roads. Naturally, most of this is expected.

Thousands of American soldiers were being sent home for reassignment or discharge, while others were being sent to reorganized army occupation units in Europe. My sector of G-1 handled officer assignment, including stateside regular army (permanent) officers looking—often desperately—for a good job in Europe. Otherwise, they were discharged. Most placements had to do with field-grade officers, that is, majors, lieutenant colonels, and colonels, with a few exceptions. For example, one day we received word of First Lieutenant John Eisenhower's assignment to our group, and I had to find a spot for him. Of course, that was pretty easy with a name like Eisenhower (in this case, the son of the supreme Allied commander). We found a place for him in a very secure office, a part of Vienna-area command. One day, a tall, thin young first lieutenant reported to my desk for assignment. Without looking up my first words were, "Come down from there and sit down."
After I asked his name, he replied, "Eisenhower."
I said, "We've been waiting for you."
We talked for a few minutes about his West Point roommate, Doniphan Carter, a fellow platoon leader of mine in B Company of the Eighty-seventh Mountain Infantry Regiment. I then escorted him to the front office, where the executive officer, a colonel, sat as I introduced him. When the colonel heard the name, he practically jumped out of his seat, his back ramrod-straight, and said, "You look just like your father." I had enough of that, turned, and quickly left the room.
The military lifestyle had its own culture. Humor was standardized and safe, and flip remarks were risky. Body movements were observed. "Kissing ass" was a common phrase and ridiculed, but nonetheless

practiced by many. I learned the full meaning of RHIP: Rank Has Its Privileges. My colleagues all outranked me. Though I occupied a lieutenant colonel's spot, my rank was only that of a first lieutenant. The tables of organization did not even show a place for a first lieutenant at this level of the organization, and it would stay that way. All promotions had been frozen because hundreds of officers of all ranks were looking for jobs. (The man whose job I was filling, a West Point lieutenant colonel, was in the United States looking for a stateside military assignment. He never came back.) It was a friendly and easy place to work, casual as much as rank would permit. Brigadier General William C. McMahon, the big boss as well as my immediate boss, was a very superior officer. The office saluting requirement was minimized quickly by General McMahon. I learned the meaning of the word *professional,* and he epitomized it. He also fulfilled the "gentleman" part of the well-known phrase.

The view from the top gave me a new and greater perspective on life. I observed the treatment of the people in this country we were occupying, and how they were treated affected me individually. It exposed me to the complexity of the world. I had a lot to learn and realized I was not going to be flashing across the scene as someone new or smart. I couldn't move that fast and the pressures were too big. I wouldn't get that experience back home.

We worked intensively and had little time for diversions in the cold Vienna winter. The orders of the day banned fraternization with the Austrians (though these restrictions were ignored by both officers and enlisted men). In my free time I thought of attending law school later that year. In my mind, law school, the pinnacle of educational achievement, lent itself to the business world, economic independence, and my primary interest, public service. I counted my army discharge "points" and realized, unless the criteria changed (always possible), it would be at least a year and a half before my discharge. Despite the long shot of attending school that fall, I prepared for whatever opportunity came my way. Success, as I see it, consists of guiding your own life and reacting to the coincidences that impact your life, thus redirecting it. I applied to a number of schools from Vienna: Harvard, Georgetown, Stanford, Duke, and the University of Chicago.

When I thought of my friends back home, many who had started their families, I felt older and a little left out. I kept in touch with

Rebecca, the Wyoming girl in Texas. We wrote quite often, but the six thousand miles between us diminished serious consideration. At the same time, I grew increasingly worried about my dad's health. For all these reasons I itched to get back home and get started again, yet within myself I felt a moderation of my fire-burning ambition. Combat had a sobering effect on me. I had been under fire and I felt confident: I was alive and eventually I would go home. Combat showed me how fleeting life can be.

Earlier in my assignment, in October 1945, I asked General McMahon for permission to visit my relatives in southern Italy. He allowed me to do so, and he added a personal chore to his consent. A staff sergeant and I were to drive a jeep down to Naples where we exchanged the jeep for a huge thirty-foot French-built Ford open-air touring sedan (with a top), which had been confiscated from the Germans. It all sounded quite wonderful and exciting. We would drive this huge automobile down to the toe of Italy to visit my relatives.

For the first time, in my eyes, I would see my grandmother, who left the United States when I was two years old. She lived in Calabria with my mother's two American-born sisters. They all had moved to Italy in 1924 and lived in this same area: Rosa (Rose in the United States) was in the small hilltop village of Celico, where Rocco Arnone, my grandfather, had been born and raised; the other sister, Lena, was living in the big city (ninety thousand people) of Cosenza, twelve kilometers away. They both spoke English without accent (they graduated from St. Mary's of the Wasatch High School in Salt Lake City). Lena was called "the American." She had a buoyant personality and enjoyed life. Her voice startled me; it reminded me of my mother's voice, but Lena didn't have my mother's pessimism.

Everybody in Celico was a relative, and they all knew the Arnone boy was in town. I shook all the hands and had meals with them. Everyone said I looked like my grandfather and my uncle Carmie. My aunt Rosa and her husband, Uncle Tony (a U.S. veteran of World War I!), served as interpreters for the U.S. Army, so we could talk in English. I visited my grandmother Carmela Mastroianni Arnone, a tiny bundle of energy, dressed in the customary black. She was mourning the death of my grandfather Rocco, in October, just eight months before my visit. In fact, black seemed the standard color for the women of Celico because everyone was in perpetual mourning for some family member.

Grandma proudly took me into her house, the first house with an indoor toilet in the village of Celico. They had built it in 1924 after returning to Italy with the money my grandfather had saved from his coal mining and saloons. A lovely little house, it had incredible views for miles and miles in every direction. My grandfather had loved it and from all accounts was the big man of the village—both in size and in influence—until his death. My grandmother took me to a dresser, opened a drawer, and proudly showed some savings. Tragically, she didn't realize how inflation had already devalued her money. Instead of the many dollars it once represented, it had already fallen to a few cents per lira. Nonetheless, she was happy, she had money, she had her house, and her daughter Rosa lived nearby.

These peasant people lived in a satisfactory fashion, no starvation, though limited to a tinier diet with less choice. The Allied troops—principally American—were their biggest suppliers of foodstuff. The cooking facilities often stood at the edge of the house—half in and half out —a broiler-style combination for baking bread and grilling food. Chickens were often a part of the house in a lower level. I imagined my mother as a young girl growing up there. I better understood her materialistic nature. Ideas were unimportant—money governed one's survival.

I saw a very tough, hardy people who had lived there for two thousand years. I thought, the whole ancient world has rolled over this place: the Phoenicians, the Greeks (many wonderful Greek monuments still stand, and the language of the Greek Orthodox rites is still observed), then the Romans, and later the Normans (who drove out the Saracens). Barbarossa became Frederick II there. My relatives in Cosenza talked about Alaric, king of the Visigoths, who died in A.D. 410 (after conquering Rome) and was buried in the riverbed of the nearby Busento River. People are still searching for the treasure supposedly buried with him.

Though a complex history and difficult to grasp, it meant a great deal to them. Years later, in 1977, Lena's son, a banker, introduced me to his schoolteacher wife. The first thing he told me was, "She's an Albanian *(Albanese)*."

When?

"Well, she came from the nearby Albanese village."

When?

"Well, they've been here (Italy!) three or four hundred years."

These mountain villagers would stay unchanged, if they had their choice. It illuminated my mother's feeling of inferiority in the American society of upward mobility.

My first night in Celico I did not feel well. My aunt Rosa uttered a phrase in Calabrese *(malòcchio),* which means the "evil eye," in other words, "too many good things are being said about you." I had come in an American hero, and the whole town was happy to see me. Because of this, she said, an evil spirit—which includes envy—made me sick. She cautioned me to be on the lookout for it. She requested my belt or tie. Forget her American birth. Forget her education in an American high school. I understood only because my mother had mentioned this when I was young. They took my belt into the other room, and, using oil and water, they made some mumbo-jumbo prayers and statements over it. The idea was to chase away the bad spirits. I related this incident to my mother when I got home, and she nodded; she remembered. The beliefs remained intact, and, most interesting, her sister Rosa had accepted it after moving there at age twenty. They were utterly convinced they understood my ailment and how to treat it: these symbolic ablutions were the answer.

Next day, feeling better, we decided to depart Celico for the large city of Cosenza, only to discover our exotic touring car was an enormous lemon. We couldn't even get it started. Sergeant Piersa and I got out and started to push the monster car a short distance to where it would roll on down the six or eight miles to Cosenza. My cousin Frank was standing by, wearing a suit and tie. He had been a *tenente* (lieutenant) in the Italian Army, and was also a *doctore di commercio* (doctor of commerce). Holding his cigarette aloft, he watched us, and then he got excited. He started talking to me in Italian, not the dialect. "You know you're a lieutenant. You can't push this car."

"If we don't, who will?" I answered. "And what are you going to do?"

We all pushed the car. We didn't get it started, but we got it onto the downward slope and coasted to the city. A mechanic worked on it, and we thought we had it repaired. After we left Cosenza the car really acted up. We found the roads north to Naples narrow though quite decent. At one time in the recent past they had been filled with the Allied military-supply vehicles. We saw few if any cars now, but we passed quite a few donkeys and horse carts. At some point we realized we were in trouble; we couldn't stop our lemon because the brakes were out. We had no way to even slow this thirty-foot behemoth. Up ahead we saw a man on his donkey-pulled cart, moving slowly down the center of the road. I then discovered our horn was out. I pressed as far left as possible, but there was not enough room for us. As we flew past him our right fender hit his wheel. He spun around and spilled his cargo of tree limbs on the ground. The collision slowed us to a stop. We were so upset and he was very angry, and luckily unhurt. We loaded his cart up. If he had been over another foot we would not have hit him. The impact ripped our right fender six feet back. We tied down the flopping fender and drove to a U.S. military-depot motor center near Naples.

The U.S. Army mechanics patched it up enough for us to make it to Austria, but they forewarned us: the car needed a lot of work. By the time we got to Bologna it was limping some more. The axle had slipped, and one of the rear springs had slipped against the wheel. I found another motor pool. The car had to be jacked up and the springs replaced and bolted in. I was suddenly struck with an intense pain over my side and belly. A quick trip to a U.S. hospital in Bologna brought a diagnosis of pleurisy, and they taped my body. "Rest," said the doctor. I couldn't rest; I had to return.

Against the increasing odds, we finally arrived in Vienna (our head-quarters had relocated from Salzburg) and drove the car directly to an army garage. I reported to General McMahon and told him simply he probably would not want the car. I related our tale and he was disappointed. All I remember now is our refrain—"If only we had a jeep, a wonderful American jeep."

I enjoyed Austria's history and culture, though I became cold to the Austrians. We met many in our daily living as well as in the easy violation of the no-fraternization injunction. One young educated woman consort of a fellow officer consistently proclaimed that they were not Nazis and that Hitler had taken them in. She was careless and referred to the Jewish "menace" in Austria. No Austrian ever seemed to mention that Hitler was born in Linz, Austria. Over and over we heard that the real enemy was Russia, and that we had fought the wrong people. Years later I read that although Austria composed only 8 percent of the population of Hitler's Reich, they made up 14 percent of SS members and 40 percent of those involved in the Nazis' killing operation.

I took advantage of my situation and traveled as much as time would allow. In late March 1946, as I prepared for a visit to Budapest, I received a telegram giving me emergency home leave because my father required a very serious operation. I flew to Paris, boarded a liberty ship to New York, took a soldiers' train to Salt Lake, and arrived at Fort Douglas on April 16. I reported in and was discharged, effective immediately. Just like that! After three years and eleven days, I was out of the army.

I surprised my parents by showing up unannounced on the doorstep, as they had no idea when I would arrive. My father, much to my surprise, appeared a relatively fit man. He had undergone gall bladder surgery, a very serious operation in those days. We all posed for a picture the next day with everyone dressed up. I had no civilian clothes, so I wore my uniform (that was the last day I ever wore it, April 17, 1946). I'm so glad we did that because it's the best picture of my family at that point in our lives.

Throughout the summer of 1946 I waited idly in Salt Lake City, my home, though nothing had changed. My brother Sam married Peggy Lettieri, a university classmate and daughter of a prominent Main Street merchant. Two pictures of the wedding party in my dad's Capri Restaurant show the extended family, about fifty people. I am seated between two tables wearing an absent look—the restlessness of that summer. My dream of law school was about to be realized. At the time I thought the army had slowed me down. It took a few years before I fully realized that those army years were a tremendous preparation for what was to come. World War II had one purpose: to help all humans live decent and free lives. But the summer gave me ample time to reflect on my service in the 10th Mountain Division and the Headquarters U.S. Forces, Austria. For one thing, I no longer thought of survival, but only of personal improvement.

My mother remained the same. Her same question, "And now what are you going to do?" dismayed me. I had never wavered in my decision to go to law school—since the age of twelve. In the seventh grade, we filled out a questionnaire about our life's ambitions. Forty years later, the *Salt Lake Tribune* dug out the responses and published some of them to compare reality with the dreams of youth. The newspaper article singled out my own response, which was "government man." The difference between my mother's idea of life and mine was that she thought to be the man in his mule-drawn cart was fine. I was dreaming of the American jeep.

During that long summer of waiting, I worked for the Office of

Manpower Administration, a federal wartime agency. My job as an occupational analyst was to write job descriptions, which went into the dictionary of occupations (put out by the U.S. Department of Labor). For example, I remember writing about a "lead burner": "a person who uses an acetylene torch." I was bored. When I hear ten-year-old kids today say, "I'm bored," I remember that I thought that way once—when I was twenty-four years old. I don't like to linger. I cook that way. I move around in the kitchen too fast and bump into things sometimes. Today, I have slowed down a lot, but I still have an inner feeling of wanting to move, move. I wasn't always easy to walk with because of my pace. I'm shocked when young people walk by me now. How can that be?

I dated Rebecca, who had returned to Jackson, Wyoming. But life in Salt Lake brought back thoughts of Norma. We had broken up three years previously, but the totality of what had happened was still hard for me to accept. I often replayed the night of April 4, 1943, the night before I went into active duty.

While waiting for the summer to pass, I heard from the schools to which I had applied. Georgetown, George Washington University, Duke, Stanford, and Chicago sent me either admission letters or very encouraging replies. I wanted to go to Washington, D.C., because Washington was where the action was and it had opportunities for employment. In the immediate post–World War II days, law school graduates scrambled to find employment and rarely hung out their "own shingle." My first commercial air flight came next. After two stops, I arrived in the nation's capital and, yes, I was excited. For a week or so, I stayed with a lovely old Irish American family living near Chevy Chase, but then decided to move within easy walking distance of the old Georgetown Law School—at 509 E Street Northwest—a one bedroom with a hallway bathroom, a single electric burner, plus an icebox with twenty-five pounds delivered weekly! The contrast was too much. This throwback made it easy to move to upper Connecticut Avenue with a classmate, Phillip DePumpo, for the luxury of a complete two-bedroom apartment with a kitchen and refrigerator.

I immediately liked Washington, D.C. The city has so much variety, yet beauty accompanies it all. As I wrote to Wetzel, "This is a first rate city in which a person could undoubtedly get a feeling of belonging once he got into the circle. However, that is obviously a long, and probably tedious job. Like all others, I don't expect to like the weather."

I compared Georgetown's and George Washington University's law schools and chose Georgetown because of its more distinguished reputation as the nation's fifth oldest and, at that time, with more state and Supreme Court justices and national representatives than any other school, with the exception of Harvard. I kept Wetzel posted on my progress: "School is coming along okay. I'm not doing brilliantly, but hope to be better than average, naturally. However, I'm frank to myself in realizing that there are several men in the class who have natural brilliance and reflect it constantly in their work. . . . I've never been to school before in a comparable situation."

Servicemen from the navy, Marine Corps, and army filled the classrooms. They impressed me and intimidated me with their East Coast educations, mostly at Jesuit schools. They seemed more polished than my Utah confreres or what I had experienced in the army. At twenty-four years old, I was somewhat younger than the average age of twenty-seven. My college education had been sharply shy of the full four years, with many courses lacking. I decided the other students' basic intelligence was no better, but their education was more comprehensive and thorough. It was my first experience with such sharp intellects. I no longer felt so confident about my own academic leadership. It challenged my confidence encountering such a crackerjack group of top-flight men. If the perspective I gained at Headquarters U.S. Forces, Austria, toned down my ambition, law school drilled that modesty into me all the more.

I worked extremely hard at my studies. I qualified and wrote a piece for the *Georgetown Law Journal*, which is the mark that you look for in law school. We spent hours in the various nearby federal courthouses. For diversion, we would attend hearings of the Senate and House of Representatives. I did not have to work because my tuition was paid by the Veteran's Education Act. The school allowed us to study straight through without a summer break, and being in my usual hurry, I studied straight through from September 1946 to the fall of 1948. The hot and humid D.C. summer broiled us in the old redbrick Georgetown Law School building with no air-conditioning. I stayed in the top 20 percent, which was satisfactory but not up to my expectations.

During Christmas 1946, Rebecca visited me in Washington. Shortly thereafter I announced to Wetzel that we were engaged. "I say that calmly, but feel funny inside," I wrote. "The more I see of women, the more she satisfies, and the more I want to boast about her." A measured statement without much confidence, it fitted my mood of the day when I saw friends all about me getting married. Rebecca began to collect all those things that girls collect before the big event: sheets, towels, clothes, even records and albums.

In Washington I experienced our country's polyglot mixture. As an Italian American I was more mainstream. All around me people had names like mine, and there were numerous Polish and Irish names as well. I met people of all races, religions, and colors. At that time, we had no African Americans in the law school. One day in 1947, in a lecture on jurisprudence and ethics by the regent, Father Lucy, someone asked why the school had no black students. He gave a rationale about what the alumni and other financial supporters would think. The whole class— about two hundred men—hooted him. Actually, I would characterize it as a roar of disapproval from the all-white audience. I was proud of that.

My personal perspective grew one day when I went across the street to a Woolworth's store to get a Coke. I sat down at the long counter, which had some twenty-five seats, almost all unoccupied. At the end of the counter, standing, were about ten people. They were African American. Drinking, conversing—standing. The seats were all there, untaken. They could not sit on the counter seats! The rawness of the Jim Crow sanctions hit me for the first time. While I was in the army I had seen the separation of the black troops from the white troops at Fort Benning infantry school, had drunk from separate water fountains outside of Fort Benning, and had contact with the all-black Ninety-second Infantry Division in northern Italy—but none of these hit me as that scene did that day. I was a civilian now, and segregation took on an entirely new meaning. I began to understand discrimination in its fullest form, real discrimination, not the subtle pressures that I felt growing up as an Italian American in Salt Lake City. It put my youth in context, and I realized how relatively insignificant my experiences were compared to those of other ethnic and racial groups.

One of my classmates from Hawaii, of Japanese descent, invited me to dinner on April 3, 1947. When the time came, for no real reason, I did not want to go. I called him and told him so. He sounded so disappointed, as if he expected it. I immediately suggested the next night. We would meet where he had his meals, at the International Student House, known as the I House, at 1825 R Street in Washington. A Quaker couple ran it warmly and casually. So that next night, Friday, April 4, I went. It's easy to remember the date because of what happened there.

Dear Wetz:

Where shall I start? First, about Rebecca. I've known for a long time. I was never in love with her—as love should be. However, like so many others (and with whom you never class yourself) I was looking for something and forcing myself to believe that it was something it wasn't. Every so often I would rebel, but found myself in a peculiar position. I had voluntarily placed myself into a position from which extrication would not be too easy and even more embarrassing. So—I would hesitate and hesitate. Once, I had made a firm resolve, but later discarded it in favor of waiting until I came home in order to act face to face. The unfortunate thing about that, however, was that this would have been even more unfair to her, inasmuch as the preparation would be nearly complete. So, what brought about the crystallization?

That night I met Marion Stiebel. We got talking. I thought I detected some kind of accent, maybe a Boston accent. I was not sure. Very quickly I had an overwhelming attraction to her. We met on Friday. We went out Saturday and Sunday. By the following Tuesday I made *the* call to Rebecca. That evening, I proposed to Marion. It was absolutely instant love. Setting the date became the next question.

That first night we met at the I House they showed a military documentary of the Holocaust with concentration camp scenes. Just the fact that they showed it upset her very much. Of course, I quickly found out that she was a German Jewish refugee. Her stepfather, Friedrich Oppenheimer—in every way her real father (her blood father had died when she was three) and an incredibly wonderful man—had raised her. He had been a very prominent lawyer in Frankfurt, Germany, and he served as a combat artillery officer for five years in World War I (for which he received the Iron Cross). As the tensions grew in Germany he began to worry—but only as an eminently rational man.

His wife, Marion's mother, was a quiet woman of high intelligence and poise. Her name was Eva, maiden name Kohn, and she also came from a very prominent family. Her father, Marion's grandfather, had been the director of a bank in the famed resort city of Karlsbad, Austria-

Hungary. In 1938 she told Marion that they were going to take a vacation in Italy. (She wisely knew how children might talk.) She took Marion, then thirteen years of age, and, instead, fled to Oporto, Portugal. There they met Eva's sister and husband, who had left two years earlier. Eva wrote back to her husband, Fred, telling him they were not returning. This was the only way to get him out of Germany. He belonged to that German Jewish group who could not believe what the Nazis had in store for them. His family had lived in Germany for centuries. He believed in the rule of law. After four months, they received visas to the United States and settled in Boston in September 1938. Herbert Stiebel, Marion's astute older brother, who had fled to England, later joined them.

They had managed to escape Germany with very little. At that time, Hitler's people made sure they didn't take out more than 12 percent of their worth. Marion's father paid the German government more than enough to ship all their personal possessions—furniture, china, silverware, books, even some paintings—and expressed hope they would get them. Fred had paid his 1937 and 1938 taxes, and managed to get his exit passport in three days, a testimonial to his own standing in the Frankfurt community. Privately, he doubted whether they would see their possessions again because on November 9, 1938, there occurred *Kristallnacht,* the Night of Broken Glass, the Nazi-planned violence that destroyed hundreds of synagogues, vandalized and looted Jewish businesses and homes, and killed dozens of German Jews. It was the worst pogrom Germany had ever experienced until the "Final Solution," the official Jewish extermination program, began a few years later. Much to Fred's surprise, and pleasure, in late November, the New York Customs notified them that their household goods had arrived. Perhaps they had already been shipped by the time of *Kristallnacht.*

On our second date, I told her she looked different. "Different different or different good?" she asked. I was intrigued by her very incisive kind of statements, without explanation, without trying to prove it to me or argue with me or have a big exposition on it. She would just hit right close to the point, very succinctly and precisely. That's her makeup. She has an inherent wit, with a fast tongue. A few lines and she would slice right through a person, as in the way she described me to her mother—"He's not a knife-throwing Italian." That great sense of humor was part of her charm and her acceptance: don't get into any kind of discussion with her unless you are willing to take this humor.

Marion has an inherent privacy and dignity, which I found fascinating. I saw traces of noblesse oblige, but never heard one word about "the old days." Their conduct was simple: you don't show off. Meeting Marion was also an entry into the refugee German Jewish society in America, a group dynamic that I had only read about. I found in her family little money; that had been left behind. But that material lack did not affect their mental well-being. I found a family with amazing inner strength and the deepest of intelligence—and no affectations. To this day I have never heard an envious word regarding the wealthy. Marion never— ever—distinguished people by their color or their religious belief. She has a deep spiritual base, which she rarely discloses.

Marion and I had sharp differences in our cultures and educations. Marion had been a part of the classical German education for eight years. She had studied mythology and Greek and Roman histories. Her knowledge of language—its structure and origin—was (and is) amazing. She had the same gift for languages as her mother. With eight years of Latin, she spoke German, French, English fluently, and Spanish well enough. (When we later went to Italy and she understood Italian better than I, even though she didn't speak it, I was no longer surprised.) All along I had seen the development of the intellect as a way out of a lesser life. Marion and her family had that. I easily adjusted to her lifestyle because I was most impressed with it. She shaped me, without any question, in terms of my growth. I felt you had to have this growth if you were to achieve a meaningful role in society. Marion was the completion of my effort to find a special meaning in life. I was on a "high" for months. I couldn't believe I had found such a person who brought so much to me and offered so much for our future together.

In the 1940s, the custom in certain groups was for the families of the bride and groom to meet before the wedding. Thus, I took Marion on a train trip to Utah to meet my family. This didn't work out too well. It became apparent after a couple of days that my family was uneasy. My mother—the Italian matriarch from a tiny Italian mountain town, with a very limited education—was unable to communicate easily. She asked earthy questions. Though she was the same height, but one hundred pounds heavier, my mother asked Marion if she could have kids. She was also concerned I would be "henpecked," a word she had picked up, but she did not really know its meaning. Marion's grace, her intelligence, and her civility were being ignored. What had excited me seemed to frighten my family—because they did not understand. As a result, I realized after a few days that we should leave early. I left feeling as though the trip had been a big mistake.

We were married on November 8, 1947, in her parents' Boston apartment by a Community Church minister. At the time, religion was not a great factor for either of us. Dick Wetzel, then an intern at a Miami, Florida, hospital, flew up and was my best man. No one in my family was present. Over the years, we have celebrated our meeting anniversary more than the wedding, because we have always considered that much more important than the actual wedding date.

I continued my studies and prepared for the Washington, D.C., bar exams. Marion supported us very nicely for a year with her responsible professional position at the State Department in the very hush-hush Division of Research and Intelligence, classifying foreign-language documents. It utilized her language skills with her library training and experience. She got pregnant fairly quickly, though we had not planned it that way. She stopped work just two weeks before I went to work at my first job. Loretta, our first daughter, was born January 10, 1949.

In April 1949, my parents made their first trip east for my swearing in as a member of the Washington bar and to see their first granddaughter. They met Marion's parents, down from Boston, with whom they got along remarkably well, even though they were from totally different worlds. My parents overcame any preconceptions or concerns regarding intimidation. When Marion's parents made a western trip a year or two later, they went through Salt Lake City and visited my parents for several days. My parents respected them, which is the key word here. As my mother would say in her own way, "they were educated people." And my mother respected that because she often wished she had had that herself. My dad was not articulate about such things, but he liked them. After the Salt Lake visit their respect turned to fondness.

While they were in Washington I showed my parents the city, leaving almost nothing out. Former senator of Utah Abe Murdock, whom I was working for at the time, took Pop and me to lunch at the Watergate, a famous wharf restaurant, and then gave us a personally guided tour of the Capitol, the Senate, and so on. This we didn't expect, but Pop was very pleased. We also had a long talk with Utah congresswoman (Judge) Reva Beck Bosone. She gave us tickets for the visiting Radio City Rockettes.

My dad was extremely proud that I had become a lawyer, even though he never said so. There was never a toast to success. He just glowed. He was Calabrese; you don't talk about your family, especially to your family. At home, we didn't thank one another or conduct all the other civilities that I've grown used to since then. Growing up, everything was just taken for granted. And my mother and father remained that way, especially my mother, who showed no emotion at seeing me succeed outside of the hometown. Over the years, I had seen how Pop could get quite sentimental about people who were deprived either physically or even economically. He was very touched by human misery. I guess I have some of that, as do both of my brothers. I realize that my desire to help mankind, at that point in my life, sounds fairly noble. I really felt that maybe there was something I could do that might make it easier for others. The first thing he said to me after the swearing in was, "Where is your hat?" You had to have a good hat. He said I needed a Borsalino, the brand name of the finest Italian-made man's felt hat. He bought me one and said, "You are there; you are a professional person." It meant that I had made it.

PART II

For the Good of Others,

1949–1971

The primary incentive, and hence the principal reward, of public service is service itself. . . . [The public servant] chooses to work for the government because for him there can be no greater reward than the satisfaction of applying his professional knowledge to the benefit of his fellow citizens.

—Elliot Richardson, *Reflections of a Radical Moderate*

SEVEN

IKE'S YOUNGEST

WE LIVED IN Prospect Heights, just outside of Chicago, when President Eisenhower took office on January 20, 1953. After law school I had an intense two-year period as a legal assistant to former senator Abe Murdock, a board member of the National Labor Relations Board (NLRB), where I learned the intricacies of federal labor law. I moved on to Chicago with a burgeoning corporation where my legal responsibilities expanded to include personnel management and general corporate contract negotiation. The job satisfied our family's needs, but it fell short of holding my interest as to career growth. I focused my efforts on regaining self-direction for a public service career. I contacted my good friend from college and law school days Robert W. Barker, then the chief administrative assistant to Utah's senator Wallace F. Bennett. With his help, I submitted my résumé to the Republican National Committee.

In that process I sought Senator Bennett's support, a fairly easy task since the senator's oldest son, Wally, was my close college and army ROTC friend. The senator had been a regular lunchtime patron at my father's Capri Restaurant. Bennett Paint and Glass stood around the corner, and he always came through the restaurant's back door. I hasten to add that Senator Bennett stood at the pinnacle of Utah society—a devout Mormon married to a daughter of Heber J. Grant, president of the Mormon Church. My immigrant father would never have lunch with him, but only provide it to him.

About this time—March 1953—Marion and I traveled to New York City and stayed at the Hotel Commodore. As we approached the elevator one afternoon, much to our surprise, we met the newly appointed secretary of labor, Martin P. Durkin. I had come to know Durkin quite well through my job in Chicago, where he was located as president of the International Union of Plumbers and Pipe Fitters. His selection as a cabinet member surprised most people because he was a Democrat, the only one; thus, the press dubbed Eisenhower's cabinet as "nine millionaires and a plumber." In my congratulatory letter to Durkin I indicated my willingness to assist him in his new position. I greeted him, repeated my congratulations, and mentioned my letter. He was gracious, thanked me, and otherwise said nothing. The elevator was waiting.

Some months passed. In June 1953, Secretary of Labor Durkin phoned me at home to tell me he had sent my name over to the White House for a position in the Labor Department. I was puzzled because I was unsure why my name would go to the White House. I asked if he could tell me the position.

He said, almost with some vexation in his voice, "Why, assistant secretary."

Assistant secretary! That's a presidential appointment, confirmed by the Senate, of which there were only three in the Department of Labor; it's on the top of the heap. I had just turned thirty-one. I was ambitious, but not presumptuous. In shock, I said, "That's very nice," and we hung up.

I told Marion. I couldn't believe it. I thought he might have meant assistant *to the* secretary, which did not require that kind of political clearance, but he said that it had gone to the White House.

She said, "Well, did you tell him, 'Thank you'?"

The next day I called back and made sure he understood I really appreciated what he was doing.

That day we left Chicago by auto for a long-planned vacation in Boston where we looked forward to showing off our three children to their grandparents. When we arrived, I called to check in with Secretary Durkin, and he asked me to come to Washington immediately to begin the clearance process for a presidential appointment, which included a full field investigation. There, I met with White House and Labor Department personnel people who reviewed my records. Though a resident of Illinois at that time, I had no political connections there, which alerted Barker to the need for action. The staff of Illinois senator Everett Dirksen, especially one of his key aides, approved everything before Mr. Dirksen ever saw it. With no political presence in Illinois I was unknown to them. Barker urged Senator Bennett to move quickly on this. Senator Bennett led me down a magnificent marble hallway to a big meeting room. He went in and brought out Senator Dirksen, who came over to me and gave me his support. We had just avoided all of the internecine office politics . . . happily.

Washington, D.C., was in the midst of a sea change in political management: for the first time in twenty years, the Republicans had control of the legislative and executive branches, and they wallowed in their new power. A few days later Senator Bennett took me into a meeting in the office of Senator Alexander Smith of New Jersey, the newly appointed chairman of the Senate Labor Committee. Other senators of the Labor Committee drifted in, six or eight more—all Republicans, including a new senator from Arizona, Barry Goldwater, *and no Democrats.* They discussed several unrelated items, then Senator Smith brought up my confirmation: "We have a young man here." He didn't see any need for a formal hearing. He said if they were all agreeable, they could report it out as confirmed by the committee. I walked out of the room confirmed! That could not happen today.

Though not the top position, such as a cabinet secretary, my confirmation without a formal hearing and no Democrats present showed the times and the Republicans' heady mood. My name went to the full Senate for approval on July 31, 1953. They routinely approved my confirmation and reported it out around ten in the morning. A few minutes later word came that the powerful majority leader, Republican senator Robert Taft of Ohio, had died. As a result, the Senate adjourned at noon, not only in his memory but also for the session. I was fortunate, for without that approval I would have required a recess appointment by the president, subject to a later Senate confirmation. I was sworn in as assistant secretary on August 24, 1953.

Shortly after my confirmation, which made the Salt Lake news, a letter to the editor appeared in the *Salt Lake Tribune.* The author credited an "unimpeachable source" and claimed that I was "a member in good standing of the Young Democratic League of Utah." It baffled me. I had no idea as to the motivation of a person I did not know (and I said so in my denial letter to the *Tribune*). Up until that time, I never considered myself a Republican or a Democrat. My first vote was for FDR, second for Dewey, and the third for Eisenhower. My nomination process helped me select a party. I became a Republican, and my registration has stayed the same ever since. I don't always vote Republican, especially in recent years. I vote according to the caliber of the candidate and the positions of the parties on various issues. I share the feelings of my close friend Elliot Richardson, the only person to have headed four cabinet departments. When we compared notes shortly before his death in 1999, he said, "the Republican party has left me." I had to laugh and confessed I often felt the same way. Too often, the party has not kept pace with key issues regarding civil rights, women, and the environment. I call these progressive issues, and reject the easier labels of liberal and conservative.

Two weeks after I started my job, an explosion occurred—my boss, Secretary of Labor Durkin, resigned. He left on September 9 after a disagreement with the White House over proposed revisions to the Taft-Hartley Labor Act. The under secretary, Lloyd Mashburn, also resigned in protest that same day. With the two top people gone, it left us with only two presidentially appointed assistant secretaries. Suddenly, I found myself signing papers as acting secretary of labor.

Besides fortuitous timing, at thirty-one I had at least a small reputation: I knew about the labor movement, I knew something about the unions, and I knew how to work with them. Labor was not a planned career choice, though my first two jobs out of law school focused on labor law and labor relations. Those five years gave me some qualification for the position of assistant secretary of labor—however surprising the actual fact. A flashback on the experience of those five years is appropriate here.

◦

AS I WAS finishing law school, like everyone else, I thought about employment. I wanted public service and Washington was the right place. Marion supported us beautifully but would soon give birth to our first child. World War II GI lawyers were flooding out of the law schools.

I couldn't hesitate. I had read about Abe Murdock's appointment to the National Labor Relations Board. The NLRB administered the Wagner Act, which guaranteed most American workers the right to join a union. The Taft-Hartley Act of 1947, which amended the Wagner Act of 1935, added two more seats to the NLRB, bringing it to a five-person board. One of President Truman's appointments was Murdock, a Democrat from Utah, who had served four terms in the House of Representatives followed by one term in the Senate (he was defeated for reelection in 1946). Obviously, Senator Murdock would need a legal assistant, but he had no idea who I was. The question was, how do I get Senator Murdock's attention?

I talked to my father, and he contacted a very devoted and supportive business friend, Ward Tuttle, who often helped him by either writing letters himself or finding someone who could write a letter on behalf of my father. In this case, he contacted Grover Giles, a prominent member of the Democratic Party of Utah and a former state attorney general. Mr. Giles, whom I never knew, was impressed enough with my résumé that he sent it directly to Senator Murdock with a letter of support.

In early 1948, knowing the competition after the fall graduation would be stout, I risked jumping the gun and put in a phone call to Senator Murdock's office. I was simply hoping for an appointment, but much to my surprise he personally got on the phone. He immediately told me—without ever meeting or interviewing me—he would save a place for me as one of his legal assistants. I couldn't believe my ears: I already had a job! He based it on the recommendation from Utah and my own record. Perhaps he liked the idea of having someone from Utah on his staff (as it later turned out, of fifteen employees I was the only Utahn). I started in his office in the fall of 1948. Not only was I lucky to have a job, but it also paid very well. Though I was at first classified as a "dictating machine transcriber" until I passed the bar, I was glad to have the job because Marion, by that time, had left her job and was caring for Loretta. I was sworn in as a member of the bar in April 1949, when my pay became a very respectable $4,479.60 a year.

At first my work was extremely interesting. We processed cases that had been heard by a trial examiner (called an administrative judge today) and were consequently appealed to the board. We reviewed records of hearings, read the transcripts (which could be hundreds of pages long), analyzed them, and prepared legal memoranda or summaries that recommended what sort of action should be taken. The cases were usually unfair-labor-practice complaints filed by employee unions. Other cases involved petitions by employees seeking approval of elections to select a union representative. After a year of reading nothing but these abuse charges filed against the employers, you can become very pro-employee. The employers, of course, criticized Labor Board staff as "do-gooders" and "liberals" who didn't understand the world. While clearly a prolabor board, in today's language, the facts generally dictated decisions in favor of the union, not management.

Trade unionism enjoyed its heyday in this post–World War II period as union membership soared to historic levels to include one-third of the nonfarm labor force. The unions became more responsible, and the public accepted them as a necessary part of job growth. The leaders of the day—William Green, the Reuther brothers (Victor and Walter), David Dubinsky, Philip Murray, John L. Lewis, and George Meany—were well motivated, idealistic, and also very pragmatic. No one can deny their importance as key players on the American economic stage. We owe much of our growth in this country to the improved working conditions that were a direct result of the trade unions' efforts between 1935 and the 1960s—which began decades earlier. I had always accepted the philosophy of trade unionism even though I was not a card-carrying union member (except for a brief period when in college working at Lettieri's cigar store). I equate the rights of collective bargaining with those of civil rights.

The job at the NLRB started my career in labor relations. Though it had a demanding side, it soon became routine, and I wearily read case after case of vicious management plays against the union. They weren't happy reading for young lawyers. I looked around me and could see that many of the other legal assistants were stuck there and knew that I had to avoid that pitfall.

I had some desire to return to Utah, and even imagined a run for elected office. In 1950, when at the NLRB, Marion and I had Judge Reva Beck Bosone, the congresswoman from Salt Lake City (Utah's first woman representative), over for dinner. That was big stuff! Judge Bosone, from the well-established Beck family, had married Joe Bosone, an Italian American man from the railroad town of Helper, Utah. After a divorce, she had a publicized and successful career as a judge in Salt Lake before running for the House of Representatives. She knew many in my family, and I liked and admired her. At dinner, she more or less orated and gave me instructions on how to be an important political person.

"The political life is very simple," she said. "You go home and start walking." In other words, go out in the neighborhoods and shake hands, man the ballot box, campaign for other people. "Eventually," she said, "you can perhaps rise to be a member of Congress."

I thought to myself, "Fine, that's what you did, but that's not what I'm going to do." I didn't want to be a second lieutenant on the front line again. If I ran for election in Utah, I wanted to do it my way. I dreamed of going back to campaign for the Senate or House seat, period. But the whole notion was fantasy. I had no assurance of how to make a decent living in Utah. I couldn't practice law; the system was too much against it. I was aware that the law practices of several people of Italian extraction—including that of Judge Bosone's former husband—required a real income from other sources. None were in the established Salt Lake firms.

Fortunately, the job opportunity arose in Chicago. Through a Georgetown classmate, John Woods, I signed on to help establish a new subsidiary of an old-line company, Universal Oil Products (UOP), a pioneering research, design, and engineering organization servicing the oil and chemical industry that owned some of the basic oil "cracking" patents. They formed a construction company, called Procon, which stood for Process Construction. I left my position with the NLRB and went with Procon in October 1950. Our family of four—Marion, myself, Loretta (nearly two years old), and Vincent (five months)—moved to Park Forest, thirty miles south of Chicago, into the coldest winter we've ever known. In 1951, UOP moved their extensive operation to the suburb of Des Plaines, Illinois. At that time, we bought our first home, a small house in nearby start-up community Prospect Heights. Fred, our third child, was born in Evanston on October 14, 1951.

I did much legal work as well as labor relations—not labor law, but labor contract arrangements with the building trades department of the American Federation of Labor (AFL). My income was adequate for my age and role, but never, of course, seemed really enough with a growing family. I started my longtime habit of daily reading of the *Wall Street Journal.* Comparable to my experience at the Headquarters U.S. Forces, Austria, I began to see and understand the American big-business corporate structure. I learned firsthand that the chief executive officer of the corporation is omnipotent.

I also saw intense bigotry. The group that ran the parent company, including my own boss, was from Louisiana and was known as the "Shreveport gang"—only in safe company, of course. My boss, the Procon CEO, was wonderfully supportive and friendly, while at the same time lashing out at Italians and Jews. He would say, "I do not care for 'wops' or 'dagos,' but you are all right, you are fine." He knew Marion was a refugee Jew and would say only good things about her. Of course, they didn't hire blacks ("colored" was used in those days). In fact, the personnel director laughingly said to me one time, "Why, we have colored. Look—that's the first thing you see when you come in our front doors." They were two receptionists, elderly black men beautifully dressed in dark suits, who would escort visitors to the appropriate office.

My boss was a product of his environment with speech typical of his slice of southern society. He would chuckle at his own remarks, yet he seemed unaware of how they came across. Interestingly, the big boss—the chairman and CEO of the parent company—was cultured, quiet, and refined, without any obvious ethnic or racial bias. His failure: he permitted this behavior of his team of executives. My boss, sadly, was an alcoholic. Along the way to job sites he would ask me to pull in at a bar. He would order drinks for us both. I would protest a reorder, explaining that I was driving. Nonetheless, he would order another. I would not drink it and knew he wanted only to enjoy my company. Obviously, the job situation made me uncomfortable, but it offered security. I maintained a discreet voice and manner. With Marion and three children I did not throw rocks, but hoped only to set an example for respect. It wasn't a good lesson. I saw immediately some of the very things that I had reviewed in NLRB transcripts, but this insidious discrimination would never become an unfair-labor-practice charge under Taft-Hartley.

While in that job, between the years 1950 to 1953, I worked with a good many of the international labor unions. Our biggest employee group was the pipe fitters, being about 60 percent of the labor costs in building an oil-refining plant. It was in these circumstances that I met and negotiated with the plumbing and pipe-fitting head, Martin P. Durkin. Some six months after President Eisenhower appointed Durkin as secretary of labor I joined him as an assistant secretary.

THE NEW POSITION of assistant secretary awed me a bit (never mind the acting secretary!). I stepped into a role where I supervised people who had been in government twenty or thirty years. The men who ran our biggest bureau, Robert C. Goodwin, and his deputy, Ed Keenan, were top-flight career men. During the war they had managed tens of thousands of employees (it was called the War Manpower Administration) while I had been a lowly lieutenant in the army. They seemed very dubious of me, and understandably so since I was a young politically appointed newcomer. I never cared whether they were Democrat or Republican and tried to avoid any politically stated judgment. It took the better part of a year before they showed acceptance, and by the time I left four years later we were close friends and colleagues.

Within the first few weeks on the job I was called to testify before the Senate Finance Committee regarding the amendment of the Federal Security Act. With expert assistance I reviewed for hours what seemed at first like a foreign language. My greatest concern was the committee's redoubtable chairman, Senator Eugene D. Milliken of Colorado. When I finished the presentation and answered the senators' questions, Milliken peered down at me and asked, "Young man, where are you from?" I said, "Utah." He mumbled a compliment. Later, Senator Bennett (a junior member on the committee) told me that Milliken had been most impressed.

I testified many times before various congressional committees on technical subjects. My first cabinet presentation came when I had been in the job maybe three months: a twenty-five-minute presentation on unemployment insurance, which three months earlier I hardly knew existed. The Department of Labor recommended certain actions, which subsequently the president agreed to adopt and submit to Congress. As I became more familiar with the subject matter as well as the cabinet members, I looked forward to these presentations.

There were situations where confrontations would occur. Unhappy congressmen were the most difficult to handle. One day about twenty-five members of Congress—Republican and Democrat together—paid us an angry visit. They came from the districts in the various states where the Mexican Farm Labor Program, known as the Bracero Program, employed Mexicans. I had to defend—or, rather, explain—

our work. On that day the angry House members sat there and listened to me. In the presence of Secretary of Labor Mitchell, I spelled out in detail how they were misinformed. And that was the problem—they did not know the facts, and in the quiet of the large Labor Department conference room, without publicity, they had to accept the facts. Mitchell was very pleased and phoned his approval afterward. The Bracero Program was so involved and emotional; everyone had a different take on it. The newspapers were always agog about the state of it. One day, two Scripps-Howard reporters came in unannounced. My policy was to see the press at all times. In a cryptic fashion they announced that they had just come from the Mexican border. They mentioned a town in Mexico, which I didn't know. They repeated the name of the town.

I asked what that meant.

They explained that they had been investigating the Bracero Program. They wanted to hear from me about it. I recognized their antagonism, so I immediately called to my office the men directly involved with the Bracero Program. I hoped that a full-scale session might satisfy their questions. We tried, but they had already written their story. It came out the next day as a long "exposé" of how these Mexicans were being exploited by farmers. Finally, at the end, they summed up our conversation: "Assistant Secretary Siciliano said that [the program] was working very well, and that 'we even provided church services for them at 2:00 a.m., if they wanted to go to Mass before work.'" It made me look pretty ridiculous.

These new situations were always challenging and sometimes even frightening, but I had an easy rationale—recalling my combat experience, I would tell myself that this was politics, not a matter of life or death, and you can go from there. I am surprised how many times the memory of the Italian test of fire returns. Yet it was a different set of values. In the office, my greatest concerns were learning and adjusting to the frailties and chicaneries of human nature.

At the time of my appointment, I was known as "Ike's Youngest," and I had my fifteen minutes of fame as the newspapers latched onto that. Besides being the youngest appointee, I was said to be the first Italian American to be a member of the Little Cabinet with the title of assistant secretary. One other Italian American, Judge Paul P. Rao Sr., had the equivalent rank of assistant attorney general in the Franklin D. Roosevelt administration. John Pastore of Rhode Island, then in his third year as the first Italian American to serve in the United States Senate, told me of his pleasure to see a kindred soul in the executive branch.

Now, did the country care? No. Was the public interested? No. But was I interested? Absolutely. I had broken through the glass ceiling. Italian Americans were still striving to be accepted as first-class citizens. They enjoyed prominence in the performing arts, but all too often were thought of being associated with organized crime—the Mafia. The few in public service usually served in "Little Italy" communities, while the corporate world rarely saw any Italian surnames. The notable exceptions, Fiorello La Guardia and A. P. Giannini, were just that—exceptions. At that time I was unaware of my father's trials in Pocatello.

On December 3, 1953, I went to New York City to receive on behalf of President Eisenhower the Humanitarian of the Year Award, which was presented by the American Committee on Italian Migration (the National Catholic Resettlement Council) at a white-tie dinner attended by more than one thousand people. The ranking clerical host was Francis Cardinal Spellman, assisted by Archbishop Cushing of Boston (later a cardinal). The audience treated me like a rock star. A few months later I gave a talk at a similar affair in Philadelphia. Women (from the "old country") came to my table crying.

Much of this "success" was timing. I was in the vanguard of demographic trends. After World War II, ethnic minorities had become most visible and accepted, along with their foods. Whoever heard of pizza in the 1940s except those of us who ate fried bread at home?! Today, Italian Americans serve as cabinet officers, White House chiefs of staff, congressmen, senators, and judges, while the business community crawls with Italian names. Also, coming from Utah, a state almost unknown to most easterners, made me different. Few seemed to believe that there were Italian Americans out West. I enjoyed the ease of social acceptance in Washington, D.C. ("Are you different different or different good? Or both?" as Marion would say.)

During the early family years at home, Loretta, Vincent, and Fred were all less than three and in diapers at the same time, which kept Marion really busy. She quipped that every time I received a promotion we got a new baby in the family. When she was pregnant with John, our fourth child, friends would introduce her as, "This is Marion Siciliano, whose husband is in Labor, and she almost is." My mother remonstrated to me: "You know, she's not a rabbit." We laughed at that. We never planned our family. John came in 1954 and seven years later, 1961, came "the caboose"—Maria.

When we lived in the District of Columbia (over a period of nineteen years total) we always chose to live in the city. For most of that time, we lived near the Annunciation Catholic Church in northwest Washington, D.C. Marion literally read her way into the Catholic Church at that time. Thomas Merton and his *Seven Story Mountain,* which led to other writings and authors, fascinated her. She loved the poems of William Blake. She went from one writer to another, and finally she announced that she was going to take instruction on the Catholic Church. Being ignorant about the theology of the Catholic Church, I joined her.

When Marion was baptized, she was nearly nine months pregnant with Vincent. Having baptized her, the priest then asked if we would like to be married! We received a blessing and a church validation of our marriage. Vincent came a day or two later (July 19, 1950). From that summer on, Marion became a very active practicing Catholic. As our kids grew up, we became increasingly involved in the Annunciation parish, which had a great school. All five kids were baptized as Catholics, and the oldest four attended the parish school. Marion loved the Latin mass, because she understood it. As our three boys successively became altar boys, she taught them the Latin responses to the priests conducting the mass. John, at four years old, was the youngest altar boy the church ever had; he was so small he could not move the big missal (Vincent helped). Marion started a library at the parish and wrote a different prayer for each day of the year to be said during the mass. We had many priests come to our house for years, and one of them, our very best friend, Monsignor Pio Laghi, from the Apostolic Delegation, baptized six-day-old Maria before he left his post that day for the Vatican. He has since become Pio Cardinal Laghi. That religious period was intense, and we were very attentive to the many demands of the Catholic Church.

One of the high points of our lives was the fifteen minutes Marion and I spent at the Vatican alone with Pope John XXIII (except for a big Irish bishop who translated). Pope John was an incredibly warm man— you wanted to hug him—and we were very supportive of his efforts "to bring the church up to date" *(aggiornamento)*. We thought the changes were for the best, but many disagreed. Many people remember the change from the Latin to the English mass, but most changes went even deeper in intent, if not in fact. Ecumenism became the goal. More and more disaffection came after Pope John's death in June 1963, and, unfortunately, the Second Vatican Council's edicts receded into insignificance. Today we are not so institutionalized in our beliefs. We both continue an intense interest in spiritual values, as we watch our two daughters follow the Jewish faith of Marion's family, two sons and their sons follow varieties of the Christian faith (including Catholicism and Episcopalianism), and one son follow his eastern beliefs.

Marion joined Barbara Lewis, wife of Assistant Secretary of the Interior Orme Lewis, to start the Little Cabinet Wives, which functioned as a social organization for the top presidential appointees. Among other events, they organized dances at the military installations, such as Fort Meyer and Fort McNair in the District of Columbia area. Marvelous relationships developed in those social hours, which translated into improved work relationships. The Eisenhower aura was unique—it fostered a sense of orderliness and an absence of fierce rivalry, which in part had to do with President Eisenhower's discipline and organization. These socials also developed the Eisenhower esprit, which has not been equaled since—even in the Kennedy years.

EIGHT

THE BRACERO PROGRAM

WHEN I CAME into the Eisenhower administration some eight months after its inception, the excitement was palpable. The Republican officeholders, myself included, strutted with their new power, though the realities of satisfying public needs quickly became evident.

Nor was it easy satisfying the Republicans on the Hill, who were leery of the Labor Department, or, as they called it, "the Department of Labor Unions." Despite the new Republican administration, they did not trust the politically appointed officers of the department and ascribed our actions to obeisance to union leaders. This was definitely not so, and it was a continuous job to prove that our goals were to improve the status of *all* American workers. Unfortunately, most of President Eisenhower's top appointees were business executives who appeared to have little understanding of working-class problems.

One person emerged who had the extraordinary ability to bridge the differences among the department, the unions, and the Republicans: James P. Mitchell. Some three weeks after Secretary Martin P. Durkin resigned, President Eisenhower appointed Mitchell as secretary of labor. I first met Mitchell in a greeting line with other staffers when he came on the job. Standing in front of me was a fellow who had worked in the Office of Manpower Administration with Mitchell in Berlin during the occupation period. He kept saying, "Jim Mitchell is great." An interesting scene followed. As Mitchell approached, this man greeted him as "Jim," and Mitchell's shoulders went stiff. I greeted him as "Mr. Secretary."

That episode set me thinking. He didn't know me, and I realized that protocol apparently meant a lot to him. The next morning I made an appointment to go see him alone. I went in and said, "Mr. Secretary, you don't know me. I like my work, but I realize I'm not your appointee. I herewith offer you my resignation if you want to accept it."

It was the last thing I wanted to do. I had been on the job six weeks, and we were barely settled in our house, but from what I quickly learned it seemed the thing to do. I had a presidential appointment and was confirmed in office, but he was my real boss and he had the right to fire me.

He looked at me carefully and asked me to stay.

The other two assistant secretaries, who were older (in their sixties) and had established labor union reputations, apparently felt it unnecessary to offer to resign. As former union leaders, they reflected the old department when assistant secretaries were strictly political animals who made speeches, floated around, and represented their past constituencies. Mitchell terminated them within a year. His arrival reinvigorated the department. He immediately accepted the departmental reorganization announced a few weeks before he took office, which required each assistant secretary to take on a specific management responsibility. Mitchell also knew that public service demands a different form of allegiance. My title became assistant secretary of labor for employment and manpower.

Mitchell inherited an agency crippled by its trade union identity. Privately, I referred to it as the stigmata. In the early 1950s the American labor movement was very significant, a strong and (in most cases) responsible element of the American economy. Mitchell and his top team (the under secretary and assistant secretaries) had the unending task of convincing Congress and the executive branch that the trade-movement philosophy was not an evil thing and that our judgment was not simply a reflex of the labor movement's desires. We had to interpret it, explain it, and sell it. It was here to stay. Mitchell, fundamentally, was an apolitical pragmatist without any union affiliation. Under him, the Department of Labor worked for the laboring American worker, union or nonunion. He shook up the management of the whole department. He changed the public understanding of the department's purpose, and in his nearly eight years he raised, in my judgment, the department's stature from the bottom to near the top. He also understood the labor movement cold. The trade union people—after an initial period of suspicion, then caution—greatly admired him and the department. I heard George Meany, the respected leader and president of the AFL-CIO, say publicly that Mitchell was the greatest secretary of labor the country had ever had.

His style of leadership was fascinating to watch. He could put on his Irish charm with his wonderful smile when he met outsiders. In his office his personality shifted to all business with a frozen face that intimidated people. With staff, he could be very abrupt and almost inconsiderate. As a self-made man, he believed in the underdog. Once, when we considered some people for promotion, he looked at the job description of a GS-11, not a very high rank in the public service, and he noted that he could never qualify for that position. He had no college education, and he fondly reminded the personnel director and others in the room of that fact. We all got the point: don't forget the little man— don't judge a person strictly by their résumé.

I learned a great deal about management from Secretary Mitchell. He utilized people in the best possible way and stimulated them to produce. He was a great administrator, and a very tough-driving taskmaster. He continuously gave me assignments and added to my duties, including responsibilities of the under secretary (which was a vacant position for the next year). As the *Salt Lake Tribune*'s Washington reporter put it, I frequently "had double and even treble duties as a result of vacancies in the upper echelon of the Labor Department." Mitchell knew what was going on in the department, not just the big picture but specifics about each agency's operations. Details were important, he said. He wanted people who were close to the work of the department, and its programs, and who would not just sit on top of the organization and wait for people to hand them speeches. Mitchell required the assistant secretaries to have that level of involvement.

One of my added duties concerned the cold war, a term that involved the state of political tensions and military rivalry between the United States and the Soviet Union. Life at the height of the cold war experienced some tense moments. In the 1950s the country stood on alert, and everybody was to plan for the possibility of a nuclear attack, which meant preparing a bomb shelter in their basement or in their backyard stocked with food and water. I oversaw the Labor Department's actions in the case of a nuclear attack. We would practice relocating our offices and several hundred employees outside of Washington, D.C., to a small college in Chambersburg, Pennsylvania. (Our first relocation was to a rural smaller college in southern Virginia. That was not repeated because of the conflict with the segregation practices.) We were told to leave our spouses and children behind and head for the relocation center, with the presumption that your home would be destroyed. As a newly made "widower" with no family, I was appointed as the nation's "war manpower administrator." We took the charge seriously, though joked about the unrealistic basic assumption regarding one's family. During one drill I left Marion in the middle of a play. I thought it totally ridiculous to pick up and leave your family, helpless against the radiation that would hit the city. Today we might laugh, but in those years the cold war was real.

After World War II, *automation* became a fashionable word. It had its day over a fifteen-year period as technology and the machines that preceded the computer were developed, mostly by the only manufacturer of consequence—"Big Blue," International Business Machines. We had a small, select group known as the Manpower and Analysis Group that looked at future developments and estimated where automation might take the industries of the nation. The U.S. labor force suffered shortages due to the lower birthrate of the Depression era. Automation could increase productivity, and it also produced new jobs. Because of this, we saw that the jobs of the future would require more and wider types of educational support and training. I spent a good deal of time giving speeches that forecasted the future (the newspapers liked that and picked up on it). We predicted such prosperity in twenty years that instead of two toasters, every household would have two cars and make twice as much money (something like six thousand dollars per year in expendable income).

One of the bureaus I supervised was the Bureau of Apprenticeship. This bureau encouraged the traditional form of apprenticeship as administered by the skilled craft unions, including plumbers, pipe fitters, carpenters, ironworkers, and electricians. Some of these skilled unions had apprenticeship programs that went back to the guild days in

England. A worker would train under supervision for two to four years and become a journeyman. Knowing the scope of future change, we wanted to expand it and get away from the old, traditional apprenticeship programs. Our study group recommended that the scope of training be widened to include more academic and classroom education in order to emphasize mathematics and the sciences. To reflect the change at hand, we proposed the addition of the words *and Training* to the name of the bureau, thus Bureau of Apprenticeship and Training.

Sounds simple, but hell hit us. Enormous fights erupted with the labor movement. They didn't trust us and felt that we wanted to change the nature of apprenticeship. They wanted the status quo—so much so that Congressman John E. Fogarty of Rhode Island, a former member of a building trade union and then chairman of the House Appropriations Subcommittee on Labor, put language in the Labor Department appropriations bill preventing us from using the words *and Training*. The unions had convinced him that we would dismember the traditional apprenticeship system. That killed it for a year or so, until I was able personally to convince him that this would benefit the labor movement as well as the apprenticeship program. We brought the construction trade unions around to realize that education only benefited the building trade unions. The words *and Training* were added, and the bureau received more funds. But this was only a small success. In time, the Bureau of Apprenticeship and Training, though still in existence, was later submerged and became only a small part of the massive Employment and Training Administration.

We watched these stepping-stones toward today's high technology. During those years—for the first time—more workers wore white collars than blue collars. My speech announcing this fact in Michigan in September 1956 got wide publicity. We tried to get some of the traditionalists to recognize the need for more classroom education in other fields. We realized that we had a shortage of skilled workers, and it threatened the nation's continued industrial expansion. We never, in my judgment, got the labor movement to fully understand the coming changes. They opted for the status quo, and I believe that has hurt them and their whole membership.

Secretary Mitchell's weak point was Congress. He simply did not understand its importance. The members of Congress, particularly the ranking members and committee chairmen, demanded a certain amount of attention. I called it "stroking." Mitchell delegated to me the supervision and direction of all congressional and legislative activities of the department. Working as the congressional liaison you had to be nimble and know your people. To keep me informed, I hired as special assistants to the secretary a former congressman from Delaware, Herbert Warburton, to cover the House, and Albert McDermott, a close friend and classmate from Georgetown Law School, to cover the Senate. They helped me especially in testifying on Labor Department programs, either in defense or in advocacy. I liked the contest. Even though the congressmen were sometimes pretty rough on me, I maintained very good relations with selected members of Congress, regardless of party affiliation.

One illustration sticks in my mind. Going to work one morning at my usual time, a few minutes before eight, I saw a tall man in an overcoat and fedora hat in the hallway waiting at my door. To my amazement, the man was Congressman George Mahon from Lubbock, Texas, one of the most powerful members of the House. I had worked quite well with him in department matters. When seated in my office he apologized for not calling, but he wanted me to know that he was issuing a press release that day that blasted me and criticized me for the conduct of the Bracero Program.

He then stressed that it was nothing personal. He said he enjoyed working with me, and he gave me more compliments as a public servant. More important, he kindly asked if I would not pay any attention to the press release. That made such a difference. I then read his press release. He was correct; I would have been upset that he of all people attacked me. He made it very plain that he wrote the press release to satisfy his farmer constituents and not because he personally believed their ideas about Mexican braceros. The release went out that day. It criticized me specifically as well as the Labor Department for failing to do certain things. That level of criticism comes with the job, but Representative Mahon made it palatable to the recipient, me. I could do nothing about his duplicity, but at least I understood his personal dilemma. When my own people picked it up and came tearing up to my office, I very calmly told them I knew about it and that we shouldn't worry about it.

I testified on the program before Congress (particularly the House committees) many times to answer the very critical comments that were being made by the farmers and their employer-group representatives who accused us of being in bed with the labor movement. (Ironically, the labor movement opposed the program and sought its abolishment. The church groups opposed it because they said these were "indentured servants.")

The Bracero Program became one of my heaviest responsibilities, and at times I was totally immersed in it. Created by Congress in 1942, the Bracero Program was a temporary measure to meet the wartime labor shortage in the agricultural fields of the Southwest and in other areas of the country. The braceros would pick the crops, everything from cherries in Michigan to strawberries in California. Cotton was perhaps the biggest crop. This program supplied growers with low-cost seasonal labor, and the workers returned home when the season ended.

After the war, the Bracero Program became a tool in managing the rising tide of illegal Mexican immigrants. Even though domestic labor increased after the war, illegal immigration began to surge in response to the need for farmworkers. The "wetbacks," so dubbed because they swam the Rio Grande at night, would work wherever they could find employment and stay on indefinitely. In the early 1950s the government performed an intensive and somewhat inconclusive effort, known as Operation Wetback, to repatriate illegal Mexicans. By 1954 the United States deported more than 1 million. In order to control this international mix of supply and demand, we relied more and more on the legal Bracero Program, which peaked in 1956 at 445,200 workers in thirty-eight states. The Bracero Program became a very important part of the economy, particularly in the western states. Out of their total earnings of approximately $200 million in 1957, the braceros spent roughly half of it in the United States.

The remainder of their earnings went into Mexico. Within the Bracero Program we would bring postal clerks out to the farms so that the workers could legally and easily send their earnings back to Mexico. At that time I was told that the Bracero Program was the second largest revenue producer for Mexico, exceeded only by tourism. The workers also gained considerable practical knowledge of industrialized farming and equipment.

The program took a lot of my time because it had so much political meaning, domestic as well as international. Though not involved in its day-to-day management, over four years I made numerous trips to

Mexico as the U.S. government's lead negotiator with the Mexican government, and we constantly renegotiated the international agreement and made amendments to those treaties.

The program grew in size and required more management. We had hundreds of employees throughout the United States handling bracero importation and the regulations regarding their treatment. Our staff made certain that the braceros received decent treatment and that their housing included basic living conditions—beds, running water, and toilets. We found it necessary, however, to include finite details. Because of sharp differences with farmer-user organizations, our regulations had to designate the width of a mattress and how high it must be off the floor. In working to meet the essential needs of humanity, we were caught between needs and costs—and human emotions.

That drove the farmers who employed these people crazy. Some farmers resented that we required living accommodations. The leaders of the farmer-user associations lectured me on the inanity of our regulations. While we often made adjustments here and there, it was impossible to agree with the statements ofttimes expressed to me personally. "You don't understand. These people have nothing in Mexico, and it takes very little to satisfy them here." "But they don't need toilets or beds. They don't have them in Mexico." Ironically, many of the farmers felt they were already doing the braceros a favor by hiring them.

Officials at the Department of Agriculture would admonish me about our treatment of the farmers. Some users campaigned to transfer the program to the Agriculture Department. Even in Congress, the labor and agriculture committees competed in a strong jurisdictional rivalry. The possessive inclination of the members of those two sets of committees was obvious, and it didn't really matter whether they were Republican or Democrat. The majority of the members of the Senate Labor Committee were basically more liberal, and the majority of the members of the Senate Agriculture Committee were much more protective of the "good of the agriculture industry." In any case, the Bracero Program spelled "trouble." The politicians of all sides viewed the Bracero Program as a favorite whipping boy, and it appeared to be liked only by the Mexican braceros.

The use of Mexican labor became a habit in many parts of our country. Even though our employment offices in many states recruited U.S. citizens, or at least legal immigrants, we had little success. We recruited American itinerant farm families (shades of the "dust bowl" exodus in the '30s), but these were few and becoming fewer. "Stoop labor" was on its way out since the end of World War II—at least for American citizens. Many growers protested the expense of Mexican labor ("premium-cost labor," they called it), yet they continued to ask for it. Eventually, the advocates of closure—who claimed the braceros interfered with labor supply and demand and infringed on employment opportunities and wage levels for U.S. workers—overwhelmed the government, and the program was closed in 1964 by congressional and executive branch action. Yet the demise of the Bracero Program plays a role in the enormous increase of Mexicans who have illegally entered this country since then. These same people are still picking the fruits and the vegetables, only as illegals they are without any of the protections of the Bracero Program. The labor vacuum gets filled one way or another. With the loss of the Bracero Program, we lost a means of managing two very real situations—our need for labor and the surplus of Mexican workers. (A small immigrant farmworker program was enacted many years later, but it is only a feeble effort.) My interest in this subject continued, and I had another opportunity to work on it later in life.

The Labor Department job was both exciting and demanding. I became intimate with the ways of Capitol Hill and enjoyed it intensely. One day, in 1956, when Secretary Mitchell was out of town, I got a summons from President Eisenhower's chief of staff, Governor Sherman Adams. He had me sit down and told me he wanted to recommend to the president that I be appointed chairman of the National Labor Relations Board.

I looked at him and realized I had no time to think. He was famous for his brief, staccato-style conversations wherein he spat out his words.

I remembered my two years as a legal assistant in the NLRB and immediately said, "Thank you very much for thinking of me, but I have to say no."

Surprised, he looked up at me, very focused, very sharply, and asked, "Why?"

I quickly explained that with Congress out of session, mine would be an interim appointment, which meant I would be in office for up to six months and make some four hundred decisions before confirmation. I was not convinced that Congress—meaning the Democrats (they had regained control of the Senate) and even some Republicans—would confirm me for that post. My first reason had to be substantive because I knew him. Second, I related my NLRB experience—granted, in a very junior role—and even though I liked the judicial appointment, the NLRB did not interest me nor did it offer me a future.

He looked at me and thanked me for coming over.

The next morning, Secretary Mitchell returned and summoned me. As I walked down to his office, I anticipated his position.

Mitchell asked me why I turned the offer down. My decision irritated him because with me in the position, he would have had someone who was accepted by the unions and, for the most part, by Congress. I would have relieved him of a political headache.

I gave him more of the first reason than the second. He did not accept it. He told me to call Governor Adams and tell him that I had reconsidered the offer.

I went back to my office in a quandary and not sure how to handle it. I called Governor Adams and said that I had just left Secretary Mitchell's office, who wanted me to tell him that I had reconsidered.

Governor Adams said he understood and thanked me for the call. Bang! Down went the phone (he was famous for his phone hang up). He understood from my tone that I was not really reconsidering.

On another occasion, Senator Wallace Bennett called me to his office. Since he was obviously much my senior in position as well as age, I regarded him as the Mormon patriarch he was and as a mentor who became very fond of me. I admired him, his character and considerable intelligence, though politically I was much more liberally inclined. He was not sympathetic to labor unions, and he was not sure even then why I had taken the position in the Labor Department. He made every effort to understand my background. An Italian American was somebody different, and he liked the difference. His awareness of the fact that Marion and I were not part of the Anglo-Saxon majority brought him to write a letter on my behalf strongly endorsing my nomination as assistant secretary. He closed the letter with a personal comment on the fact that I was a Roman Catholic and that my wife was a German Jewish refugee. He saw this as an important asset to the administration. He recognized the Eisenhower administration's makeup—overwhelmingly white, Anglo-Saxon, Protestant, it had a dearth of "ethnic" types. Senator Bennett was an early proponent of diversity.

On this occasion, his thoughts of diversity had carried over to the state of Utah. He asked if, after the Labor Department, I would like to go back to Utah. He wanted a non-Mormon active in Utah's Republican Party who perhaps could even run for office on the Republican ticket. He noted that I had name recognition due to my well-known and prominent status as a student at the university and because the Utah papers closely covered my Washington career. This idea intrigued and interested me. In college I had dreamed of running for public office in Utah. I knew the mores of the state, and was always careful that my own motivation would not conflict with them. Senator Bennett, as the son-in-law of a president of the Mormon Church, assured me that I was accepted. But already, without knowing the full extent of it, I was quite a different person from my days as a teenager, a college student, and a soldier. In Washington, D.C., I had achieved a different success pattern at an earlier age than I had ever envisioned. It set my career on a different course. Even though returning to Utah held some allure, my greatest concern remained the means of making a living in Utah. The senator inquired into a few possibilities, but nothing happened.

One day in July 1957, just after we returned from our summer vacation, I received another phone call to visit Governor Adams. He told me that the president was about to issue an executive order that would create a significant new position in the White House, special assistant to the president for personnel management. It was one of the topmost positions in the White House, besides chief of staff and the deputy chiefs of staff. He offered me the job, at the request of the president. I immediately accepted.

NINE

INSIDE THE WHITE HOUSE WITH
PRESIDENT EISENHOWER

I HAD NEVER talked to President Eisenhower one-on-one until I went to the White House and became his special assistant for personnel management. The first thing that most impressed me was his ability to completely concentrate on the speaker. An astonishing listener, he paid attention to every word. I saw this technique . . . it was more than that, it was genuine. It just came with him. He sat in his chair, leaned forward, and though he might move about a bit his movements were not abrupt. His face intent, he absorbed himself in the person speaking. This world-famous leader showed so much devotion to what that person said, and not in any sense deviating from his fixation on this one person, as if he had all day to hear you out. You were inclined to forget, if you could, that he was president of the United States.

I moved over to the White House when I was thirty-five. The president was almost sixty-seven, and all of the principal men in the White House were in their fifties and sixties. They were highly qualified leaders, mostly in business or the military. I felt right away that my experience and insights learned at Headquarters U.S. Forces, Austria, would help me interface with this enormous generational difference in the White House. When President Eisenhower introduced me as his special assistant to his cabinet some members were curious, but after four years as an assistant secretary I was known to most of them. He then compared my new function to the inspector general function of the army, which has wide-ranging autonomous power. This caused some cabinet members to look at me again, though with a raised eyebrow. In truth, the inspector general is vastly different from a special assistant to the president. The first causes fear in the army ranks at all levels of command—due to explicit authority to back its use of power. The second causes interest and respect, but no managerial concern. What none of the cabinet members knew that morning was that the presidential executive order creating my position did have some specific authority that went beyond the ordinary staff role.

President Eisenhower demanded careful and thorough briefing. He had obviously had thousands of hours of presentations in his military career. He became impatient if your presentation was not expedient. He barked his requests if he felt you did not get it out in a coherent, logical fashion. And he always used last names in a group setting. Once, he called me by my first name. In a presentation that I was about to make to the cabinet, he said, "And now Rocco's going to explain this." I almost choked.

In his press conferences some looked upon him as "fumbling, bumbling Ike." Many times I think this was a deliberate behavior. He was so accommodating with his power position that he didn't have to explain anything to anybody. He used his power without strutting, without ego. He had immense self-confidence. Long before he became president he had worked with some of the great men of the century—Churchill, Stalin, de Gaulle, Montgomery, Roosevelt. In smaller groups, I saw his intelligence and wisdom, and realized that he downplayed them in a public setting.

President Eisenhower naturally organized his White House with a military type of hierarchy, though it had a very civilian feel to it. He delegated great authority to his cabinet officers and to his assistants, and he expected them to come up with solutions to problems in their areas. His leadership style was best described in Fred L. Greenstein's insightful book *The Hidden-Hand Presidency: Eisenhower as Leader:* President Eisenhower "employed his skills to achieve his ends by inconspicuous means." I watched this in process and participated in it. That "hidden-hand" ability elevated him in my opinion. This able, extraordinary person never looked for credit, nor did he want people around him aggrandizing themselves. I soon realized that almost all the people in the White House had this same makeup. It reminded me of the famous phrase by the 1930s Brownlow Committee on Administrative Management that suggested the president have assistants who possess a "passion for anonymity." I consider it the strength of Eisenhower's White House.

Another personality strength that I admired was his temper. In smaller sessions Eisenhower would get angry or he might even explode. He would gesticulate and words would spit out of his mouth—he spoke with great force, and he often cursed with "damn" and "hell"—but he was never personal. He didn't chew anyone out; he chewed out the situation. Somehow or other, you felt he was just blowing steam. He knew when and how to display his anger. I learned a real lesson: I thought, this is an incredible man who can be upset and cuss, but he isn't angry with me.

One time I went into his office with a very simple bill that said when a holiday fell on Sunday, federal employees would have Monday off. The White House staff was sharply divided as to whether he should sign it or veto it. I went in with David Kendall, who was then the president's special counsel and speaking for the Bureau of the Budget against its signature because it would cost many millions of dollars every time federal employees received a day off. Also against it was the traditional business philosophy: They have enough holidays, and if by accident a holiday happens to fall on a Sunday, why, that's too bad. In support of it, I spoke for myself as well as the Civil Service Commission. President Truman had signed an executive order that, when the holiday fell on Saturday, federal employees were granted Friday off. This bill seemed to be the natural consequence of that approach. As a matter of progressive employee relations, it should be signed. This bill had passed with little dissent, and it seemed very obvious, from a political point of view, that it would pass over his veto. President Eisenhower, up to that time, had never had a veto overridden. I carefully avoided emphasizing that political point. He knew that, and he would have resented a straight political argument from me.

The president pondered it. He scrounged a little behind his desk. (Sometimes he would get up and walk around the desk, and you almost felt like you should get up, too, and walk with him.) He "grumped" around, and that is the only word I can use. He looked at the two of us—we had no clue as to which way he was going. Finally he said to me:

"Give me the damn thing. I'll sign it." I slid it over to him for a quick signature. Jerry Kluttz, a daily columnist on federal civilian personnel for the *Washington Post*, found out that I had pushed for its approval. He and Joe Young of the *Washington Evening Star* in their columns referred to it as the "Siciliano Holiday." The name has long since been forgotten, but the holiday subsequently became a part of federal law.

President Eisenhower witnessed my swearing in to the White House position on September 23, 1957, the same day he ordered federal troops to enforce desegregation in Little Rock, Arkansas. As he watched, I had no idea what weighed on his mind (nor how the issues involved at Little Rock would intersect my life). The *New York Times Magazine* had interviewed me for a major story because my new position signified such change in governmental management. But then something really big happened: *Sputnik.* After the Russians put that first satellite into space, our country went wild with uncertainty, unhappiness, concern, even fear. The Russian Bear became a scary international threat—to even mainland U.S.A. As a consequence, the *New York Times Magazine* scrapped the article.

This job offered challenging new frontiers because this area of responsibility had not existed before. The job's importance showed on paper, so I had the job of trying to make it important in fact. My function, as described in Executive Order no. 10729, gave me much planning authority not normally associated with the White House, as well as direct effect in some governmental operations. The position was also unique because I had a small staff of four professionals (something else that had not existed in the White House before, except for the national security adviser).

I worked very closely with the cabinet officers and agency heads. As part of my responsibility, I attended all cabinet meetings, usually held every Friday. Because I was not to sit at the cabinet table, I deliberately chose to sit behind Vice President Richard Nixon so I could look straight across the table at the president. Each week I hurried in to get that particular seat or one like it. After a time I noticed others had the same idea: Lewis L. Strauss, the chairman of the Atomic Energy Commission, and Allen W. Dulles, the CIA head. I watched the president closely, as all of us did. He couldn't keep his face always frozen— his mobile face could flash a grimace or a grin. Being privy to the events in the White House kept life exciting: the intricacies of the cold war unfolded right before our eyes. I especially remember the briefing on Mao and the course of the Chinese "Cultural Revolution" (of the late 1950s), among other top international issues.

I am thankful my job did not include political assignments, so presidential appointments did not concern me. I oversaw the aspect of the public service that the general American public had little knowledge of yet was so needed. The federal government employed 2.3 million Americans in roughly one thousand different occupations. At that time, we had about seventy-seven different pay and compensation systems—sixty-one blue-collar or wage-board systems and sixteen white-collar systems. These systems had no reconciliation of the differences among them, nor had any real work been done, on behalf of the president, to make sense of competing systems. Later, in testimony before the House Post Office and Civil Service Committee, I am quoted in the *Washington Post* as describing the Classification Act, which was used to fix the salaries of a million employees, as a "jumbled inconsistent statutory mess which has been developed in a piecemeal fashion by successive patches of legislation." At the cabinet meetings I listened as one department laid out plans that affected the employees of another department. The agencies were sporadic in their interagency planning, due to jurisdictional pride, as I called it. My job was to try to coordinate, to some degree, this incredible web of unequal pay systems for a more effective executive branch. The emphasis, I quickly learned, was on the words *to try.*

One of my primary concerns was to bring to the average federal employee the realization that the newly appointed Republicans were not cold, callous, and unaware of the needs and wants of the American public. Twenty years of Democratic Party rule was a long time, which made it possible for contentious feelings and mistrust between the Republican appointees and the civil servants. (Unfortunately, I question if anything has changed as we enter the twenty-first century. The attitudes seem the same, regardless of the party in power.) Part of the realities of this relationship stemmed from the 1920s through the 1950s when both governmental unions and management were highly adversarial. This had been complicated in house because of a letter from President Franklin D. Roosevelt regarding the role of trade unions in government. He penned this famous letter, which stood like an order, sometime in the 1930s, wherein he roundly scored attempts to organize federal employees. He basically said, stay away from our door. Some twenty-five years later, this letter still circulated in the White House.

Nonetheless, union memberships had been growing in the various departments. The postal department stood out with an especially powerful union. The civilian worker unions in the Defense establishment became organized (in a lesser degree), and in some instances, such as the Department of Commerce, management and employees worked out their problems through collaborative committees. As the union pressures grew, employee relations achieved star billing and top management could not delegate it to second-level officials.

For decades the unions had wanted the president of the United States to issue an executive order recognizing their status and need for cooperative labor-management relations in government. President Franklin D. Roosevelt's letter moved in the opposite direction, and no succeeding president showed any sign of addressing the issue. With my new position, I thought we could improve the situation. I used my specific delegated authority per the job description in the executive order and began working with the many federal employee labor organizations. I met with their leaders and spoke at their conventions. When people filed grievances, usually procedural in nature, we would see that they were handled. My professional staff, headed by the always level-headed and knowledgeable Joe Winslow, worked with the Civil Service Commission and its investigation department to ensure due process. Shortly after I stepped into the job I realized that President Eisenhower held the same position as the preceding presidents; whether or not he saw the need for change, I recognized that philosophically he would be uncomfortable establishing a new policy. If we couldn't get a presidential executive order, I thought a policy letter should be issued to all the executive agencies under my signature, which spelled out the already established policy to recognize labor unions, procedures for the conduct of grievances, and meetings with the trade union groups that represented the federal employees. The government had to stop ignoring the employee organizations and collaborate with them, which would make the government more effective, economical, and efficient in its performance.

I found the idea of putting such a letter on White House letterhead, though, to be a difficult sell within the administration. Secretary of Labor Mitchell was opposed, and he thought, as I knew he would, that the issue fell within the province of his Labor Department. And Maurice Stans, director of the Bureau of the Budget and a very conservative person, opposed it. So I had the job, as I saw it, of convincing the powers-that-be before going to the president. My staff and I drafted a statement with which I was able to convince the one person who counted the most in this whole effort, Sherman Adams, the chief of staff. Surprisingly, he easily accepted my rationale.

I asked if he wanted me to explain this to the president.

He looked at me, hesitated (which was unusual), and said that he would do it. He wanted to avoid a full-dress battle with other agencies, that is, circulation of the draft to all agencies for their comments. This would invite certain death. I, too, wanted to avoid that and said so to him. Privately, he could argue the strong point that the letter merely put a presidential imprimatur on procedures that were fairly well established (though not by every agency). The president personally approved my letter, and I issued it on June 3, 1958.

The letter effectively reinforced the authorized procedures as written into law in the *Federal Personnel Manual* by the Civil Service Commission four years earlier. In essence, this approach, advocated by Harvard and most public affairs schools, emphasized human relations and a highly participative management: it sought collaborative rather than adversarial collective bargaining. We wanted to dispel the longtime strongly felt practice, as sanctioned by President Roosevelt's letter, that federal managers should frown on—even oppose—employees joining unions. Simple, yes, but it upset the status quo in the federal agencies.

Here we had, for the first time, a fundamental philosophy of acceptance by the president of the United States of America of employee-employer relationships (trade unions) in the public sphere. Yet, after all that, the unions remained unhappy because, though it was "a progressive step," it fell short of what they wanted. "We need something stronger than a mere letter, not even signed by the President, to effect a workable labor-management program in Government," wrote James Campbell, president of the American Federation of Government Employees. But they couldn't miss the point that the letter came out on official White House stationery, signed by me—not a staff assistant but among the select few allowed to use the words *to the president*. The phrase conveyed an authority not unlike a Roman Catholic cardinal (but not the pope!). Note: This action would be lost in today's White

House, where there are some eighty-plus special assistants "to the president." The letter received great attention in the constituency it was meant for. It received approval in the union papers and in their meetings around the country. In a short while, they smartly began to treat it as a presidential executive order in their effort to correct gross violations of good employee-management relations. It reached its full appreciation later that fall. On September 26, 1958, in his regular column in the *Government Standard,* the same James Campbell wrote, "I'll take my crow with mushroom sauce and wild rice. As a side dish, I'll eat my words. I refer specifically to the statement I made to the press last June commenting on Rocco C. Siciliano's memo to agency heads on employee-management relations." He noted: "Well the Siciliano memo has done good" and that, while it appeared to be a restatement of policy already in place, "it has caused just about every department and agency to take a fresh look at this area of personnel management. . . . It has brought directly to the attention of Cabinet members and agency heads their responsibilities for the development of a climate which encourages union-management consultation in the Government Service."

As the assistant secretary of labor at thirty-one years of age, I reached my fifteen minutes of fame as "Ike's Youngest." I was also impressed when told that I was the first Italian American to serve at this level in the executive branch.

The Labor Department changed dramatically with the appointment of James P. Mitchell as secretary *(seated)*. He shook up the management of the department and attempted to change the public understanding of the department's purpose. *Standing, left to right:* Assistant Secretary of Labor Harrison Hobart, Under Secretary Arthur Larson, Assistant Secretary Rocco C. Siciliano, Assistant Secretary F. Ernest Wilkins, and Administrative Assistant Secretary James Dodson, in 1954.

One of my responsibilities at the Labor Department was to attend, every Saturday, legislative policy meetings at the White House. The political analyses and exchanges were vigorous, testing, and easy to enjoy. Occasionally, President Eisenhower would drop in. I am on his left and Chief of Staff Wilton Persons is on his right.

President Dwight D. Eisenhower witnessed my swearing in (by Judge George W. Latimer) to the new position of special assistant to the president for personnel management, a position that required much innovation and proving. A formidable challenge was the issuance of a policy letter supporting the right of federal employees to be active in labor union organizations, contrary to an earlier edict by President Franklin D. Roosevelt.

On the day of my swearing in at the White House, my son John, age three, had a terrible cold. President Eisenhower reached down and said, "What do we have here?" The press ran this photo widely across the nation. Also, left to right, Loretta, Fred, Vincent, and Marion.

"Take me out to the ball game." May 29, 1959, Washington Senators game. I did not want to go—was very busy—until Ann Whitman (the president's secretary) insisted I should come. I'm first from the left in the first row, next to David Kendall, chief counsel; to the president's right is George Allen. Right of the president is Calvin Griffith, Washington Senators owner.

I arranged the first policy meeting of black civil rights leaders with a president of the United States in the White House. *Left to right:* Lester Granger, National Urban League; Dr. Martin Luther King Jr., Southern Christian Leadership Conference; E. Frederic Morrow, White House administrative officer; President Eisenhower; A. Philip Randolph, international president, Brotherhood of Sleeping Car Porters; Attorney General William Rogers; me; and Roy Wilkins, president, NAACP. Wilkins's smile, like his letter, conflicts with his later criticism.

THE WHITE HOUSE

WASHINGTON

June 25, 1958

MEMORANDUM FOR THE PRESIDENT

As an aftermath of your meeting with the Negro leaders, you may be interested in the following observations:

1. The Negro leaders were more than enthusiastic about their reception, the length of time granted for the meeting, the willingness to be heard and the willingness to speak, and the intense and sympathetic attention given them.

2. Immediately afterwards, they met with the press. Their accounts of the conference were faithful and honest. After much give-and-take, with repeated attempts to evoke criticism from the members of the group (particularly from Mr. Wilkins), a comment was made that they appeared to have been "brainwashed." Mr. Louis Lautier, only Negro member of the National Press Club, finally asked Mr. Wilkins (with some sarcasm), just what had occurred in the meeting which brought about the change in Mr. Wilkins' attitude from that of a month ago. Mr. Wilkins, visibly irritated, made no real response.

3. After a number of conversations with knowledgeable people, I am convinced that this meeting was an unqualified success -- even if success in this area is built on sand.

Rocco C. Siciliano

Memo to President Eisenhower re: Civil Rights leaders meeting.

The family—Fred, Loretta, Vincent, and John (Maria yet to come).

Governor Sherman Adams, President Eisenhower's chief of staff, square-dancing with Marion in 1957. Adams had an idiosyncratic, abrupt character, but I was not disturbed by it. Without him, Eisenhower's administration lost a principal mover and shaker of operational efficiency. This photo was reprinted many times in national publications.

At home with the family.

With President Kennedy in 1963. The National Civil Service League, of which I was vice chairman, annually recognized outstanding public servants. The award winners had a chance to meet with the president. The two men here are Bernard L. Gladieux, chairman, and James Watson, the executive director.

Pictured are the three primary advocates for civil rights change in the Eisenhower administration. They are (to my left) Fred Morrow, largely unrecognized today for his life and work; Herbert Brownell, attorney general, responsible for much of the civil rights progress in the 1950s; and Max Rabb, a key negotiator and liaison with the African American community during the first five Eisenhower years. This photo was taken at a 1990 Eisenhower reunion at Columbia University.

At the White House on April 14, 1964, the National Civil Service League presented to President Lyndon B. Johnson the winners of the distinguished public service awards.

The saucy and animated Harry Bridges, of the International Longshoremen and Warehousemen's Union, was at the top of his game when I was president of the employer organization, Pacific Maritime Association, in San Francisco.

My confirmation hearing on January 29, 1969, as under secretary of commerce (later changed to deputy secretary) with Senator Wallace F. Bennett *(right)*, the senior Utah senator and my mentor, and Senator George Murphy of California *(left)*.

Secretary of Commerce Maurice Stans *(right)* and I with President Nixon. As Stans's deputy, I accomplished much, but comparisons with Ike kept interfering and I chose to leave.

Maurice Stans and I hosted a rare gathering for former secretaries of commerce on June 7, 1969, including *(left to right)* Admiral Lewis Strauss, Averell Harriman, John Connor, Charles Sawyer, Stans, Sinclair Weeks, Alexander Trowbridge, C. R. Smith, and me. Working with Stans made life bearable for me in the Nixon administration.

The strangest presidential meeting I ever attended! I had no real idea of its purpose in advance except a clue given to me by Peter Flanigan, who (in answer to why we were invited) said: "The President wants to talk about you Eyeties." That is when I learned Secretary of Transportation John Volpe, on Nixon's left, would be there. What followed was a mystical monologue.

Marion and I at a dinner in the John Quincy Adams Room, State Department, on April 15, 1970.

Marion and I square-dancing at son Vincent's marriage to Susan Campbell (in a park near Stanford University). Vincent is laughing in the background.

The Italian ambassador Egidio Ortona awarded me with the government of Italy's second highest order (for a foreigner), Commendatore (Knight Commander), on May 21, 1971. Also John, Marion, and Maria.

Marion was responsible for our outdoor adventures, including trips to many of the great rivers of the American West. We paddled these sports yaks down Green River in August 1971, just after we had moved to Los Angeles. Little did I know that President Nixon had implemented a wage-price freeze and was making plans for me to serve on the Pay Board.

TEN

WALKING ON SAND

ONE OF THE most important people in the Eisenhower White House was Sherman Adams, the former governor of New Hampshire and now chief of staff. I met Governor Adams during my time in the Labor Department and frequently communicated with him at the White House. I greatly admired him. I loved the twinkle in his eyes, and he showed warmth—even in his abrupt speech. One day I walked into the dining room (called the White House Mess at that time, but when the last word took on another connotation it then became the White House Dining Room) where Governor Adams sat eating with a guest. He signaled to me and asked me to join them. Through such a spontaneous introduction I met Governor Luis Munoz Marin of Puerto Rico. Another time I met the poet Robert Frost. Governor Adams did have eccentric behavior. For example, he never said "good-bye" on the telephone; he would just hang up. That bothered a lot of people, who referred to him as curt. In the many meetings I had with him, sometimes several a week and most of the time with other staffers, I saw the respect he had for people. True, he did not want you to speak unless you had something to say. His abrupt nature had no intent of discourtesy. He had much to do and he wanted to conserve his time. I thought he was truly a gifted man: a great administrator, facilitator, and decision maker. I don't think there's any doubt that Governor Adams only reflected what the president wanted.

Inside the White House, I found Governor Adams available and easy to approach. He fulfilled the key role for a successful administration, and he had the ability to make decisions. His broad understanding of the issues gave him the capacity to know when *not* to make decisions. Governor Adams directed the policy-making process that fostered internal debate between those staff people who supported a policy and those who opposed it. We engaged in tough, rigorous, candid debates in which the president often took part. Governor Adams also operated as a facilitator between the cabinet and the president. Eisenhower's administration utilized the cabinet government as no other, and under Governor Adams the Eisenhower administration thrived. His strong chief of staff position contributed to Eisenhower's legacy, which many other presidents have tried to follow.

During those years, the country's economy flourished and people generally enjoyed life. But the 1950s, being bookended by the global upheaval of World War II and the riotous '60s, were never as tranquil as *Leave It to Beaver* reruns would suggest. The United States was in transition and great confusion, all compounded by the Red Scare. As good White House staff officials, we tried to be anonymous in our behavior, though not always. One early evening Marion and I went to the Capitol to meet Barbara and Jack Martin (a veteran Senate hand, legislative assistant to President Eisenhower, and later federal judge). As we rode the senators' elevator from one floor to another, Senator Joe McCarthy of Wisconsin got on, looking worn and distracted. He showed the after-effects of his Senate censure (along with giving his name to the dictionary term for one who accuses another of disloyalty without any proof). He got off at the next floor, with Marion's words suddenly ringing after him, "Wash the elevator." I heard it clearly. Who else, I don't want to know! We exited at the next floor. I attempted to remonstrate with Marion, reminding her of Eisenhower's behavior, which was to ignore McCarthy. Fortunately, no press was nearby. Marion looked undaunted and satisfied.

Besides the hostility of the cold war, other incidents kept the threat of war imminent, as George Colburn has presented in his documentary *Eisenhower: The Dangerous Years:* a leftist coup in Iran, the Suez crisis of 1956, American marines landed on the beaches of Lebanon, Russia launched *Sputnik,* the downing of an American U-2 spy plane, the Hungarian revolution, the Korean War, the military defeat of France in Vietnam, a major crisis in Berlin, a calamitous summit in Paris, the Cultural Revolution of the '50s in China, and the proliferation of nuclear weapons.

Amidst all this tumult, Eisenhower, with his "hidden-hand" style, fought for stability. I believe he understood the temperament of the country and how fast we could accomplish any changes as well as how to downplay those things that he felt the public could not readily accept. He clearly felt the country was unprepared for drastic measures—as he defined them. This style caused Eisenhower to be labeled a gradualist. He did not want to make any giant leap forward on any issues, but he insisted on consistent forward movement. Most certainly, the international issues loomed large in the 1950s, but domestic civil rights gave the administration almost as much concern. In 1954, the Supreme Court unanimously decided against "separate but equal" in public schools *(Brown v. Topeka Board of Education)* and in 1955 ordered school districts to proceed toward desegregation "with all deliberate speed." In 1896, the U.S. Supreme Court, in *Plessy v. Ferguson,* had annunciated the "separate but equal" doctrine, which the *Brown* decision reversed.

The *Brown* decision provoked white segregationists, and they responded with a rampage in the South. White Citizens Councils assembled to support the oppressive status quo of Jim Crow of the South. A manifesto, *Warning of Grave Dangers,* proclaimed that civil rights legislation threatened liberty. Then, case by case, the pressure built. Several white men brutally murdered a fourteen-year-old black boy, Emmett Till, in Mississippi, which was followed by no rectification, no justice. Whites harassed blacks, even killed them, "to keep them in their place." Riots exploded around individual circumstances, such as when, in early 1956, a young black woman, Autherine Lucy, tried to enroll in college. The black people stood fast and fought for their basic rights of first-class citizenship. This reign of terror brought about more devoted action by the black activists. Then, in Montgomery, Alabama, when Rosa Parks refused to give up her bus seat to a white man, she ignited the boycott led by a then relatively unknown Baptist minister, Dr. Martin Luther King Jr.

I remember, when I first moved to Washington, D.C., in 1946, my shock at seeing black people standing at one end of a Woolworth's lunch counter while many empty seats were available. I quickly learned that

African American citizens could not get a seat at a Washington, D.C., restaurant also patronized by whites. They couldn't go to any of the D.C. theaters, and they couldn't go to any of the public swimming pools, except when segregated. Washington, D.C., was effectively a southern town, governed by a congressional committee stacked with southern senators and congressmen. But the District stood under federal jurisdiction, so Eisenhower used it as a model city for desegregation. He did it in his first year in office without any legislation (which the southern senators would inevitably filibuster—as they did with most such legislation). He pushed to implement President Truman's executive order that the armed forces be desegregated, he brought unprecedented numbers of blacks into the executive branch, and he put into effect a nondiscrimination clause that prohibited government contractors from discrimination on the basis of race or color. The Civil Rights Act of 1957 managed to get passed (it was weak, but a beginning); this was the first federal Civil Rights Act since the Reconstruction era. It protected basic voting rights, the Civil Rights Commission was created, and the role of the civil rights section was elevated to that of an assistant attorney general in the Justice Department. The Civil Rights Act of 1957 divided the black community because the segregationists in the Senate had compromised the act (in particular, Part III, which called for the enforcement of "constitutional rights other than voting rights," was dropped).

In May 1958, Governor Adams called me into his office. Maxwell Rabb, the secretary of the cabinet, had resigned the month before. Rabb also served as the White House minority representative (back then, presidents never assigned anyone full-time to minority issues). For five years Rabb had handled the requests, problems, and protests of the black community. Adams handed me a file and said that "diverse colored" leaders were calling for a meeting with the president. He asked me to review their requests and give him my opinion as to what we should do.

I felt it a questionable honor to be assigned such a complicated issue. On the one hand, Governor Adams knew I would not create trouble nor would I make waves. On the other hand, they undoubtedly knew that I would handle it the way I saw fit. My staff and I were immersed in seventy-hour workweeks addressing the multitude of personnel issues that had emerged as soon as my position was created—the problems affecting 2.3 million federal employees. I was in the midst of writing a labor-management letter regarding recognition of federal employee unions, which I thought would be my most significant act as assistant to the president. We were also analyzing the effect of a major pay increase. My function had some but no close relationship with minority issues, which involved intricate social justice problems and fundamental constitutional rights.

Though Governor Adams knew some of this, I could not say no to him. He had made sure that I understood that this was terribly important to the president. I took the assignment and in a few days realized it could eclipse all my other projects. It was front page. Almost immediately, I found it surprising that the president, at that time in office for just over five years, had never met with black leaders in the White House. He had met with members of the business community, employee organizations, educators, and church groups; almost any other civic public organization had always had easy communications with presidents of the United States, except the black community. I found numerous telegrams and requests from Adam Clayton Powell, Martin Luther King Jr., A. Philip Randolph, Roy Wilkins, and leaders of many other African American groups. All were seeking a visit with President Eisenhower in the White House. A few weeks before I received the assignment, the president had spoken to a "summit meeting" of black leaders at the Dunbar Hotel in Washington, D.C. But he had not, as such, sat down in a formal policy conference in the White House office with a group of black leaders. No president had ever done that.

Max Rabb, successfully in his mind, held off the black leaders from seeing the president. He tried to satisfy their concerns with letters and personal visits. Rabb, a very adroit, smart man with an effusive, outgoing personality, had the best of intentions with respect to wanting people to meet with the president or government leaders, but the pragmatism of the times said you do not force a civil rights issue onto the president of the United States. Rabb's response to the African American leaders had always been, "Don't worry, your message is getting through because I'm taking it in." I quickly realized that this "know your place" role was finished, and I had to change it.

I went through the letters and found a recent request from the Reverend Martin Luther King Jr. At that time, he was the up-and-coming leader of black civil rights. He had gained national recognition for his role in the Montgomery Improvement Association and their successful bus boycott. He had met and discussed civil rights with Vice President

Nixon and Labor Secretary James P. Mitchell. Recently, he had been highly praised for his closing speech (known as the "Give us the ballot!" speech) at the Prayer Pilgrimage, a 1957 march in Washington, D.C., to commemorate the third anniversary of the Supreme Court's *Brown* decision. After that speech the black media, such as *Ebony* magazine, proclaimed Dr. King as the new leader of black men, though he was not yet a household name.

After thinking it through, I went in to see Governor Adams, and I proposed the president meet with a few of the black leaders. He asked whom I would call, and I picked Martin Luther King Jr. because he seemed to be responsible and measured in his approach. Adams listened to my request and supporting reasons. His only questions were how many would attend and who in addition to Dr. King. He agreed with my recommendation that no more than four should attend and left it up to me to work out the actual attendees with Dr. King. The meeting took only a few minutes. He said, "Go ahead." He did so in my presence without leaving his desk or calling President Eisenhower.

I sought out Fred Morrow, the first African American to ever attain a professional status in the White House, who served as the administrative director of the Office of Special Projects. Morrow had been in the White House for several years with offices only 150 feet from mine. Up until that point, we knew each other only casually. I told him about the proposed meeting and asked for his help, and he started to educate me. That's when I really came to know him, a very conscientious, sensitive, and keenly intelligent person with a rich, crisp voice suited for the lawyer he was. He took his responsibilities in a dual fashion: he served his president and his race. In his own words, he didn't want to be a "race saver," but he knew he stood as "a symbol of achievement" for the eighteen million black citizens he represented in the White House.

Fred Morrow and I were both realizing first-ever opportunities that came as a result of World War II. The war effort assimilated the recent ethnic immigrants: the Italians, Greeks, Poles, Irish, and others. They went from being viewed as inferior "races" to being accepted as ethnic Americans, as long as their skin was white. At the same time, the war created a seedbed for the civil rights movement. During the war blacks migrated to jobs in the North, which increased their numbers in the middle class and brought them political clout to push civil rights issues. With the black minority growing in its political influence, both the

Democrats and the Republicans were beginning to address these issues; the 1956 campaign was the first time presidential candidates addressed civil rights issues. The increasing black vote brought the issues to the surface. Some thought I served the president as a symbol of an ethnic group. I gave speeches to Italian American groups, and I received awards and recognition for my first-ever achievements. In a minor way, I served as a role model, but not a soldier. Morrow fought for equal rights every day of his life. As an Italian American, my status in American society had been greatly resolved by the war. As an African American, Morrow and his issues were brought to the headlines by the war.

Fred Morrow had worked with Max Rabb and had tried to arrange this meeting on previous occasions, though he was, in his own words, "powerless to do anything." When Rabb left, Governor Adams asked Morrow to handle all the White House correspondence involving civil rights and black affairs (my assignment focused solely on this particular meeting). Morrow was in a very conflicted situation, caught between being dutiful to the president and effective in his representation of African Americans. He felt his impotence deeply, and I could only sympathize. (He tells his own story eloquently in his books, *Black Man in the White House* [1963] and *Forty Years a Guinea Pig* [1980]. He directs his painful recriminations to the society of that time as well as individual experiences. His sorrows touch the reader, and all Americans should recognize his successes.) He and I hit it off. His judgment in this situation was essential. He understood the players and knew the political realities. Of course, we would meet Dr. King together.

I returned to my office and called Dr. King in Alabama. I identified myself and told him I knew of his requests to meet with the president. I said that sometime when he was in Washington I would be glad to meet with him and we could discuss his requests. He jumped and immediately accepted. He said he would check his schedule and get back to me. Later that day, his secretary called back and set an appointment for Monday, June 9, 1958, at two o'clock.

I also discussed it with the new attorney general, Bill Rogers, and asked if he would come over to the meeting. He was unable to attend, and instead Judge Lawrence Edward Walsh, the deputy attorney general, would be there.

On June 9, Dr. King met with Fred Morrow, Deputy Attorney General Lawrence E. Walsh, and me. Dr. King came in quiet, poised, and expectant. I recall his physical appearance and manner as, in one word, controlled. We had three things to discuss for the meeting: what to talk about, when to do it, and whom to invite. We set no parameters for the meeting with the president. We couldn't. We asked Dr. King, and he felt, as I wrote in a memo to Governor Adams, the "subject matter would be largely confined to some potential problems of school integration which might occur this fall. He mentioned Virginia, Dallas, Texas, and Little Rock." It was evident to me that more important than the agenda, in Dr. King's mind, was the mere fact of the meeting. As Dr. King expressed in a letter he had written the year before: "[I]f it does nothing else [such a meeting] would at least give persons of goodwill in general and Negro Americans in particular a feeling that the White House is listening to the problems which we confront."

Our biggest topic concerned whom to invite. Along with Martin Luther King Jr., we quickly agreed on A. Philip Randolph, the vice president of the AFL-CIO and long-standing head of the Brotherhood of Sleeping Car Porters. Then in his seventieth year, Randolph—the Old Lion—stood as the longtime undisputed spokesman for change and integration in the business place. Most Americans knew and trusted him as a respected citizen. As for the others, Dr. King felt we should definitely include Roy Wilkins, the executive secretary of the NAACP. The nomination of Wilkins didn't bother me, but Fred Morrow and I knew some people in the White House had feelings about him because he had been most outspoken and critical of President Eisenhower.

The person of real concern was Congressman Adam Clayton Powell of Harlem. A Democrat, he had announced his political support of President Eisenhower. His position as a longtime national figure and a congressman of some prominence warranted consideration, but Morrow and I did not think he should be a part of the group. Powell was under tax indictment, so serious political reasons existed for not including him. His dominant nature concerned me. He would try to take the meeting over and would have made it into a political football. I felt that with him present, it wouldn't be a thoughtful, progressive type of meeting. Dr. King easily agreed not to have Powell. In my judgment, Dr. King was relieved.

Though we left Powell out, he later pushed his way into the limelight by portraying himself to the press as the brainchild of the conference. This put the White House in a difficult spot, so it became necessary for Jim Hagerty, the White House press secretary, to rush a story into print to deny Congressman Powell's claim. Later, Powell leveraged this attention by demanding that a black woman—he suggested the president of the National Council of Negro Women—be added to the delegation.

We recommended that the three black leaders meet with the president as soon as possible. Governor Adams was all for it, and the president agreed to it. I called Dr. King to tell him that the appointment was set for Monday, June 23. About two weeks later, Dr. King came to my office a second time. Assistant Attorney General for Civil Rights Wilson White came over from the Justice Department. We confirmed the three participants and added Lester B. Granger, the executive secretary of the Urban League, a strong and forthright advocate of black economic progress.

Everything went smoothly for me (I was also very preoccupied with getting the labor-management letter out on June 3, 1958, with its enormous aftermath). Morrow, by his account, had a very different experience. Down at his end of the hall he responded to bags of daily mail and talked on the telephone, day and night, to countless people across the country who wanted to be part of the delegation (it went so far that he left town to escape the phone calls because people had discovered his unlisted home phone). For Morrow, with the participating leaders chosen and the date set, it was finally over. We could get on with the meeting, which we all greatly anticipated.

The morning of the meeting, June 23, 1958, Attorney General Bill Rogers, Fred Morrow, and I met in advance for a final review prior to briefing the president. I suggested we caution the president on two words—*patience* and *tolerance*—that he had recently used in a speech to black leaders. The black community considered them patronizing—for example, "with patience and tolerance your status will be improved." We all agreed that he shouldn't take this tack.

We went in to brief President Eisenhower. He appeared expectant and recognized the meeting's importance. He did not seem entirely comfortable as to what was expected of him. As always, his essential decency was evident. I explained that the men were going to present a program of action to which they hoped he would agree. We did not expect verbal fireworks but knew that they would make specific proposals. Though unfamiliar with the details, we knew that uppermost in their minds would be a request for a White House conference on civil rights to be preceded by a presidential pronouncement on the dangers of continued segregation. Everything went well, except the mention of the two words—*patience* and *tolerance*. I kept looking at Attorney General Rogers to make this semantic suggestion; after all, he was the ranking officer. He remained silent and for good reason. Fred Morrow was not going to move into that territory. Finally, I spoke up.

"Mr. President, there are two words that generally cause some negative reaction, that I might suggest you not use when you meet with them. These two words are *patience* and *tolerance*."

He looked at me and snapped, just as he could do, "Well, Siciliano, you think I'm going to avoid good English words?"

I struggled on, saying that this could help avoid causing the wrong reaction. Even though this was a minor explosion, I had become familiar enough with him and these little outbursts that I felt it could be done and that he would soon forget it. Morrow flashed a look of appreciation. I did not say that after some 350 years, black citizens in America were tired of hearing those words used by well-meaning white citizens. I was not that bold.

The leaders came in. Before the meeting I found out from Dr. King that they had been up most of the night preparing their remarks. I knew they regarded this meeting as an epochal event, and even though they had only thirty minutes they decided that rather than have one spokesman they would each speak for about five minutes. Introductions were brief and the atmosphere was formal. I sat slightly behind Wilkins. You were not supposed to take notes when outsiders met with President Eisenhower, but I could not help it. I moved my chair back and turned myself sideways. I took an envelope out of my pocket and laid it on my knee, making notes as they spoke.

The men eloquently described in careful detail the "forces in our nation's life [that] are changing the pattern of Negro-white relations." Mr. Randolph was the nominal leader of the group. In his resonant voice, Mr. Randolph prefaced their written statement by strongly commending the president for his many efforts to advance the political and economic status of African Americans. He spoke strongly and favorably about the president's action in the Little Rock episode. Then he read their nine recommendations contained in the full statement. Though the fuller prepared statement was given to the president, they did not specifically refer to it. Essentially, each speaker spoke without notes.

Dr. King concentrated on the first three recommendations, which were designed to help mobilize the spirit that, in turn, would aid in the fight for abolishment of segregation. He asked for a presidential pronouncement of desegregation "that the law will be vigorously upheld" in order to give the nation a moral boost. He also requested the president conduct "a White House conference of constructive leadership." He saw a need for the president to come out as a moral leader, which would help with the social, political, and economic reprisals that existed in the South and prevented the goodwill of white southerners from being expressed. He also requested that "a program of education and action" be developed and made available to "appropriate government agencies."

Mr. Wilkins commended the president on his armed services integration, which was nearly complete, and his involvement in the passage of the previous year's Civil Rights Bill. He urged that the administration seek again the inclusion of Part III of the Civil Rights Act, which had been deleted during the heat of the debate, namely, "that constitutional rights other than voting rights may be enforced by the United States attorney general." He was "dismayed, distressed, and angered" by the Lemley court decision of the previous week, wherein the district federal judge in Arkansas had given the Little Rock Board of Education a stay of two and one-half years before integrating its school system. The decision had given segregationists a map, meaning that this decision explained to the segregationists how best to defeat school integration (the Lemley decision was overturned shortly thereafter). He also supported the necessity of protecting the right to vote, which he called the "most effective and bloodless way" to solve this whole problem.

Mr. Granger recalled to the president that, in his lifetime, he had seen three different phases of Negro activity in the field of civil rights: "during his World War I days, during the time of the depression, and today." He said he had not known of a period "when the bitterness of the Negro showed 'more signs of congealing' than today."

The discussion was careful but warm—even passionate—and always civil. There were no strident tones, yet the black leaders were urging that more needed to be done from the executive offices. Attorney General Rogers observed that bitterness might exist *because* of the very fact of progress: in prior years, speeches were made but progress did not follow, so hope never built up, but during the Eisenhower administration some of the hopes had been realized, thus the bitter reactions. He assured them that occasional setbacks or delays should be regarded only as temporary. The attorney general said his office was defending the laws by aggressive court action whenever the legal facts were sufficient to ensure a successful conclusion, and he emphasized how unwise and damaging it would be to institute court action in every individual complaint situation. In addition, he noted the lack of a written preface on their statement given to the president that reflected Mr. Randolph's oral presentation (wherein he commended the administration's accomplishments), and thus their statement gave no appearance of appreciation for the gains in recent years. Last, the attorney general recalled Mr. Wilkins's willingness to abandon Part III of the proposed Civil Rights Bill during the debate.

The president said that "he was extremely dismayed" to hear that after five and one-half years of effort and action in this field, these gentlemen were saying that bitterness on the part of the African American people was at its height. He wondered if further constructive action in this field would result only in more bitterness. Mr. Granger, seconded by Mr. Randolph and Mr. Wilkins, hastily assured the president that the bitterness was not directed at the president or the administration but only at the communities in which progress was slow or stopped, and that the bitterness consisted of individual reactions where such obstacles were met.

The president said that there might be at first blush some value in convoking a White House conference, but added his doubt that it would produce anything. Mr. Rogers emphasized again that the president had directed him to take aggressive actions in all matters affecting the federal authority. The president agreed and then emphasized the importance of voting rights.

Throughout the meeting the president sat absorbed by these speakers—his eyes and posture showed that intense concentration. He listened very carefully. He went from the first, to the second, third, and fourth. He gave them his total attention, which is what I believe made the meeting such a success. As a result, the meeting went well beyond the scheduled thirty minutes, lasting about fifty minutes, which was unusual. And he never used "the words," nor suggested their meaning in his comments to the leaders.

I wrote a memorandum to the president two days later, in part saying, "The Negro leaders were more than enthusiastic about their reception, the length of time granted for the meeting, the willingness to be heard and the willingness to speak, and the intense and sympathetic attention given them." I described briefly the meeting in the adjoining "Fish Room," where they met the press. The black press showed up in force, making up a significant number of the sixty reporters. They shot questions—some angry—at the four men. The four leaders were united in saying that the meeting was very successful. My note to the president states, "Their accounts of the conference were faithful and honest."

This response disconcerted the press, because they wanted conflict: "What did you say? What happened? Had the meeting changed your attitude?" one reporter repeated this to Mr. Wilkins, who had publicly criticized the president a month earlier. Mr. Wilkins became visibly irritated. "Efforts were made to bait Wilkins in the press conference inasmuch as he seems to be the most militant of the group," I wrote in the memorandum, "but I would say that he held himself under control." After much give-and-take, with repeated attempts to evoke criticism from the members of the group (particularly from Mr. Wilkins), Louis Lautier, the first black member of the National Press Club, fired a sarcastic comment, "What went on in there? You fellows brainwashed or something?"

The next day, Lautier's article in the *Washington Afro-American* stated, "Ike leaves 4 leaders 'impressed.'" He quoted Randolph as saying the group was "greatly impressed by the general attitude of the President concerning civil rights." Randolph continued, "[President Eisenhower] feels very deeply that this whole problem of achieving first-class citizenship for colored people must be completed." Then he echoed what Dr. King had said earlier, that "the conference has put a new hope into the hearts of colored people, that as a part of the great American family they have greater assurance of belonging to this family as equals in order that they may utilize the gifts, talents and genius to make America great and strong."

Following the press conference, I went to my office and dictated a memorandum for the files, using the envelope notes and my conversations with Fred Morrow. Because of this, I had a fairly complete report as to what took place, including some verbatim remarks.

I agree with Fred Morrow, who wrote, "the meeting was an historic one." Beyond being the president's first face-to-face conference with black leaders since he took office, for the first time in history a president discussed civil rights policy with black leaders in the White House. For them as black leaders, the meeting had real weight as a very eventful occurrence. It fulfilled Fred Morrow's prediction in a memo he had written two and one-half years earlier to Max Rabb (on November 29, 1955):

> [Such a meeting would be] a demonstration to the whole country that the responsible leaders, white and Negro, have a deep concern about this situation, and wish to sit down and talk about it intelligently and dispassionately. . . . Meetings of this kind always have a steadying effect upon responsible Negro leaders, for they are able to go through the country and assure Negro citizens that the head of the nation is concerned about their welfare and will utilize the prestige of his office to prevail upon all to exercise common sense and common decency in dealing with the problem. By the same token, it notifies any racist element that the Administration frowns upon their un-American tactics, and will use the Office of the Attorney General to bring to justice any infractions of federal laws.

Martin Luther King Jr. appeared as the intellectual soul of the group. Though young, he served as the ideological linchpin that held the group together. He had spoken to me of the importance of such a meeting, especially the symbolism of the White House Oval Office. At the time of the meeting, Dr. King had been heralded in the black press as the true visionary of the civil rights movement. In my judgment the meeting helped establish King as the clear political leader of the black community. Five years later, in 1963, the crystallizing moment of his "I have a dream" speech at the March on Washington—which was broadcast on television into the homes of millions of Americans—brought him widespread, popular recognition for his leadership.

This meeting between President Eisenhower and the black leaders has been criticized, usually because of Eisenhower's reputed "failure" to use the presidency as a pulpit for moral leadership. I disagree with those assertions and believe the meeting represents tangible evidence of President Eisenhower's personal concern. He understood so well the temper of the time. He enveloped his fundamental fairness in a pragmatic approach that he thought 1950s American society—as a whole—would accept. He may not have been able, at that point in his life and career, to address it in the fashion the black leaders requested, but without a doubt he supported their efforts. As he said in 1959: "If it is going to be true to its own founding documents [the U.S. government] does have the job of working toward the time when there is no discrimination made on such inconsequential reason as race, color or religion."

I feel hindsight commentators criticize this "failure" because it is easy to hang modern-day labels on people of another time and place. Equally difficult, if not impossible, is for the historian to understand the reality of the mood and the temperament of the country at the time.

Taylor Branch wrote a key book on civil rights, *Parting the Waters: America in the King Years, 1954 to 1963* (1988). He wrote this comprehensive treatment so well it won the Pulitzer Prize. Branch describes my role in arranging the White House meeting about as well as anyone, but he gets some facts wrong, such as labeling me as "an oil company labor lawyer." I have some very strong disagreement with some of his language, his portrayal of how the people behaved, and their opinions. He editorializes and spins nuances that aren't accurate with what I saw and lived (including my "abrupt resignation in 1958"—a gross error, considering I resigned at the end of 1959). It is one of the better descriptions written of the meeting, though some scholars have yet to recognize the purpose and the consequences of the meeting. I felt then and I feel now the meeting's consequences were most helpful to the advances of the civil rights movement.

Branch concludes the meeting was "an empty still life framed but devoid of substance." His scenario dismisses the whole subject and indirectly singles me out to support his position. Why Branch writes these things, I don't know—he never talked to me. I can only assume he tried to cement his disapproval of the significance of the meeting by citing "evidence" to give his dismissal of the meeting some corroborative reassurance.

Branch refers to "usual, ferocious infighting" preceding the meeting. Perhaps he has made the assumption that because it had happened earlier, it must have happened again. It did not. Fred Morrow, as I mentioned earlier, does note in his book that there had previously been tension in the White House. When I arranged the meeting, everything went very smoothly. The same erroneous assumption must be at work when Branch claims Sherman Adams "tried to block the meeting." The basic protocol inside the White House with Governor Adams as chief of staff made a meeting impossible without his support. In this case, it was very strong support.

Nor was the meeting a bargaining session. Branch states that King had an advantage over his three colleagues because "he was the only preacher on his side," and though his colleagues were "skilled bargainers . . . Eisenhower was far from ready to bargain with them." At no time before the meeting, in the conversations and sessions I had with Dr. King, did he suggest he and his colleagues would come armed with demands and wanting agreements. On the contrary, Branch misses the epochal nature of the meeting because, for the first time in the history of the United States of America, black leaders discussed civil rights policy inside the White House. As a result of this meeting, they sought and received the universal acknowledgment of their leadership of a national movement, which, though well under way by 1958, was still to see more explosive times in the years ahead.

Branch, obviously, gets much of his information from the written record. In Roy Wilkins's autobiography, *Standing Fast*, Wilkins describes the meeting with some sarcasm, especially directed at Attorney General Rogers. Instead of noting that these were Wilkins's later perceptions of the events, not the general consensus at the time, Branch describes the meeting as having some tense exchanges. Wilkins's latter-day version has become a source for scholars, but his account has dramatized the affair. Fred Morrow's account of the meeting (in *Forty Years a Guinea Pig*) contradicts Wilkins's assessment by describing the meeting as "cordial." I don't doubt that Wilkins's feelings were valid, though he hid them well at the time.

The meeting was a success from the administration's point of view, as I think my own memo at the time indicated. The black leaders thought so, too. At the press conference, Wilkins remarked that if the president had immediately agreed to their request, he would have doubted the president's sincerity. "We were greatly encouraged by the attitude of the president," Wilkins added. Their perspective at the press conference is evident in the unabashed smiles on the front page of the following day's *New York Times*.

Branch selectively uses the Wilkins account. In Wilkins's autobiography, after he reveals his deepest feelings, he acknowledges Eisenhower's further efforts. The president "incorporated some of our ideas in the civil rights legislation that he proposed to Congress the following year." And in a note he sent to the president two days after the meeting, on June 25, 1958, Wilkins further reveals how attitudes can fluctuate:

Dear Mr. President:

I wish to express to you my personal appreciation of your courtesy in receiving the delegation of which I was a member on June 23 and the attention you gave to our presentation of the views of Negro American citizens on the present situation in which they find themselves.

In view of the extreme pressure of world affairs affecting the welfare of our country and the peace of the world, it was generous of you to devote an extended interview to us.

While the disabilities under which they live loom large in the minds and hearts of millions of Negro families, they are loyal Americans and realize that their problems, while important, do not enjoy priority over the problems facing the nation in its international relations.

They feel, however, as we attempted to indicate, that their situation has an important relation to international policy and that this and other aspects of their citizenship difficulties will have your careful consideration, as well as such action as is deemed appropriate and effective.

Respectfully Yours,
Roy Wilkins

The president retained his view: You can't legislate goodwill. He thought that time would take care of this, that in a generation or two we would find equality. As Martin Luther King Jr. observed in his autobiography, "President Eisenhower was a man of integrity and goodwill, but I am afraid that on the question of integration he didn't understand the dimensions of social change involved or how the problem was to be worked out."

True to his style, President Eisenhower moved firmly but quietly on other fronts. In my opinion his greatest contributions were the appointment of judges to the federal benches in the southern regions (in sharp contrast to Presidents Truman and Kennedy). As my colleague Arthur Flemming once said, "I feel that possibly the outstanding and most lasting contribution that the Eisenhower administration made to the civil rights movement was its strict adherence to high standards in appointments to the Federal Judiciary. . . . Herbert Brownell and the role that he played in finding some of these judges and persuading the President of the United States to appoint them. . . . [T]hese people really put the civil rights movement in this country on a solid foundation."

My responsibility for this one civil rights aspect of minority concern covered a brief time. It came to fruition without the interference of White House politics simply because of timing. To attempt such a meeting any earlier would have been foolish. The landmark *Brown* case ruling really set the change in motion. Domestic turmoil and internal politics had blocked real progress in the following years, but by 1958, as Taylor Branch describes in his first book, attitudes were improving.

I concluded my memo to President Eisenhower with this statement: "I am convinced that this meeting was an unqualified success—even if success in this area is built on sand." I feel better today, though much has yet to be done; we have seen the enormous progress over the past half century establish a foundation. In a twist of definition, I have come to conclude that tolerance—the very word I advised President Eisenhower not to use in talking to black groups—is the one thing we still need, desperately. Tolerance of those who are different from each of us is sometimes the most difficult human challenge. Southern California, where I have lived since 1971, has become one of the most diverse regions of the world in terms of its polyglot population. Old hatreds and new disputes still crop up and challenge our ability to get along. Conflicts of all gradations continue, but as time passes, I am even more optimistic.

The White House meeting with the black leaders has had a continuing influence on my life. Being a part of that, watching Martin Luther King Jr. and his colleagues advocate the equality of every human being, was for me a defining moment in the history of the American government. I think that Sherman Adams was the only one in the White House to hear Fred Morrow's lonely voice. I was privileged he called me and believed strongly in Morrow's plea.

At this time (July through September 1958), the Eisenhower administration suffered its worst personnel tragedy—Governor Adams experienced intense scrutiny for accepting gifts, including the infamous vicuña coat, from an industrialist friend. Many public officials have done this without losing their objectivity or their jobs, but not this White House chief of staff, who had many enemies willing to attack him. This taciturn model of probity and propriety had stumbled, in their eyes, and they wouldn't allow him to stand up. He had no constituency, except the president who said: "I need him." Overwhelmingly, his defenses were crushed, as he was personally. I was among his loyal colleagues who watched him lose a great deal of weight and age perceptibly in those few months. This man, who had kept his emotions under careful control, just withered away. He resigned in a dramatic radio-television speech on September 22, 1958.

The Eisenhower administration's forte—a decisive chief of staff—became the Achilles' heel once we lost the quick, accurate, incisive Governor Adams. After that, the staff oftentimes became a debating society. We went from man to man; we had to check, check, check in a line of command that worked in a circle. What would start as a two- or three-man discussion would grow to six or seven of us, and when a new man walked in with his own particular philosophy and objections, things took too much time. No one took the brunt of responsibility or, when need be, the blame (which Governor Adams did habitually); we became muddled down by minutiae. We all recognized that the president had been ill, and he had several ailments, but some of the staff had an attitude of complete protection. The idea was to conserve the president's time by presenting a consensus view with a consideration of the pros and cons. In getting there, however, we listened to all viewpoints, which led to an excessive amount of consultation. Quick decisions on anything became impossible. For example, the holiday bill, which I argued successfully for the president to sign, was a relatively minor matter to go to the Oval Office. With Governor Adams, we would never have gone in to see the president. Governor Adams would have simply sent it in with a note saying: Here are the two positions. I recommend you sign or I recommend you not sign. After Governor Adams left, a great many things drifted in to the president. The White House machine stalled.

Governor Adams's replacement, his deputy chief of staff Wilton Persons, was a retired major general who in World War II handled army congressional relations. He was a well-informed and fine person, but he did not approach the job like Governor Adams. He was much more permissive, and he allowed these interminable discussions. He was very charming, gregarious, smooth, and shrewd, with a great storytelling ability and an extremely conservative outlook. He came from a prominent family in Alabama, where his brother had been governor, and was a noted segregationist.

He clearly would not support any of my further efforts regarding the minority folder. At the same time, I was continuing my work on the enormous subject of labor-management relations in the government, which included ongoing issues addressed in my labor-management letter to all government agencies issued in early June 1958. I decided to focus on the specific priorities set out in the executive order, which created my job. I went in to see General Persons and told him I had completed Governor Adams's assignment on the question of the president meeting with the black leaders. Persons made it plain that he did not want to get involved with minorities or in civil rights. Accordingly, he appeared happy to hear me speak of the challenges of my personnel management assignment. I returned to my full-time duties.

Fred Morrow said of General Persons's assignment: "A man with all the training, tradition and emotions of an aristocratic Southerner finds himself the number-one man on the team of a President whose Administration has done more than any other to advance the cause of the Negro in the field of civil rights. What a dilemma!" It bothered me considerably because it signaled the end. Fred Morrow would be left alone. No one else would be asked to assist on minority issues. The request for a national civil rights conference was, of course, ignored. The administration shunted minorities aside for the remaining part of President Eisenhower's term. They regarded this area of concern as safely assigned to the Justice Department under the recently created post of assistant attorney general for civil rights. Though from my position I could not accept that responsibility, it bothered me that no one with enough influence in the White House seemed to care about it. Fred Morrow, certainly, continued his efforts in a yeomanly manner through the administration change in January 1960. He still remains unrecognized for all his valiant efforts and quiet leadership. Many times I have read and reread Morrow's personal summation from his book *Forty Years a Guinea Pig*. He says it best:

> I further resolved that I could never be disloyal to Dwight Eisenhower. Despite his myopic view on civil rights, he was straining every nerve to serve to the best of his ability the interest and the welfare of all the people of the United States. In every decision he had to estimate what was best for all the people, and while he should show concern and deep interest in the ignoble plight of 10 percent of the population, his ultimate decisions had to be based on what he determined was best for the welfare of the whole. To me,

this was a fair and honorable point of view which in no way dismissed the President's derelictions as regards the Black.

Besides these difficult decisions, in just over two years as special assistant I felt we had accomplished much: in addition to my labor-management letter, we got training-authority legislation passed that enabled top-flight civilian career people to get masters and other graduate degrees (just as in the excellent medical and military training programs), which was not as easy to get as it sounds today; we secured the first comprehensive major medical program for federal employees; we proposed an affirmative, comprehensive compensation proposal—the first ever submitted to Congress by any president; we got a 10 percent classified-employee pay raise; and over time, we decompressed the pay scales, which contributed to the federal government's ability to recruit better workers.

Meanwhile, something very exciting came along. President Eisenhower's Advisory Committee on Government Organization, a small "think tank" that advised him on the federal government's organization and management, proposed the idea of an Executive Office of Personnel Management (OPM) headed by a director. (Almost unknown in its operations, the Advisory Committee on Government Organization was made up of Milton Eisenhower; Nelson Rockefeller; Don Price, later dean of Harvard's Kennedy School of Government; and Arthur S. Flemming, director of the Office of Defense Mobilization and later secretary of the Department of Health, Education, and Welfare.) Significantly, for the first time, a major governmental organization would be concerned with the welfare of the federal employees. The organization would have merged the duties of the Civil Service Commission and my special assistant position and would have dissolved those two entities. As Eisenhower contemplated the OPM's creation, Senator Joe Clark of Pennsylvania introduced a bill to create it by legislation.

Everyone accepted the theory of the proposal. I urged that there be no exclusions, which is problematic in government service because many agencies want to be exclusive; thus, it received heavy opposition. The people who objected were good friends of mine, such as Maurice Stans, then director of the Bureau of the Budget, who made sure it never became an official presidential proposal. I was fighting an inbred system. An idea, no matter how good, represents the unknown, and a real substantial reorganization such as the OPM proposal represented a jurisdictional nightmare.

By this time, in the last two years of his second term, President Eisenhower seemed reluctant to take on new initiatives. I knew the creation of the OPM would require him to submit it to and wrangle with Congress. Obviously, he would allow the next president to do it. I remained convinced beyond any doubt of its need. Those people interested in management and government, such as the Committee for Economic Development's Committee for the Improvement of Management in Government (on which I worked), studied this problem. In July 1964, it issued a report calling for exactly what President Eisenhower's Advisory Committee on Government Organization had proposed years earlier. Finally, in 1978, Congress, after lively debates, enacted the Office of Personnel Management (I was happy to testify for its creation), and President Carter signed it into reality.

The job in the White House was the closest I came to doing something for humanity. The issuance of my labor-management letter in June 1958 and the Eisenhower-King meeting—the most important things I did while in the White House—couldn't have been done without Governor Adams. The difference with the OPM proposal was that without Governor Adams, my best efforts could not overcome the inertia. Nothing I could do would make it happen.

Even though President Eisenhower once referred to my position by the army term *inspector general,* that was impossible. I wish I could have acted with the unquestioned authority of the inspector general. Working in the White House was the most challenging, satisfying, and frustrating experience. I was not unhappy, and I knew I could never duplicate that powerful surrounding. But I knew my place, and that was it—you had to know your place. In that environment, I had found the limit of my power as to what I could accomplish. I had authority spelled out in the executive order, but it overstated the realities of what I could do. We didn't have *power.* For that reason, I wanted to get away from my splendid situation. I accepted a private law firm opportunity and left government service at the end of November 1959.

ELEVEN

CASTING ABOUT

TWO TOP GOVERNMENT positions had only whetted my appetite. At thirty-seven years old, I wondered about and ached for what next to do. Vice President Nixon had seemed a shoo-in for the presidency, but I did not want to work for his administration. It was time to establish my legal career. My accomplishments gave me a self-confidence that I had not previously known: I no longer felt I had to prove anything. I just wanted to take advantage of my skills as a lawyer.

While I was casting about for job opportunities, my college friend Bob Barker, who had helped me get into the first Eisenhower administration, invited me to join his law firm, Wilkinson, Cragun, and Barker. Though they were not a big-name Washington firm, they were people of substance with an excellent reputation, known as the "Indian claims law firm." The Indian Tribal Claims Commission Act, passed in 1946, gave the American Indian tribes the right to file suit against the U.S. government for payment of forfeited lands, among other things. Dr. Ernest Wilkinson was the pioneer, and he heavily promoted passage of the act while with a famous New York City law firm: Hughes, Hubbard, Blair, and Reed (former chief justice Hughes's law firm). Wilkinson, his brother, Glen, and John Cragun handled the leading and famed case, the Ute Indian claim, which when concluded became the largest judgment against the U.S. government ever awarded at that time—more than $30 million. It established the firm, and it made Wilkinson rich. Though Dr. Wilkinson went back to Provo, Utah, to head what was then a small school known as Brigham Young University, he continued to play a key role in the firm's progress.

The law firm on Jefferson Place was a brief two-minute walk from my office in the Executive Office Building (now named the Eisenhower Executive Office Building). The firm's primary effort was in prosecuting some seventy or eighty Indian claims cases. These required years of litigation, and no income before their resolution. The firm hoped I could attract non-Indian legal work to help the ongoing office costs. Widening the scope of its business was easy to understand but not easy to do. As a White House assistant in those days, I had been really anonymous. The art of legal "rainmaker" eluded me, and I don't claim any great success. Actually, my first paid legal task was to write the bylaws for a newly established farmers' cooperative. Doing work usually assigned to a junior lawyer, I struggled to smash my ego and not think about the White House. Fortunately, business improved when I secured a very important client that became the firm's largest fee-paying client, the American Society of Travel Agents (ASTA). Other representation required becoming a registered lobbyist for a Central American sugar group. Later, I became managing partner, which was more of a headache, making sure the lawyers were content in their working arrangements. When my senior partners offered to add my name to the masthead, I declined. I was unsure, unsatisfied, and did not want such a sign of permanence.

As I endured the pains of practicing law, all hell broke loose in Washington, D.C.: John F. Kennedy upset Vice President Nixon in the 1960 election. The Kennedy atmosphere—his youth, intelligence, and good looks, along with the collective brainpower of his young crowd—was "electric." Robert Frost described the epidemic of goodwill at the inauguration as "A golden age of poetry and power. Of which this noonday's the beginning hour." Dream clouds floated from the White House. I watched as Kennedy's administration swooped in and attempted to reshape the progress of American society. From my office one block away, I could look down at the White House. I read the headlines in the newspaper and could imagine the rooms wherein these ideas were discussed and decisions made. My private personal concerns that I had worked on when I was in the White House suddenly became headline issues. Certainly, some of these issues were forced on the Kennedy administration—such as civil rights—but others came as a result of the youthful exuberance of the young testing their powers. I felt envious. Much younger than the Eisenhower assembly, they were my age, thirty-seven, and some were even younger than when my appointment had caused comment as "Ike's youngest." Kennedy, himself, was forty-three years old.

Thus, I was excited when a Kennedy emissary, Dick McGuire, walked over from the White House and offered me the Republican vacancy on the Civil Service Commission, then the top organization (with three members) affecting all federal civilian employees. Though flattered that they had thought of me, I rejected it. The commission, a major player at the time, was a dead-end because I would have been the minority member. Furthermore, the authorized salary, twenty thousand dollars a year, was five hundred dollars less than what I had gotten fifteen months earlier at the White House.

For some months, I squeezed into the role of labor arbitrator, hearing and deciding labor disputes between employers and their employees, the latter being represented by labor unions. I traveled about the region hearing labor disputes in mostly small towns. I liked it because it put me in direct contact with the workingman's situation. My decisions here, however, were not as lopsided in favor of labor as when at the National Labor Relations Board. Eventually, I had to stop—not enough income for the law firm.

As I redoubled my efforts to bring in revenue for the firm I began to see a discrepancy in my compensation. My partners were good people and first-class lawyers, but they followed a very complicated compensation system regarding the distribution of fees from the various Indian tribal claims, which rewarded those with the most years in the firm. I would never qualify because I could see the end of Indian claims litigation, while ASTA was our largest current cash-flow client. (The right to file claims under the Indian Claims Act had expired some years earlier.) More important than the money, I found to my surprise that practicing law did not excite me.

In 1964 I received a call from a high school friend, John Strike, then a member of the University of Utah Board of Regents. He had submitted my name for consideration as the president of the University of Utah. I knew the job's requirements, including the fact that the school had never had a non-Mormon president. The offer intrigued me, and any hope I had was based on the modest population diversity in Salt Lake City's as well as Utah's political histories. A mayor of Salt Lake City, Louis Marcus, was Jewish. I knew former governor George Dern was non-Mormon. The second Jewish governor in the history of the United States was Utah's Simon Bamberger. Were they ready for a non-Mormon president who was also a noneducator? Strike insisted that they were interested. I traveled west for a series of interviews, and I met with the senior faculty. A few of them knew the family name from my father's restaurant or had heard of me because of my prominent governmental positions, but I knew what was on their minds: What does this man know about running the university? He is not an educator. At most he is a lawyer, and a Washington lawyer at that. I met individually with a number of members of the Board of Regents, but I did not meet with the board sitting in camera. That bothered me, and I knew I was not going to get the job. But my quiet hope was in where it might lead; in a dreamy way, I still thought of elected politics. Returning to Utah as the university president, and doing a good job, also held promise for my psychological makeup: the culmination of a lifelong agitation. I could finally say, Aha! Now you have been accepted by this community in which you were born and grew up. Of course, I spoke my dramatic inner conversation to no one. Marion expressed total disinterest in Utah, then, now, and always. I understood why, and think with hindsight she was completely correct. I received five of twelve votes, and I learned the lead person of my opposition (a Mormon Church spokesman) had indicated that he was unsure the university was ready for a non-Mormon president. (In 1968 I was happy to be among the first group of people appointed to the University of Utah's National Advisory Council and have served on that council to date.) Marion was very pleased at this outcome.

My law firm workdays were long and arduous. Legal work was the track record of most people when they left the White House, but the financial reward, one of the primary reasons to do it, was eluding me. I left the White House with a great sense of accomplishment. Even though I narrowly lost the presidency of the University of Utah, in part due to an identity issue, in the larger sense I no longer had that tugging identity as an Italian American. The five and one-half years with the law firm had little career significance. I was treading water. I learned the business of law firms, but I missed the variety of the challenges in government, especially akin to those that I experienced at the Labor Department where I managed people and programs. I always said I wanted to help people; Marion said I wanted to be a boss. While I searched for the right job that would satisfy my ambition and my family's needs, those five and one-half years were wonderful for our family's growing period. Maria had joined Loretta, Vincent, Fred, and John. I bought a lot of groceries and spent much time in the kitchen.

The following year, 1965, a search firm approached me regarding the position as president and chief executive officer (back then, *CEO* was a rare term) of the San Francisco–based Pacific Maritime Association (PMA), which represented the ship owners and the stevedore industry. On their behalf, PMA negotiated the contracts with the International Longshoremen and Warehousemen's Union (ILWU), which had about fifteen thousand longshoremen who loaded and unloaded ships in all the ports from Vancouver to San Diego, as well as some half-dozen offshore unions sailing the U.S. flag fleet. Not only were we very happy to move to San Francisco because it had always been one of the great cities we loved, but the job also offered very good money—more than three times my draw at the law firm. And I welcomed the change, a complete change. I saw PMA as a perfect management opportunity. I was the boss, I saw what a CEO was, and I learned I could really run an organization. I learned a different leadership style. Missing was the established hierarchy of the army or the U.S. government. This position required a lot of give-and-take, and constant searching for an acceptable middle ground.

I worked with the ILWU's leader, Harry Bridges, one of the great controversial labor leaders of the twentieth century. A very intelligent and witty man, he also had showmanship in his makeup. At times, his technique reminded me of an actor. His own negotiating team (some five to twenty men sitting behind him) would laugh and urge him on, and even once in a while they would clap. He had a noted easy, free speech, which he laced with humorous expletives about employers, big business, and the ship owners. His humor concealed a razor-sharp mind and predetermined objective: his own life reflected his desire to improve the lot of his fellow workers, the longshoremen. He was among the lowest-paid national union leaders; this I could not forget. Harry Bridges had incorruptibility and integrity—the union reflected this style of leadership. His ethical lifestyle made it unlike a trade union, where normally you have some mischief, collusion, or graft; it just didn't occur with Harry Bridges's group.

Bridges's ILWU was a pleasant contrast to the half-dozen other maritime unions we worked with—the West Coast offshore unions who manned the American flag fleet. We did not have "the muscle" to counteract what was called "job action" (a walk off the job in violation of the written contract). Whether it was, as examples, the "brand" of coffee available for the men or the demand to increase the per-daily contribution to a pension plan, job actions would follow. The labor-negotiated agreement was ignored. My members, the leaders of the companies that belonged to PMA, had a simple attitude: We can't allow that to happen. Once the job action started—stop the press—give them what they demanded. No employer wanted a strike when idle ships cost ten thousand dollars a day. We could do nothing but meet their request. Of course, as soon as we did, the domino effect set in with other unions. Legal action was unrealistic, even though the violation of the contract was clear. Well, that was hardly negotiation.

Looking at these negotiations from the union point of view, which you have to understand, you can't argue with them. A union leader told me that the way the industry was going, certain steamship companies could be out of business the next day. The pot of money that was presently in the pension plan would not cover the benefits. The only thing you could argue with was their tactic. Why press the issue now? Why not wait until we can negotiate? But "timing" is a weak argument.

This went on and on over a period of nearly four years. It really became quite disheartening for me because even though I received adequate compensation (including a substantial increase) and the members liked my management, I felt helpless. Our members would go to only a certain point and then expect me to be a miracle man and bring the unions around to a compromise position. We could not satisfactorily compete with the unions. The employers would not stand up. They would all nod their heads and say: Yes, we should take our chances and take our lumps. But when it came to a ship being held up in harbor, they just did not want to take their lumps because it was too costly. For the first time, I saw management succumbing to inordinate demands of labor unions, in this case the offshore maritime unions. The federal government subsidies were shrinking, and the American ships flying the

U.S. flag were pricing themselves out of the market. It was a rough four years. Foreign flag carriers, with dramatically lower costs and non-U.S. crews, were taking over the maritime industry.

◆

WE LOVED San Francisco. We lived in the city on Clay Street, which I had been told not to do. Philip Arnone, my mother's brother and a favorite of mine, was a realtor and had urged us to move to the suburbs when we arrived there in 1965. Unbeknownst to us, thousands of young people—the flower children—were streaming into the city at the same time. We found it a fascinating time, but it concerned us, especially because we had three teenagers. We wanted to be in touch with the events, so we went out at night to observe the thousands of young people. Many hundreds were sleeping on benches, in doorways, and in churches. In the Haight-Ashbury section we saw a large Methodist church with maybe two hundred kids sleeping on the floor. We couldn't believe it. Fortunately for us, we maintained close communication with our kids, or so we felt. They stayed in school and did very well.

In 1968 my very close friend from White House days Maurice Stans became Richard Nixon's campaign finance chairman. Stans raised enormous sums (in those days) for Nixon's campaign. Every now and then, he would come through San Francisco and we would have lunch or dinner with him. I can still remember telling Maury, "Why are you doing this? Nixon will not get the nomination. And if he does he will not be elected." I was certain about that. He shook his head and said he thought he was doing the right thing.

When Nixon won the election, Maury Stans called to tell me I was being considered for secretary of labor. Eventually, I heard that two of us remained. Soon thereafter, the AFL-CIO president, George Meany, whom I had known since 1953, called to tell me he had just left the president-elect's New York office where he had endorsed my selection as secretary of labor. I thanked him for his support and help, realizing that he was just making certain. He probably called the other man and said the same thing to him.

Two years later I discovered why I did not get the appointment. Maury Stans, Arthur Burns, and I had lunch in early 1971. I had worked closely with Burns during the Eisenhower years when he served as chairman of the Council of Economic Advisers. I admired him and thought of him as an academic mentor. That day Burns said to me that he had one regret, namely, that he stopped my being named secretary of labor! He had voiced his support for George P. Shultz, a respected economics professor at the University of Chicago, whose only ties with labor were as an arbitrator and economist. In my case, as a practitioner with the labor movement as president of PMA, Burns thought I could be susceptible to the influence of the labor unions. I was shocked—obviously. He apologized for that because by that time he was very unhappy with George Shultz, who had moved on to become director in the much more important and newly created Office of Management and Budget. (Later, of course, George Shultz had a notable and rewarding career in two other cabinet posts.) Years later, in the 1994 publication of *Haldeman's Diaries*, I discovered that in June 1970 Nixon had again considered me as labor secretary, this time as Shultz's successor. Unfortunately for me, Shultz, understandably, argued that his under secretary, James Hodgson, should replace him. Hodgson, long one of my closest friends, was a good choice. Under President Ford, Hodgson had an outstanding career as U.S. ambassador to Japan.

I never became a cabinet officer, obviously one of my hopes. Though in a different era, I am reminded of my disappointment that promotion to army captain was not possible at the end of World War II. I saw my army performance review in Headquarters U.S. Forces, Austria. I worked among field-grade officers, mostly above major, and as a first lieutenant I filled the post of the chief of officer personnel, normally occupied by a lieutenant colonel. I had my eye on the captain's silver bars. I wanted to go home a captain, but the army had a freeze on promotions. My review said, "superior in every way but sometimes satisfied with ordinary results." The words are still frozen in my mind. When I got home I received the Secretary of the Army's Special Commendation Award, stating that I had served as chief of officer personnel (actually, it should have said "acting"). You can only live with these disappointments and remember no one else really cares. I remember in law school, repeating my explanation to myself, "If you have ambition it can't be inordinate." Even if I had made it to the cabinet level, I'm convinced that it would not have appeased my ambition because there are limitations in every level of endeavor.

In December 1968, I received another phone call from Stans, who had by then been announced as incoming secretary of commerce. He said that I would receive a call from President-elect Nixon offering me a position. Obviously, I asked what it was. Stans told me the position was deputy postmaster general. I very quickly declined. He asked me why. I viewed this number-two position as an enormously complicated and controversial one involving retrenchment and reassignment of the largest employer in public service (beside the Defense Department). It had (and has today) received all kinds of public criticism as well as experiencing internal dissension. I had no intentions of undertaking a massive public labor-relations position based on staff reductions by the thousands.

He sort of paused, because he had held that position for a time under President Eisenhower, and then he said, "You know, some good men have held that position."

I laughed and said I was aware of that, but asked him to please not have Mr. Nixon call me. I thought that would end my opportunities with the Nixon administration.

In the first week of January 1969, I was in New York City on PMA business and took a room in the Waldorf-Astoria Hotel. Early the next morning I woke up to a phone call. Maury Stans said the president-elect wanted to see me. I asked him what this was all about. He assured me it was worth my time and asked that I come down quickly. I went out and got a cab and went to the Hotel Pierre, where the president-elect had his New York office. In the taxi I figured it out: deputy to Maury Stans (at that time called under secretary, today known as deputy secretary). I immediately accepted. I called Marion and announced we were moving back to Washington. I accepted the job of under secretary of commerce. I took a huge pay cut to go back into government, but I welcomed the challenge, variety, and responsibility of this position. Also, I had a great respect for Maury Stans, and I knew that I could work well with him as his second. I returned to my job in San Francisco, resigned immediately, left my family there, and took on the job in Washington within a week of the offer. The Senate Commerce Committee gave me a quick honeymoon confirmation. The acting chairman of the committee, Senator John Pastore, a fellow Italian American from Rhode Island, had been in our home for dinner in the Eisenhower years. He introduced me and welcomed me back to government. There were no questions, only compliments, including one from Senator Ted Moss of Utah. My mentor,

Senator Wallace F. Bennett of Utah, was by my side (as was Senator George Murphy of California). The committee reported it out immediately, and I was sworn in on February 5, 1969.

Marion was quite ready to move back to Washington. We had lived there for a twelve-year period, and four of our five children were born there. Marion and I always had an easy, mutual sharing of my goals and ambitions. During that time we saw many marriages fail; often the wife did not know how to manage the husband's ego or he would not share his career with her. Fortunately for me, I had Marion, who is terribly unimpressed with the Washington glamour. She kept me down on solid earth. She was interested in my work and followed it very closely, without having to get into all the details. What a relief to be able to discuss my work with someone at home. She got to know many of the people with whom I worked, and she has an uncanny ability to judge people. She has a direct, instinctive style; she abhors digressions and she wants to quickly resolve any indecision. We had many strong disagreements about people. I describe my own style as deliberative, forgiving, and judicial. But in the area of people judgment I learned that my caution was often a failing—and Marion was most often correct. In that respect, Marion has been vital to my successful career.

Then—in the ending '60s and early '70s—came the big anti-Vietnam protests. Just recently, my oldest son, Vincent, sent me a newspaper clipping of the *San Francisco Chronicle* from 1970. In a large, prominent front-page photo, a young man holds up a barbed-wire fence for a young lady as she crawls through the fence. In the background, police move students and smoke billows. The caption identifies the people as a Stanford protest group. Then I looked again, and I recognized the young couple as Vincent and his girlfriend, Susan, his future wife. I instantly remembered a telephone conversation we had with him at the time Nixon had ordered the Cambodian "incursion" in the spring of 1970. By that time, Marion and I were back in Washington, D.C., and I was in the Commerce Department. After we had discussed school matters and closed the conversation, he said, "Oh, yeah, we had another demonstration today. We got away from the police just in time! Good night."

After we hung up, Marion and I looked at each other and asked what was going on. We couldn't complain, because Vincent was nearly a four-point student. He received a B.A. in human biology in three and one-half years with a footnote on the diploma saying that he had also completed all academic requirements for a B.S. in engineering except for the resident hours requirement.

About that time, I happened to be going to California to make a speech, and I took time out to visit Vincent and Loretta, who were both at Stanford. Their father, a Nixon cabinet official, was coming to visit. They carefully told me how to dress—don't wear a tie. A man in a dark suit, a white shirt, and tie was suspect on the Stanford campus. The actual scene startled me: groups of protesting students gathered everywhere, many flaunting the ultra-ultra protest dress. Loudspeakers boomed at any convenient meeting place—under trees, on patios, and on building steps. I couldn't believe it was a college campus. I read about the student protests in the papers day and night, and saw it on television. On campus, I experienced it unfiltered. I saw people whose eyes flared, and who were obviously angry. Fortunately, I didn't see that in any of my own kids. This struck me deeply, and when I returned to Washington, I told anyone who would listen, though I never got close to President Nixon. I couldn't influence anybody. Maybe if I had been in the Defense Department, or in the White House, but not in the Commerce Department. Stans just shook his head; he felt Nixon could do no wrong.

The anti-Vietnam protests aimed to change the government's decision, and they probably saved some lives. This interesting process works in our democracy. I have long considered the idea of change and how one can instigate it. Knowing where you can work best is crucial to being effective. I knew James Farmer slightly, one of the big four of the Civil Rights movement in the '50s and '60s who was the founder and leader of the Congress of Racial Equality. Appointed by President Nixon in 1969 as assistant secretary in the Department of Health, Education, and Welfare, he felt blacks needed to be involved in government so they could have more input in shaping national policy on race. Yet Farmer became disenchanted with the government process and quit his post in 1970. He left because he felt Washington bureaucracy moved too slowly. He returned to a position in which he felt more comfortable—working from outside of government—through peaceful agitation.

I understand this preference because the processes of government are slow. With so many layers involved in decision making, issues aren't resolved in a crisp way. Instead of two or three people getting together, you have two or three agencies—large organizations, eventually supervised by the White House. A good example is civil rights. The Justice

Department coordinates with the White House, which coordinates with the pertinent officials, such as Farmer, in lesser levels of the cabinet agencies. At times, people can become frustrated because they feel impotent. They discover they are not in a position of real power or even close to someone who is in real power. They hear the word *coordinate* until they become ill. These procedures drive a lot of well-meaning and eager people to quit in disgust.

This process actually suited my temperament very well. To me, human nature, being what it is, rarely agrees to rapid change. I don't see how a nation that is growing in complexity can change overnight. Moderation becomes even more of a necessity, as our people become more diverse in race, ethnicity, belief, and behavior. In this environment, even though the cause may be right and the course of action just, it may take time to implement a good and necessary idea. Even so, I like to be in there, working on the issues—whatever they might be. I don't think of myself as an ideologue. When Stans asked me to join the Nixon administration it didn't occur to me that these people were too conservative or too liberal. As a political appointee, I thought of public service with all the vagueness those words convey. Who knows, maybe I can be constructive and properly influence the country's direction. From the day I left the Eisenhower administration, went to the law firm, and then went to the impossible job in San Francisco—trying to establish some career outside public service—my real goal was to get back to Washington, into public service. When Stans began calling with possible job offers in the Nixon administration I was instantly interested. No to the post office and yes to under secretary of commerce.

Maury Stans appeared to be a very contradictory man in many ways. As a conservative, particularly in financial and business matters, he had gained great respect around Washington for his ability to balance the post–World War II budget under Eisenhower. At the same time, he was socially liberal; he did not forget that he was the son of a Belgian immigrant who painted houses in Minnesota. You would never know this about his background from the way he dressed and the careful way he spoke. Though he was brilliant, he had a very astringent personality, so private that it was hard to break through. He had no ebullience in his makeup. He envied people who had a natural charm and would talk about that trait in his own careful way.

Stans and I had worked closely together ten years earlier when he was the director of the Bureau of the Budget and I was special assistant to President Eisenhower, so by this time our relationship had become close and trusting. Our discussions were intimate and open, with a lot of synchronicity in our approaches to problems. I was the only one who would tell him when he was off course or if I did not agree with him. Many times, privately, I simply disagreed. He never used his rank and I didn't always prevail, but we would have a full discussion. Many times he would half smile, shake his head a little, and agree. If I did not convince him, he had, at least, heard a different viewpoint. He was a very good listener, and I was too, which was one of the reasons he wanted me there. He knew that he could completely trust me and I would never embarrass or upset him.

I attended all cabinet meetings as acting secretary when Stans traveled, which he did a great deal. The Department of Commerce compares to a large business conglomerate, with more than twenty separate operating bureaus and organizations and about thirty-seven thousand employees. The functions varied, from the Office of Foreign Direct Investments to the U.S. Travel Service (which no longer exists); from the National Industrial Pollution Control Council to the Economic Development Administration, with regional commissions in the Ozarks, the coastal plains, the Four Corners, the upper Great Lakes, and New England; and the Census Bureau. As in my previous position at the Department of Labor, I spent a good deal of time on the Hill. I felt very familiar with those people on the Hill. My contacts with the White House were close, especially with Bob Haldeman and to a lesser extent John Ehrlichman.

In the enormous nineteenth-century-style Department of Commerce office building, Stans's office and my office abutted each other without any secretarial corridor and thus no secretaries between us. Of course, we kept the door that joined the two offices unlocked, and we passed freely either way. Although two holes had been drilled in the door frame earlier, they had been filled with putty. They dated from the Roosevelt era, and years later, when Secretary of Commerce Luther Hodges came in, he was forced to have as his under secretary Franklin D. Roosevelt Jr. They did not get along, and Hodges had the holes filled and the door locked. I suggested to Stans that we drill those holes open again, and he agreed. Through the holes I could see Maury, his desk, and his sitting-couch area. With that one look I could tell where he was and who was in there with him. The other hole permitted him the same view of my office.

One day Stans asked me to fire the commissioner of the Bureau of Patents. The commissioner holds an important position in the American business-community life, though not well known. The commissioner was being asked to resign because of the patent bar seeking a new face for a new administration. I had the job of explaining to a very decent and competent person why he was being asked to resign. I gave him honest reasons for our action and also tried to make sure that he kept his head high as he left my office. I have always tried never to be brutal in respect to anyone's dismissal. I later had much more experience in this field of management, and it's never a pleasure. As soon as the commissioner had left my office, Stans walked in and asked how it went. I knew he had watched. He had a lot of concern about people's feelings, but he, himself, did not express them very well, and he certainly did not know how to handle this kind of situation. Like so many men in top jobs, and I have seen this in the corporate world as well as the government, Stans could not fire anybody. He wanted me to do that, and I did it. He used to tell me that was my job, because he said I was the "people person." Maury felt he was policy, not management. I was definitely management.

My job also consisted of supervising some internal reorganization of the Department of Commerce. The public at large, as well as Congress, has had a very poor sense of what constitutes the Department of Commerce, or what it is about. For example, what was then called the Weather Service had some twenty constituencies. We wanted, of course, to become known as a more effective cabinet department, a challenge with a potpourri of agencies. In one of my own accomplishments, I oversaw the creation of the National Oceanic and Atmospheric Administration, known as NOAA (sounds like Noah), which became a conglomerate of the Weather Bureau, Marine Fisheries, and other related bureaus. Most important, we selected the leadership of Dr. Robert White, a career man. Even though he had an exemplary reputation, some senators wanted to know if he was like his brother, Theodore White, the famous journalist who wrote the books on the presidency, that is, a Democrat. I successfully secured support from key senators of both parties and from White House doubters.

By the time we moved back to Washington in 1969, it had flared with its own disorders and the atmosphere remained pretty grim. I thought it had become much more polarized. Riots had erupted at Fourteenth and U Streets. African Americans felt that they were isolated in D.C. and had not been given equal treatment as citizens of the states. The District was badly ignored. When we arrived in January 1969, the only program available was the Economic Development Administration, and it was inadequate. We were anxious to do more in that field, and, almost immediately, Maury Stans proposed the creation of the Office of Minority Business Enterprise, known as OMBE, which President Nixon created by executive order on March 5, 1969. Because it was created by executive order, it had no sanction or funding from Congress. We had to borrow monies from other agencies in the Commerce Department, where we were legally permitted to do so. We went to the Small Business Administration, an independent agency but, nevertheless, under the strong influence of the secretary of commerce. It, in turn, sponsored what we called MESBICS, Minority Enterprise Small Business Investment Corporations. The heavy emphasis was on the black community, and it was often called the "black capitalism program." Under MESBICS people could secure bank-guaranteed funds to establish businesses. The ratio of success was pretty poor, and critics in Congress immediately accused us of wasting government funds, but those that succeeded provided jobs. Stans believed that the only way to help the minorities, particularly the blacks, was to improve their economic life. Stans deserves, and got, recognition for his leadership.

The Commerce Department is made up of many disparate groups, which Stans tried to bring together. We had numerous meetings. We had retreats. We had papers, almost too many papers, of unity and relationship to one another. Stans tried to make the groups feel that they were part of a family, though in truth the cases of real relationship, or a reason to have one, were few. We both agreed on this approach, and he expected me to carry this out.

Another one of our achievements was a streamlining of the Maritime Administration, then a part of Commerce. Though the American flag fleet was shrinking, people felt we should have an American fleet in the event of war. I understood the Maritime Administration because of my nearly four years as president of the Pacific Maritime Association. I recruited a new director, Andrew Gibson, a very knowledgeable, experienced person from that industry. He and I worked on this large reorganization for the maritime industry, the first large maritime package in years, which involved a lot of money. The White House, despite heavy money constraints, nevertheless allowed us to propose legislation to Congress in the fall of 1969, just eight months into the term. It surprised Congress, but they very easily approved it with both parties claiming credit. Nixon could do it; Democrats could never have overcome the Republican opposition.

But the dark side of Nixon's administration came up in that same effort. I viewed President Nixon as either a captive or a captain. I have concluded that he was no captive; he was the captain of a crew with which I disagreed. We were putting together the Maritime Advisory Board, made up of private citizens who were from that industry. With my experience in the maritime industry I felt quite secure in my knowledge of who should be on the board. I had numerous phone disagreements with Charles Colson, a special aide to President Nixon, who tried to have his way in the appointment of this advisory board. I rebutted those attempts when I felt he was misinformed or crudely political. I insisted on people with content who could make an objective contribution. Colson adamantly argued for a particular labor leader who had quite an extensive criminal record.

I asked if he had seen the FBI's full field investigation on this person.

He replied that the individual could help get money and votes.

I knew the person and felt he should not be on our advisory board. I prevailed only because of Maury Stans, who had their enormous respect for having raised nearly $30 million for Nixon's first election. When I explained to Stans why we could not have this individual on the board, he agreed. Because of my relationship with Stans, the White House top staffers were very careful with me. They did not push him around, or try to. Because of this, in addition to my status as an "old White House hand," I did not have any fear of the White House. (After Stans and I left Commerce, the individual in contention was appointed to the advisory board.)

Today's hindsight makes it plain that President Nixon personally welcomed this administrative intrusion by his key staff people. I could not accept the simple test being advocated—that policy does not turn on content, politics are votes, and votes determine policy. This behavior makes Nixon seem like a confused man. What happens to "principles"? I don't know of Nixon's principles—like those of most people, they probably did not stay fast. The unfortunate result is that the Nixon era has a black mark on it, even though it was most progressive in some areas.

People sometimes forget the progressive thinking and actions taken with respect to minorities, including American Indians and their unique status. Nixon had reasonably advanced labor policies. Of course, we all know about Nixon's successful international efforts with China. He exhibited a unique type of leadership wherein sometimes he acted opportunistically and sometimes after careful analysis. I remember the discussions that led to the Consumer Product Safety Commission. Toys were hurting kids and needed safety devices. The public looked for governmental oversight, and the pertinent legislation easily passed. During the same time period, the Occupational Safety and Health Administration (OSHA) and the Environmental Protection Agency (EPA) were formed, though with much more involved, intensely diverse opinions. Who creates these major programs: Republicans or Democrats? Nixon was there and picked it up. Today, people are sometimes surprised that a Republican administration created the EPA. Nixon's tactics were outstanding: Take an issue that is important to the country, even if it is typically a Democratic issue, and do something about it. Nixon had the ability as a leader to perceive the need and—as a pragmatist—followed it. If not at first, all presidents become pragmatists. He was very successful with the Consumer Product Safety Commission, the EPA, and OSHA, though he had a failure of epic proportions when he took radical control of the economy in 1971 by first freezing wages and prices, followed by the creation of the Pay Board and Prices Commission. I served on the Pay Board and witnessed how politics gone bad hurt the country. For me, the Pay Board is of such magnitude and interest it gets its own later chapter.

As a person, though, Nixon was a total enigma. I could not figure him out. One day I got a phone call saying that the president wanted to see me. I asked what it was about. The White House aide said he didn't know. I asked Maury Stans if he knew anything about the president wanting to see me. Stans was surprised and had no idea. I called the White House aide and asked who else would be attending the meeting. He mentioned a couple of staff men, one whom I had known well, Bryce Harlow (one of the great men of Eisenhower's White House), and Peter Flanigan. I could not reach Harlow, but I talked to Flanigan on the phone and asked him what the meeting was about. Flanigan could be supercilious, and he thought he was being funny; he said the president wanted to talk about "you Eyeties." I assume I know what he meant.

I arrived at the meeting and found John Volpe, the secretary of transportation, former governor of Massachusetts, an Italian American whom I had known since the Eisenhower years. Present were Bryce Harlow, Peter Flanigan, Charles Colson, and Richard Moore, assistant to the attorney general and an old friend of President Nixon.

I have never attended such a strange meeting. The president sat behind his desk in a very far-away kind of mood. He looked down at his desk and spoke rapidly. "What do you do," he asked John Volpe and me, "to help get Italian Americans to become Republicans?" I was astonished. He then looked directly at each of us. He didn't really wait for any reply—then or later. He wandered, wandered quite a great deal, aimlessly, clearly not wanting a reply or comment. He talked about other ethnic groups—the "Pollacks" (not so flattering), blue-collar people, and Irish Catholics. He talked about how these groups should "be worked on." Notably, he did not mention African Americans. He went on and on and on. I said very little because I really did not know what to say. About thirty or forty minutes later he finished his mystical monologue. I was thankful he made no mention of a further meeting. We walked out, and John Volpe and I looked at each other, shook our heads, and nearly simultaneously said, "What was that all about?" It must have been a catharsis for Nixon.

As usual, the White House photographer came in and photographed the meeting. This one is worth having on my office wall. Volpe is on the left side of the president's desk, and I am on the right side. Colson, Moore, Flanigan, and Harlow ring the front of the desk. Colson and Harlow, in typical fashion, are taking notes. I have often wondered what they wrote. Flanigan is looking his urbane self, as if saying, "What else is new?" And the president's clean desk has an empty "in" box.

This behavior by Nixon, with an abject senior staff, heavily influenced me to move on. I recognized the value of men such as Haldeman and Ehrlichman but realized that they were in impotent positions much of the time. The pressures from the lesser White House staff made me very uncomfortable. By the end of the first year and even though I enjoyed being the number-two man in a major cabinet agency, I began to plan my departure. I became disenchanted and then disillusioned. The only reason I stayed was because Maury Stans allowed me to run the department as the chief operating officer and gave me total support. He never once insisted that we go along with what the White House wanted. On the contrary, we acted together in our advocacy, and prevailed most times. The Nixon White House—at least in the business and economic areas that concerned the Commerce Department—contained a miscellaneous collection of rare talent and raw power players. Unfortunately, with little of the structured supervision and professionalism that I remember in the Eisenhower administration, it was wasted. Stans had to leave to raise funds for Nixon's reelection. I knew I wouldn't succeed Stans with my status in the White House. I figured that I better get out before I got thrown out. I finally told Marion that we needed to prepare ourselves for early departure. After two years, I wrote my letter of resignation to President Nixon on February 12, 1971. I intended to leave promptly, in two or three weeks, but as it turned out I stayed for almost three months because Stans asked me to stay.

During my departure, Bob Haldeman, Nixon's chief of staff, asked me to come over for a "good-bye talk," or an exit interview. We had a good relationship, and our sons, his oldest, Hank, and John, my youngest, were close friends at St. Albans and were each other's best man at their respective weddings years later. We talked uninterrupted for the better part of an hour. I had a litany of concerns, and I carefully explained the difference between the six years that I had spent in the Eisenhower administration and the two years in the Nixon administration. Of course, my comments were heavily weighted in favor of the Eisenhower administration and not at all complimentary to my experience in the Nixon years. I had a difficult diplomatic task of making my points without being insulting.

Uppermost was the morale of the more than twenty-five top presidential appointees in Commerce, many of whom I had helped recruit, and how disjointed they had become from the administration. As the department's general manager I knew the assistant secretaries and heads of agencies very well, and their complaints to me were the same: They didn't feel they were a part of the Nixon administration. They didn't know what was going on. They felt they were being ignored. I told him about the social activities involving Eisenhower's White House, the presidential family, as I called it, and the Eisenhower "Little Cabinet Wives," with which Marion had been so involved. We were engaged on a social basis, and that promoted a cordial work atmosphere. Also,

Eisenhower's White House functions brought assistant secretaries and other top officials to the White House several times a year, which included spouses and gave appointees a sense of belonging to the administration. Many presidents before and since have done this. The Nixon people had dinners, but they rarely included senior officials of some of the "lesser" cabinet agencies. Haldeman made a note of that (though I later had a feeling my remarks were being taped). If nothing else, such inclusion would help the marriages, which always need help when you move to Washington.

My principal point, however, was the need for freedom to manage our appointed functions. I knew of people "planted" in the departments to report "intelligence" to White House staffers, but my pet peeve was the White House staffers' direct instruction to key Commerce employees. They gave specific directions on what to do, set time limits, and even said, "Ignore your supervisor." These phone calls from the White House were a dynamic power play that intimidated the employees and disrupted the management process. Responsibility without authority was becoming endemic, all because of White House staff actions. I freely developed these thoughts with Bob Haldeman and felt satisfied that he had the courtesy to hear me out, though I was skeptical as to how much it achieved.

Throughout my career, I left nearly every job before the appointment ran out or I would have been forced to go. I wanted the personal choice of time and place. I have always done that, beginning with the National Labor Relations Board. You can't rest on your laurels, and I kept looking for resolution to my characteristic restlessness. I had strong negative feelings when leaving the Nixon administration, and my restlessness actually caused me to leave before his administration self-destructed in the Watergate scandal.

During my last days in Commerce, I was surprised when Attorney General John Mitchell called me from Key Biscayne, Florida. He said he was "in the sun" with President Nixon, and the president was asking if I would accept an appointment as a federal district judge in California. I had always viewed a lifetime judicial position as the culmination of one's career—the ultimate public service accomplishment. I immediately expressed my thanks and said no. I couldn't afford it. I envied my friend Elliot Richardson because throughout his life he had the means to immerse himself in public service.

In just a twelve-year period—from thirty-seven to forty-nine years old—I had three very meaningful job situations, but more challenges were ahead. My career had started off with a big bang, and these later years, though not always completely satisfying, were at least worthwhile and educational. Some job opportunities fell flat because they were not financially rewarding or did not meet my other larger goals in life. I wanted successes, not just for myself, but something that could be shared by the people with whom I worked and, I hoped, the larger public. I couldn't find it managing lawyers or when asked to get on my knees before a labor union. The under secretary position came much closer, where I did things that benefited people, but I was forced to realize my time was limited. Job contentment exists in varying degrees. Like happiness, it is rarely constant. Change is always in the society in which one lives, and we, as individuals, are only a very small part of it.

The brightest note was that these were family years and a time of growth in the home life with Marion, two daughters, and three sons. We have had a rich family life, with enjoyment and loving experiences.

The Department of Commerce job changed my whole life by giving me the credentials to enter the Los Angeles business arena where I found greater responsibilities that led to ideal opportunities.

TWELVE

NIXON'S PAY BOARD
A Public Administration Disaster

OVER THE YEARS, river running became one of our family's favorite vacations. We spent our days outside on some of the great rivers of the American West: the Snake River, the Middle Fork of the Salmon, in Cataract Canyon on the Colorado, Oregon's Rogue, and the ultimate river trip, the Grand Canyon on the Colorado. Once on the Snake River, we included a new "child" in our family, Kim Siciliano—her "adopted" name. Actually, it was Kim Agnew, a lovely girl whose father was then vice president. We did the name change to avoid the necessity of Secret Service men joining us on the river. Discovering and arranging these trips was Marion's work. She has always loved the outdoors and has an advanced taste for adventure. On the river she was the respected skipper, aka "Joe Cool," a nickname lifted from the *Peanuts* cartoon. In 1971 she scheduled us for ten days in Desolation Canyon on Utah's Green River, one of our most memorable adventures. Each one of us piloted his own craft, a strange seven-foot-long "sports yak" that looked like a pregnant kayak. Over those ten days of running rapids in the beautiful mountains and desert of eastern Utah, we learned the all-important skill of reading the river. With her emergency medical kit always handy, Marion acquired another name as well, "Dr. Sweetie."

The meanders in our lives had been many in that time. In just a few short years we had moved from San Francisco to Washington, D.C., to Los Angeles. After I left the Nixon administration in early 1971, the Green River was a comfort, a place to reflect on my recent and very successful transition out of the public service into L.A.'s private sector as president of an established and respected corporation. My new job was an exciting change with a host of challenges, and it also paid well. I was nearly fifty years old, and, at that time, we had no retirement savings and very limited funds for continuing our children's college educations. That financial necessity always ran crosscurrently to my deep-seated desire for the public service, though I must say—parenthetically—that President Nixon's political style certainly made me question my passion for public service in government. Unbeknownst to me, even while I was on the river he was creating another chance to prove that to me.

Two weeks on the river is a short, intense withdrawal from the daily affairs of the world. No newspaper, no TV, no radio (and certainly no cell phones back then). As an avid reader and interpreter of society's daily events I realized that when we launched the boats I would never know what I might miss, what pieces of the puzzle would fall into place while I was on the river. The world spins on without you, though, really, how much can change in two weeks?

We came off the river in August 1971 and discovered things had changed. President Nixon had announced his New Economic Plan, which immediately froze all wages and prices in the country. He delighted the country with his bold—perhaps drastic—move, which took our economic policy in an unprecedented new direction. Upon returning to my office in L.A., I discovered Nixon wanted to appoint me to his newly created agency, the Federal Pay Board (which along with the Price Commission was the essential component of his New Economic Plan). With my chairman's and chief executive officer's consent, I accepted the position.

The United States was a very restless and noisy nation, and President Nixon was at a low point as the leader able to bring the nation out of its confusion. He had promised to get us out of Vietnam, yet he had increased the fighting. Student protests against the Vietnam War became more intense after the tragic killing of students at Kent State. His relations with Congress were souring. The economy was hobbled by "stagflation," with 6 percent unemployment and about 5 percent inflation; labor strife threatened his hopes of cooling inflation; and the international economic picture was the worst it had been since World

War II, a threat to the United States' international economic position. Nixon's approval ratings had dropped below the 50 percent mark. All these issues were directly related to his reelection campaign for 1972: if we were still in Vietnam, and, especially, if the economy didn't improve, he would not see a second term.

To make things worse, in early August, a crippling steel strike was narrowly averted with a contract for a 30 percent wage increase over three years, and railroad workers won a 46 percent wage increase over forty-two months. This wage-price spiral became a key driving force of inflation: as workers received raises, producers raised prices to absorb the increased costs, but productivity failed to keep pace. Some areas of the country suffered deeply from strikes, such as the longshoremen's strike on the West Coast shipping docks (ironically, against the very group that I headed as president of PMA; this was their first strike in twenty years). The American public braced for the worst and wanted something done about it.

Economic controls were being proposed from various corners in Washington. The secretary of the treasury, the Federal Reserve chairman, and the Council of Economic Advisers chairman advocated some type of policy to check the wage-price spiral. Twelve Republican senators prepared legislation to create a wage-price review board. The Democrats, and several of their presidential hopefuls, forced the issue with the president. The public liked the idea of changing the economic policy to address the issues. President Nixon stood firm with his laissez-faire principles, which was a promise of governmental nonintervention and individual enterprise. He specifically stated his opposition to wage-price controls.

Knowing this, the Democratic-controlled Congress pulled a fast one. In August 1970 they passed the Economic Stabilization Act, which authorized the president to control wages and prices. They, in effect, offered him the diabolical solution. Remember, this was considered a peacetime economy, and there was no real war crisis at hand. For a president of the United States to go in this direction was unbelievable, particularly a Republican president. The Democrats offered it simply to embarrass him, not believing he would ever use the authority given to him. They then could blame him for the economic problems.

They were probably the first to fall off their chairs on August 15, 1971, as they watched a distraught President Nixon announce on all three TV networks, "The time has come for a new economic policy for the United States." Nixon presented his New Economic Plan, a multi-faceted attack on unemployment, inflation, and international speculation against the dollar. He attempted to spark the economy out of stagflation. Among a number of other controls, President Nixon initiated his plan with a ninety-day freeze on all wages, prices, and rents, known as the wage-price freeze. His announcement surprised America, and the people loved it; they felt their government was protecting them. The freeze stopped inflation dead in its tracks, and Nixon was regarded as an economic hero. The stock market rallied. President Nixon had stolen the issue from the Democrats, and it gave the economy enough of a thrust that, along with his detente, he began to move up in the polls.

I don't think the significance of what took place in the summer of 1971 has ever really sunk into the American population's mind. At the time, President Nixon claimed that it was "the most significant monetary agreement in the history of the world" and that it was the most important weekend in the history of economics since March 4, 1933 (when FDR closed the banks). We were treading on new ground, and people were deeply concerned about the future of the American economic system. You have to be an economist to understand the new economic policy in all its complexities, but the freeze raised doubts and questions about how to control inflation after the freeze.

After the freeze (Phase I) came Phase II on November 14, 1971. The Cost of Living Council oversaw the Price Commission (which controlled price increases) and the Pay Board (which controlled wage increases). Phase II, a more flexible program, aimed to maintain economic stability through economic restraints while we came out of the freeze. Our orders were to bring the inflation rate back down to 2 percent by the end of 1972, half of the prefreeze rate of inflation. In order to do that, we had to set limits on pay increases. For the most part, we were charged with controlling the leaders of the inflation race, that is, the biggest corporations and unions, such as the steelworkers, the coal miners, and the longshoremen. I have kept a set of drinking glasses that reads, "Phase II: I'm for that!" During Phase I, no one could get a pay raise. At least during Phase II, there was hope.

Almost immediately, things took a wrong turn. We set the ceiling for pay raises at 5.5 percent, a compromise between labor (6 percent) and business (5 percent). Then the first major case we negotiated was the coal miners, who were threatening to strike. They are historically one of America's most individualistic workforces. We did not question whether those men would work; they would not. The consequences of a major strike by the coal miners would have been disastrous on the fuel-supply situation for many major cities, and it would have had an impact on the economy of the country. We granted the coal miners a 17.5 percent pay increase, more than three times our preestablished limit. It was very controversial.

The Pay Board was a tripartite board of fifteen members with five representatives, each from the public, business, and labor sectors. I was asked to represent business, inasmuch as I was a corporation president with extensive governmental experience and hands-on experience with labor problems. The president and executive branch hoped that the Pay Board's balanced representation would bring some sort of harmony among those three groups, a sort of government-endorsed collective-bargaining panel. While labor and business traditionally fought each other, the public members quickly alienated both labor and management members. The *Wall Street Journal* summed it up: "The Pay Board is headed for another confrontation."

One of the most difficult and emotional issues was retroactive pay boosts. The freeze had initially stopped the inflation-causing wage-price spiral, but during Phase II we had to decide who would receive retroactive payments for contracts made before and during the freeze. For instance, hundreds of thousands of teachers had signed contracts for raises before the freeze that would go into effect after the freeze. We had initially set standards that prohibited retroactive payments unless certain conditions were met. One of those conditions, "where severe inequities existed," allowed the labor members to argue for broader interpretations. Using the teachers' issue, the labor members tried to establish a precedent for granting most other retroactive payments. I, personally, felt the unions had a certain plausible explanation of their position, and certainly their argument about contractual integrity was valid. Initially, the board voted labor down on retroactivity, ten to five, though the issue was far from resolved. It came up for more votes with different language. I collaborated with another business member, Ben Biaggini (chief executive officer of Southern Pacific Corporation), to write up a compromise, but it was to no avail. We lost by an eight-to-seven vote.

The questions and issues just got more complex. If someone was granted a wage that can increase due to their productivity, do they also get the 5.5 percent raise? We wrestled over tandem settlements, which were usually smaller concerns that followed the decisions made on larger wage packages. Another volatile issue was executive compensation. Labor was adamant that executive compensation be the same as that of rank and filers. There were heated debates over how to treat stock options and executive perquisites. And what about an executive's increase in responsibility? Well, what kind of responsibility? We were asking questions: Is that a real increase, or is that an increase just to get a pay raise? We quickly became a very complicated organization. There were so many exceptions, promotions, and underrecognized-but-now-wanting-recognition types. In that sense, it was totally a joke.

I expected the negative reactions from the business members, of which I was one. We had a more difficult time, much to my surprise, with the public members, who always seemed unanimous in opposing any issue. On many issues the board was divided—bitterly so—between labor and public, with the business members being the swing votes. The debate was so divisive because of the different philosophies at the table. Labor, obviously, felt we had no legal authority to derail contracts with pay increases during the freeze. The public members argued that it was unfair (more "severe inequity") to give the unions (two million affected people) their retroactive pay and not the rest of the population. Everyone agreed that as part of the economy as a whole, the number of people and amount of back pay involved were not enormous. What it came down to for both sides was a matter of equity, morality, and principle. As one member said, "We're writing the script for this whole thing as we go along." With these opposing ideals and no precedent to follow, it needed a leader.

President Nixon appointed Judge George H. Boldt as chairman of the Pay Board. Boldt, at sixty-seven, had been a senior federal district judge with twenty-five years on the bench. Though well known for overseeing several historic trials, he knew nothing about labor-management relations in the United States. His legal expertise did not extend to these issues, which were public policy in its most involved, intricate sense. He often stated that he didn't know which way to vote on particular issues. He presided over the meetings and withdrew his vote, except in cases of a tie. This landed him in the midst of the most contentious issues, such as retroactivity and tandem payments, which came to a tie vote several times. He was unable to bring about a working majority from the three groups. The Pay Board drifted aimlessly for several months, and Judge Boldt baffled us with several contradictory decisions. Admittedly, it would have been difficult for any leader to coordinate the inherent, conflicting forces of the Pay Board.

The leader of the labor contingent was George Meany, president of the AFL-CIO, the nation's largest union organization (about one-fifth of the nation's workforce). I knew Meany from my Labor Department days of ten years earlier. He called himself a "plumber" from the Bronx, this pudgy curmudgeon with a constant cigar in his mouth. Always respected, he often shook his bald head vigorously and hid his shrewd intelligence behind a typically cantankerous character. He seemed to ignore his age, then in his seventies, and was very aggressive. *Newsweek* said Meany, at this time, "may well be the most powerful man in America."

Meany was always suspicious of President Nixon, who was courting him for votes. In fact, union labor was the only interest group in America opposed to the wage freeze. Meany called the wage-price freeze a "Robin Hood in reverse—robbing the poor to pay the rich." He felt that the whole economic program favored big business and that the setup of the Pay Board was a way to control inflation at the expense of the workers. One of the sore points was that President Nixon had not limited profits, interest, or dividend income during the ninety-day freeze period. The labor contingent quoted numbers that backed their claims: corporate profits had soared 19 percent in the second half of 1971 (under the freeze) over the comparable period in 1970, more than three times our base wage increase. In his mind, these were things that were unfair to the American worker. Meany and the other labor representatives repeated their desire to adhere to any control system, just as long as it was applied equitably to all parts of the economy. That's why Meany wanted to be on the Pay Board—so he could have direct input. But with the way things went, the labor representatives became increasingly stubborn. This refractory attitude continued until Meany and three other labor members walked out.

Throughout the life of the Pay Board, we grew and grew and grew, from a small group of fifteen until we had several hundred employees. Still, that was not enough employees to cover the needs of the entire United States. There were no field officers. Every single request had to come through us in Washington, D.C. It was an enormous bottleneck.

We were, in effect, becoming an IRS or Federal Trade Commission, or one of those longtime established governmental agencies, and we weren't prepared for it. We could not conceivably handle so much weight of decision. We were fighting a paper war, and it became impossible. People wanted exact answers for every situation, and the only way to achieve that was to create a massive bureaucracy, which no one really wanted. Herb Stein, chairman of President Nixon's Council of Economic Advisers, referred to this when he wrote in *Presidential Economics,* "An attempt to make the controls work in those conditions would have required the exercise of government power over the economy on a scale that hardly anyone wanted."

Each board member was deluged with special messages and phone calls from corporations. We endured pressures from union, health, and medical groups who demanded urgent attention and special treatment. Anybody who thought they knew somebody on the Pay Board tried to get through to them. I was constantly approached by people who thought I should meet with so-and-so because of problems in his corporation.

In a lengthy *New York Times* interview feature (on December 12, 1971), I voiced my displeasure with the Pay Board's operations. I was not convinced that we could accomplish the administration's goal of reducing inflation to 2 to 3 percent, by the end of 1972. I discussed the varying philosophies on the Pay Board. The public members endorsed the all-or-nothing approach. Bang! Close the door on retroactive payments. Another was the bubble theory. Initially, as you move from an unregulated economy to a regulated one, you have to allow the bubble to grow and gradually smooth it out over a year or so. My approach was to squeeze the bubble, but not to pop it. Other business members shared this approach. Of course, how hard you press that bubble was the tough decision. All these philosophies were rendered useless when we faced the individual cases. We did not, obviously, press anything with the coal industry for its own individual reasons. And we faced other issues with different criteria, though of equally great consequence, such as the ongoing longshoremen's strike.

In the *Times* interview, I noted that one of the great achievements of the Pay Board was that we were "still working together amidst all the dire predictions that we were going to fall apart, and that labor would walk out, is pretty clear evidence that everyone recognizes the need and the critical position of the nation." But the longshoreman contract put us to the test. In February 1972, the longshoreman union on the West Coast docks ended a 134-day strike by agreeing to a contract that totaled a 21.6 percent increase—almost four times our 5.5 percent ceiling. The way in which Judge Boldt managed this issue brought truth to the "dire prediction" of our failure. Judge Boldt presented labor with a decision that reduced the contract by one-third (to a 14.9 percent raise). He told the labor contingent that he had the support of the business and public members—in other words, a guaranteed ten-to-five confirmation. There was no negotiation, no listening before the decision. Ironically, I had headed the employers' organization, the Pacific Maritime Association, from 1965 to 1969. The longshoreman West Coast leader was Harry Bridges, one of the nation's most effective and idealistic labor leaders.

The decision, in the eyes of labor, was a political maneuver. It confirmed their fears that the Pay Board was an instrument of the Nixon administration. Meany considered the decision a double cross, because President Nixon had guaranteed an autonomous board. Meany felt the Republicans had simply played with labor, and that the Republicans were biased in favor of the business community. He knew a Republican administration would be so inclined, yet Meany felt betrayed. He really wanted to meet personally with the president. He wanted to pick up the phone and call Richard Nixon. Well, that was not possible. That offended him from the very start. He wanted to be treated as an equal to the president of the United States; after all, he was the leader of 24 percent of America's labor force. As their leader he didn't want to sit and argue with fourteen people who he thought were nincompoops. Meany chafed in such a subservient role. In my judgment, he made a mistake in accepting the Pay Board appointment. He, a powerful public figure, had been put in an anomalous position of subservience in a federal administrative agency.

Meany got in a big snit over the whole idea of the Pay Board. I think he viewed the longshoreman issue as an opportunity to leave. He and the other labor representatives had successfully lobbied Congress for retroactive payments. Congress passed a bill that required payment of nearly all wage and benefit increases that were suspect under the ninety-day freeze, as long as the amount was not unreasonably inconsistent with Pay Board standards. With that in the bag, he was able to make a public protest over the failure of the Pay Board to approve the longshoreman contract. He never got over his feelings of mistreatment and personal abuse. As he quit, he took three of the labor members off the board. The one union member to stay on was Frank Fitzsimmons of the Teamsters Union, which was not a part of the AFL-CIO at that time. When Meany pulled out, the Pay Board lost the tripartite arrangement, and President Nixon formed an all-public board of seven by retaining Frank Fitzsimmons and me and dismissing the other four business members.

As a business member, my principal correspondent was Donald Rumsfeld, a longtime friend who was then counselor to the president and chairman of the Cost of Living Council. In 1958 I had offered Don a position in my White House office, though he instead returned to Illinois in successful pursuit of public office. Authoritative and crisp in manner, he had a warm and sensitive inside. We discussed all the matters that we were heavily involved in, but never did he ask us how we would vote. He would relay what the president was thinking on certain issues, but there wasn't any direction. We preferred it that way. We did not want (or expect) to be told what to do, because we would not have done it.

Such vindictive politics among the various organizations can make a worst-case scenario for public service. In that position, you recognize that you're a political pawn, but you don't want to behave like one. Most of us were skeptical of the policy of controls, as the economist Herb Stein later wrote, but we were trying to do honest and constructive work in the best interest of the country. Even the most conservative member, the noted economist Dr. Neil Jacoby, who was ideologically opposed to price controls and invariably antilabor, was there trying to make it work. Fitzsimmons was the exception. Fitzsimmons rarely attended meetings, he was very political, and his motive was transparent. He buttered up to President Nixon for more favorable treatment. Later that summer, the Teamsters backed Nixon for reelection.

As a board of seven, the five public members became the new majority. The strong man and effectively the leader because of his brilliance was Arnie Weber, a Ph.D. economist from the University of Chicago (a practitioner of the Chicago School, and later president of the University of Colorado and of Northwestern University). Judge Boldt gave Weber full rein. Because of Weber's humor, he could turn a joke out of anything and make us all laugh, and we needed that. His aggressiveness was always so well tuned to the realities of the group because he understood his colleagues, who were mostly Ph.D. economists. The public members were all very principled, intelligent men, though their backgrounds were fairly remote from the practical day-to-day issues that we were addressing. Their academic backgrounds gave them little understanding of the realistic economic pressures of workers, and they were unfamiliar with the country's labor practices. Their highly qualified first-class minds made decisions in the abstract, and they were satisfied. I got tired of hearing about "the big picture" or "ten years from now." The "hypothetical issue" offers nice speculation, but people were asking for a raise. Today! Too often the public members felt they didn't have to live with our decisions. We were not an established regulatory agency. We had no constituency—a union or a corporation, not even Congress—to follow up on the impact of our operations.

We, the seven, were all part-time, but it soon became full-time, and that was not enough. This was a part-time agency, and it was a temporary arrangement. The system simply became overburdened. We were deciding on a case-by-case basis whether labor contracts would be recognized. Thousands of applications from all types of businesses were pouring in, asking for special treatment or recognition. There was no way we could tackle these individual problems. We had all kinds of exceptions on exceptions on exceptions, and we kept changing the regulations. Meanwhile, businesses figured out how to negotiate the loopholes in the regulations.

My boss in L.A. began to get nervous, just as I did. When I accepted the Pay Board appointment I had only six months' experience at my new job. Suddenly, I was working as much in Washington as I was in Los Angeles, which was much more than anticipated. Pulling double duty made Marion unhappy. We had a large family, with three kids in college, John was finishing at St. Albans and applying to colleges, and Maria was in elementary school. I confided to Marion that I was in the same morass I was in before we moved to California.

On my trips to Washington I would always find chaos at the Pay Board. Our collective spirit and will were falling apart. The Pay Board became a cauldron wherein administrative minutiae and political dogma masqueraded as effective public policy. The Pay Board failed to implement laws and regulations equally. Individual case decisions became public policy—even though we tried (as the Supreme Court attempts to do) to limit the scope and effectiveness of the decisions only to the situation before us. The Pay Board was not part of the executive, legislative, or judicial systems. It was remarkably similar to the Office of Independent Counsel, which was not renewed in 2000. That office, according to the last man to hold the position, Robert W. Ray, "didn't belong anywhere, it just stood out by itself." This, he told the *New York Times*, "offered him little institutional protection." The Pay Board had become a combination of all three branches—with omnipotent powers—and we acted as if our powers were not even reviewable by the federal courts. In spite of what George Meany thought, the White House and President Nixon were not directing policy. We were leaderless and rudderless. What came out was administrative pulp. A favorite expression: "Let's make an exception." A common greeting: "I gotta get outta here." The Pay Board was a tiny, temporary bureaucracy created by presidential executive order, which was ordered to control the entire American workforce. We were asked to do too much. We were unable to implement laws and regulations equally. The challenges were too many, and our solutions were evanescent.

One night during dinner I told Don Rumsfeld that a quick, peaceful death would be the best thing for the Pay Board and urged him to help its demise. It was very clear to me that sooner or later it would collapse. Accordingly, I sent in my letter of resignation to President Nixon in early December to be effective January 31, 1973. President Nixon accepted my letter with thanks. By coincidence (and to my surprise), President Nixon dissolved the Pay Board effective the end of January 1973, the same day I requested to terminate my service. For the record, I actually worked every day of its existence, even though I had resigned some six weeks earlier.

The philosophical concept of governmental controls is anathema to most Americans, certainly to the business and labor communities. Yet Nixon attempted it, and that's about all you can say: it was an attempt and it failed. It required much more care. Nixon misjudged the national economic problem, and he misused his power in mandating the wage-price controls. He did it without the knowledge or participation of the American public. To establish an administrative agency of the U.S. government requires a thoughtful, traditional legislative process, with the approval and support of Congress. I recognize that with a Democratic Congress, Nixon's chances of success were slim—thus the executive order. As Stephen Ambrose writes in his Nixon biography, "[Nixon] liked surprises, and back channels, and secrecy. . . . Nixon was not working with the bureaucracy, but against it; he was not bringing the public along with him, but thrusting changes on it. These techniques made it questionable that Nixon's changes . . . would have the staying power." This proves all too true when you realize the decision to freeze prices, wages, and rents was done with no clear idea of what would follow the ninety days.

The wage-price controls were intensely political. President Nixon was in a sinking boat—his approval ratings were dropping because of Vietnam and a sputtering economy. When you view the Pay Board as a political maneuver, it accomplished two things: it took fire from the Democrats during the election year, and it stymied inflation through the election, thus giving President Nixon reason for reelection. He dramatically catapulted the nation's pessimism into short-term optimism, which established an image of action. After his reelection, his defeated opponent, Senator George McGovern of South Dakota, credited the wage-price controls with making Nixon "unbeatable."

The nation suffered for it. As with Vietnam, the wage-price controls were "a temporary measure that treated the symptom of inflation while leaving the causes untouched," says Ambrose. Instead of offering real solutions, Nixon reacted politically. While the economy glimmered briefly, by 1974 inflation was on a rampage, and in 1975 prices were as high as if the controls had never happened. In those two years the nation experienced its deepest recession since the 1930s, succeeded by the worst inflation in the postwar era. By the time President Carter took office, inflation was 18 percent. And the Nixon administration had worried about it going up to 3 and 4 percent! "The lesson of that experience is not to play political games with lethal economic instruments," concludes Herb Stein. Because of President Nixon's quixotic management style, the Pay Board was allowed to become the most fruitless effort of all my public service in government.

When the news about Watergate broke, we were certainly shocked, but President Nixon's style might have forecast it. Even so, it was painful to watch. I had close friends and coworkers in the thick of it. My good friend and boss at the Commerce Department, Maury Stans, was indicted on charges unrelated to Watergate itself, though the press never made the distinction (until years later in a full-page apologia by the

Washington Post). H. R. "Bob" Haldeman, the able Nixon loyalist, had his trials, and prison followed. Marion always admired Martha Mitchell, then the wife of Attorney General John Mitchell, who understandably fared so poorly in the Watergate investigation and trials. Marion stood up for Martha's honesty and outspoken independence, and we watched her subsequent decline with sorrow. Watergate was a blow to the nation—a national nightmare—and the average American's view of public service plummeted, as it should have. This would take decades to heal. In those days, L.A. was as close to Washington as one could want to be. So I turned my attention to other public service endeavors closer to home.

PART III

Toward a Better America,
1971–

Intellectually, as well as politically, the direction of all true progress is toward greater freedom, and along an endless succession of ideas.

—Christian Nestell Bovee, 1820–1904

THIRTEEN

THE BOTTOM LINE AT TICOR

IN THE SPRING OF 1970 I traveled to Los Angeles and spoke at a conference on minority business enterprise. While I was in Los Angeles a friend made appointments for me to visit a couple of prominent businessmen, and so I began a quiet job reconnaissance. The first meeting failed quickly; the nationally known businessman hardly had time to say hello. With some reluctance I approached the second, the prominent leader of an old-line southern California corporation, headquartered in a magnificent old structure in downtown Los Angeles. I hesitated in the lobby as to whether I should even go up. Los Angeles did not rank on my list of favorite places to live. My corporate experience had been sour as a young man in Chicago. Public service, yes, even the law, yes, but I always had some question as to big business. At that point, though, at almost fifty years old, I knew I had to start somewhere to gain some financial security.

I got on the elevator and rode it to the top floor, where I met Ernest J. Loebbecke, the CEO and chairman of the board of TI Corporation of California. I arrived at two o'clock and by the time I left at five o'clock, our meeting had swept away all my reservations. In those three hours we became good friends. As it turned out, my timing coincided with his search for new leadership in the company. When I went back to my hotel room, I called Marion and told her, "This sounds crazy, but I think I have a job." At least I appeared to be on the track to one. Over the next few months I met with Mr. Loebbecke two or three more times. Following my resignation as under secretary of commerce, the TI board elected me president of TI. I started in April 1971. While I never thought of being a president of a major national financial firm, it appeared to be an opportunity for real growth. Mr. Loebbecke made it very plain that if everything worked out well, I would succeed him as CEO. That was the challenge.

I had never heard of this strange-named company, but I quickly learned that it meant a great deal to the people of southern California. President Nixon knew it well and, upon my resignation, complimented me on my appointment. I learned why upon moving to Los Angeles. Mr. Nixon had been a partner in a leading Los Angeles law firm, which used the services of TI. The company had built its large office building at 433 Spring Street in 1928, in the days when Spring Street was *the* street—the Wall Street of Los Angeles, with TI known as the "Supreme Court of Spring Street." One of its founders, Henry O'Melveny, was also a founder of one of L.A.'s great law firms, O'Melveny and Myers. It had for many years offices in the same building. As I stepped into the job I discovered TI held a position as a top power broker of the greater L.A. region.

The Title Insurance and Trust Company was founded in Los Angeles in 1893. Known locally as TI (pronounced as two letters), they initially provided basic title insurance—an American invention. If a property title proved defective, TI would pay for any loss. TI pioneered such insurance in California and popularized its use. It redefined the role of the building industry, and it went on to gain a reputation for similar innovations in other related businesses. It created the modern escrow and widened the dimensions and use of the trust business (its trust department was the oldest in California). Because of TI's intimate connection to the real estate business, its financial fitness served as an indicator of the region's overall economic health. During the 1960s, California grew by one thousand people per day and passed New York in population, with Los Angeles County becoming the nation's most populous county. Much of this growth was suburban, and so TI grew with it.

My boss, Ernest Loebbecke, used that tremendous expansion to grow the business outward throughout the nation. He started with the company in 1934, and over his forty-three years he held the various positions of treasurer, executive vice president, president, CEO, and chairman of the board. He guided TI to a nationwide expansion (which included every state except Iowa, which did not allow title insurance). We became the largest title insurance company in the nation, with huge operations in the larger cities such as New York and Chicago. In its rise to national economic prominence, TI became the leader in California, with offices in all of its fifty-eight counties.

By the time I joined it, TI had become a holding company in the financial services field with about ten subsidiary companies. Shortly after arriving, I helped to change the name of the holding company to TICOR, with seven major units. The TICOR Title Insurers, known as the TICOR Title Group, was the largest such business in the nation. We operated the TICOR Print Network, a group of financial printers located strategically about the country (New York, Chicago, Houston, and Los Angeles). We also owned the Los Angeles firm Jeffries Bank-note, a financial printer, which printed American Express Travelers Checks and, occasionally, money for South American countries. Con-stellation Reinsurance Company, a reinsurance firm based in New York, accepted insurance risks from other insurance companies. A home-protection company called TICOR Home Protection protected new buyers of homes against certain kinds of defects. Realty Tax, a service company, provided real estate tax information to the lenders, such as Bank of America. Later we formed TICOR Life Insurance Company, organized under the Utah laws and based in Salt Lake City, which enabled me to put the retired senator Wallace F. Bennett, an experienced business leader, on its board of directors. I enjoyed doing something for a man who had meant so much to me.

Shortly after I arrived, we formed TICOR Mortgage Insurance, the last of the new subsidiaries. This type of insurance covered residential loans with low down payments and proved tremendously successful. Within three years, the fourteen underwriting offices nationwide had written policies covering $2.14 billion in loans. Many years later, TICOR Mortgage Insurance, however, would end up being a shining star that would fall from the skies—and bring disaster to the whole TICOR family.

Nothing in my background seemed to prepare me for this. I had no experience in the financial management field, I knew very little about printing, and I knew nothing about title or mortgage insurance. Yet I had to fill the head positions of subsidiary companies, the internal operation of which I knew little about—one of the most difficult personnel management situations I faced. I had no time to learn the details of how to write a title policy, but I had to know how to evaluate the supervisors of those who did. In essence, I hoped my new job played to my strengths in people management and supervision.

In some respects this job reminded me of my under secretary of commerce position where I oversaw some twenty agencies and thirty-seven thousand employees. As a conglomerate, TICOR had about ten thousand employees, and I worked with the men (later I inserted top women executives) who ran these companies—the chairmen, CEOs, and presidents. Those executives reported to me, just as in Commerce. Comparatively, and to my surprise, I felt government had the greater workload. Success had a different measure—the "bottom line" defined business success. The company must be efficient and profitable. Our stock traded on the New York Stock Exchange, and the daily price quotes showed us where we stood in the eyes of the shareholders and all the pressure groups. Rating agencies eagerly told the world how they viewed our business. The test of the bottom line is simple to grasp. On the other hand, public service rarely operates with a "bottom line."

We always loved living in Washington, D.C., but after living in San Francisco we had kept our California residency. We knew we would return. Our doubts about Los Angeles did not last long. Though its size, vitality, and diversity make it difficult to comprehend initially, after three months Marion and I felt at home, and she called it "the best place we had lived." We bought a house in Beverly Hills on Rodeo Drive because the school system was one of the best in the state. Our little old house, built in 1932, stood on the "flats" of Beverly Hills, a part of the L.A. basin that had once been bean fields. It nearly qualified as a "Beverly Hills teardown." We quickly found out that the unfamiliar phrase meant the electrical system did not work and the plumbing was in tatters. Most of these original Beverly Hills homes had served as beach homes for wealthy Pasadena homeowners. About the time we bought the house, the trend had become for buyers to tear down the old beach homes and build new and larger places. We didn't have the money to do that, but over the years we have restored it so that everything works nicely. Our street, Rodeo Drive, has undergone much commercial ballyhoo, almost like Fifth Avenue. The trend has continued; people buy the old homes, tear them down, and build posh, palatial homes surrounded by manicured gardens. Many are done in good taste, but not all. Nonetheless, we quickly fell in love with the area and our home.

As the children became independent, Marion developed her own career as an artist. She had begun to paint in 1969 while we lived in Washington, D.C., experimenting with color and pastel landscapes on paper. She stretched canvas over wooden frames to create abstract two-dimensional shapes, sometimes with creative holes in the canvas. Described as hard-edged geometrical acrylic on canvas, her abstract creations are inspired by the simple logic and symbols in everyday life. Even her sharp sense of humor comes through in her art. In our first few years in Beverly Hills she painted the house in this style, which certainly brought us in closer contact with our neighbors. Today, her art is well recognized; she has participated in numerous national galleries, both solo and group, exhibited in Berlin, and is represented in many permanent collections.

When I became the CEO and chairman of the board of TICOR on January 1, 1976, I achieved what I always wanted—to be a boss. During my tenure, TICOR experienced some of its best, most profitable years, with a peak in revenues of $459 million in 1979 (the highest in company history), all in the face of bad indicators that affect the business—a shrinking real estate market, a recession, and double-digit inflation. The company benefited from its long reputation of efficiency and integrity. In a significant change, I moved the company from its longtime home on Spring Street to a relatively new building at 6300 Wilshire Boulevard, which was a sign of the times as many businesses left the downtown area and moved west. The building also proved a great investment for the company (we bought the building for $19 million, and my successor sold it years later for more than $60 million).

Over the years, TICOR had amassed the state's largest library of historical real estate transactions. The years of business made our vast title plant the dominant primary source for these records, preferred even over the county records. We had accumulated more than thirty thousand photographs along with related papers that documented the Los Angeles region's growth from the 1860s to the 1930s. In 1976, I donated this photograph collection to the California Historical Society and invited them to maintain a regional history center on the first floor of our corporate office building, without charge. The collection served as the single most important pictorial resource on the history of southern

California. Making it available to the public was in accord with TICOR's long-standing community relations posture.

During the 1970s and 1980s, diversification became a popular tenet of business growth. People argued that diversification offered corporations protection and stability. At least, most believed that at the time. TICOR was a small conglomerate, and in 1979 I began the process of merging TICOR with another insurance company, which would have made us much larger and given us much greater presence in the financial insurance field. But the pressure to do this concerned many of our competitors. Other companies had viewed TICOR, with its success, as a potential takeover for at least ten years. Up until that time, we had managed to stop it from happening. Then, one Friday afternoon, a man from a financial securities corporation in Texas came into my office. I called him "the hawk." Friday seems to be the day when these things happen: he announced his intention to take us over. Other corporations had been buying large amounts of our stock, and this company already owned 10 percent of our stock. I told him that I would consider his offer, even though I didn't like it—I viewed it as detrimental to our shareholders and to our own plans for growth.

He said he would keep it quiet, but as soon as he returned to Texas he announced the offer to the press. I know he announced it to put pressure on me. I received several calls from angry shareholders asking such questions as: "By what right are you refusing such good money?" and "Why are you waiting? I can make ten dollars per share." By law, I could not reveal our thoughts and analysis in progress, even to major shareholders; it would be unfair to all other shareholders. I had to sit there while they chewed me up and down without telling them our plan of action. To sell a venerated, old-line California company like TICOR to a Houston-based company would have been very regrettable. We had thousands of employees and had been in business ninety-five years. Ironically, we had just announced a pending agreement with another recognized company that would increase our assets and offered greater strength and growth for the future. I told these irate stockholders things like: "We're studying it. We have our board considering all possibilities." After spitting out an obscenity, one threatened a lawsuit. To say the least, in this situation shareholders are rarely sympathetic to management.

Behind closed doors we viewed the Texas offer—a combination of stock and money and reliant on TICOR's own resources—as totally unwise. My board unanimously felt we had to avoid this hostile bid, making an unfriendly takeover battle imminent. I had to find a way to bring TICOR into a safe haven. Almost immediately upon the news breaking, I had received a call from Ben Biaggini, who said he was wearing his "white hat." To hear from Benjamin Biaggini, the CEO and chairman of the board at Southern Pacific Corporation—an enormous company, much more than just a railroad, the largest private landowner in California—gave me some confidence. Ben and I had served together as business members of the federal Pay Board, and we sat on the policy committee of the recently formed California Business Roundtable. Ben, a formidable person with a keen mind and authoritative manner (pity those who thought of him as just a big Texas railroad man), enjoyed a great deal of power in California, and national prestige as well. He asked if I needed any help. At that time I said no. Almost immediately, however, arbitrageurs purchased our stock in anticipation that the publicized offer would go up. I received more calls from them challenging our right to say no to the Texas offer. In no time we estimated that 60 to 80 percent of our stock "was in play." I called Ben.

We met on a Saturday in my offices, and Biaggini brought his president with him. Southern Pacific had interest in the financial services area because our real estate cycles stood apart from their transportation business cycles. The consequences would make us a subsidiary of a much larger corporation. Southern Pacific was "old California"—even older than TICOR—and a company with which we felt very comfortable.

In the negotiations, Biaggini offered me thirty-five dollars a share —in cash. We needed more than that, but his president resisted. I asked Biaggini to join me in my office, alone. I explained to him that their offer needed to conclusively repel the Texas predator. He understood and raised the offer to forty dollars a share. Within an hour I had sold the company, and it became a wholly owned subsidiary of Southern Pacific Corporation. In late February 1979, the directors confirmed it. For the TICOR shareholders, the Southern Pacific deal brought more per share, in cash. It delighted them. It relieved me that TICOR maintained its corporate identity. To give a sense of the size of the deal, our value of $514 million brought Southern Pacific's total assets to $4.85 billion. I went on the board of Southern Pacific Corporation, and Biaggini and two of his senior officers came on my board.

TICOR became part of Biaggini's empire, and he became my big boss. We remained relatively independent because of our relationship. I describe Ben as "old school." He proudly honored his word. He rarely required reports or anything in writing between us. He just asked me to call him if anything came up. I continued on with my ideal situation, being my own boss, reporting primarily to my own board of directors. This arrangement had its defects; for example, we could no longer act completely independently and develop our own capital. It limited us in what we could do in terms of growth. While I could sell companies as long as I told Ben about it, I couldn't buy companies. Southern Pacific viewed us as a "cash cow" and used the profits of some of our subsidiaries, such as TICOR Mortgage Insurance, to pay off interest on their bonds. While this was a common practice in the 1980s business world of mergers, I knew it would limit TICOR's success in the long run.

On March 1, 1981, I hired a new president, Winston Morrow, previously the head of Avis, the car rental company, which had been a subsidiary of International Telephone and Telegraph Corporation (ITT), until ordered by the government to be spun off. I continued as chairman of the board and chief executive, with Morrow to be my successor. I didn't realize it at the time, but my decision would before long bring me into partnership with Howard Geneen, the founder of ITT. Geneen first spun the word *conglomerate* as a means of describing the aggressive acquisition of companies under one central management. I didn't like the merger mentality. Although brilliant with the numbers, Geneen showed little compassion for the thousands of people in his employ. He performed business like a game of Monopoly. He acted as if no lives were connected to the dollar signs in his eyes.

Everybody started to have real problems with the economy in 1982, including the Southern Pacific empire. Finally, in 1983, as Ben Biaggini began to merge his company with Santa Fe Industries to form Santa Fe Southern Pacific Corporation, he agreed to allow us to become independent again. Four of us formed an investment group for a leveraged buyout to take the company private. Morrow had brought in Harold Geneen, his old boss, to head the buyout effort. I raised no objection, but it bothered me. Too late I realized my inabilities in corporate takeovers. Geneen had a reputation as the master at knowing what to do—buy them and make them succeed, or sell them. I stayed on as a part owner of this new group, of which I had a very substantial percentage and position, though my title, chairman of the Executive Committee, was a make-believe type of job. In reality, I sat on the side. By the time we completed the buyout in February 1984, I had entered retirement.

The next year, 1985, the company suffered its worst year as one of the subsidiaries failed, which began the fatal unraveling of the TICOR reputation. TICOR Mortgage Insurance, the company that I had helped create, became entangled in a savings and loan scandal. According to *Forbes,* the company had "the largest risk exposure in one of the nastiest and most rumor-plagued thrift scandals to come along in some time." TICOR Mortgage had to deliver on mortgage insurance policies of $153 million. The magazine went on to taunt Geneen, "the master of minutiae," for letting this slip past his attention. Even the president of TICOR Mortgage Insurance (one of the many who lost his job in the scandal) was apparently unaware of the situation. The rub-off effects immediately spread a dark cloud of trouble over all of the TICOR family. All shared the same name and the same logo. The other companies started to suffer, even after TICOR Mortgage closed its doors.

I watched this traumatic event from the sidelines with great pain. I am now somewhat philosophical about it, but at the time, it bothered me greatly. In a few years the entire TICOR empire failed, piece by piece. I lost not only my financial investment, which I was prepared to lose, but also my contribution to that company of which I was so proud. It hurt to see the destruction of an existing old-line establishment that had thousands of employees whose lives depended on it. My longtime secretary, who retired when I did, spent forty-two years at TICOR. Her family—her sister and brother-in-law—was one of the many families who had worked all their lives for TICOR companies. The sadness was epidemic. We could not believe our company, which had played such an integral part in Los Angeles, and the nation, suffered such a downfall. The company eventually did go into total bankruptcy a few years later. The assets were sold piecemeal—the various subsidiaries, the real estate. So there went TICOR, which was almost ready to celebrate its hundredth year in 1993, but by that time it was out of business.

When we moved to Los Angeles we had hardly any personal resources. We had just managed to keep together twenty thousand dollars, which we used for the down payment on our home. We borrowed money from my father-in-law for the necessary home renovation. Even though my salary with an occasional merit bonus made life easier, my days as a corporate executive were twenty years too early for the huge corporate salaries (plus stock options) that became the norm in the following decades. As always, we lived very carefully. Three, then four (and then five) children in college will do that. Though well paid, I was always concerned about building a self-sufficient estate for retirement—at that time, 1971, about fifteen years away.

That changed when I met TICOR board member Davre Davidson, a very modest and quiet man with a keen financial mind. A self-made man, he and his wife were one of the originators of the "impulse" buying technique—in this case, the sale of bags of potato chips and peanuts for twenty-five cents at restaurants, drug stores, and markets. Initially, they worked out of the backseat of their car. From that Horatio Alger start, Davre built a business empire with the Philadelphia-based ARA Services, now Aramark, a worldwide food supplier to such entities as universities, prisons, national parks, and the Los Angeles Olympics. I confided in Davre; he knew my personal financial situation, and he offered key personal advice. After he put me on his board, he recommended that I keep my board fees exclusively for building a tax-deferred retirement account. I did that with the ARA board fees, and other corporate boards on which I served. These, in time, became significant sums, which helped considerably in retirement planning.

Throughout my years with TICOR, my reputation as a leader in business and governmental affairs brought numerous boards of directors offers to my door. They included very large corporations, such as Pacific Enterprises, a holding company controlling the Southern California Gas Company, the largest gas distribution system in the United States, where I observed the operations of an ultralarge corporation. I became a board member of United Television, controlled by Chris Craft, which operated some dozen TV stations. I served on the board of American Medical International, a pioneer in hospital management and a very large company (with forty-five thousand employees) controlling the management of more than one hundred hospitals in the United States and abroad.

In these various meetings, I not only learned how others managed their products and services, but I also saw different operational styles, some I disliked and others I emulated. The boardroom provides a provocative atmosphere. People of totally different backgrounds and experiences shoot ideas back and forth. That's the great value of the experience, if it's a well-selected board. During that time, boards began to mirror the population. Some of my boards had more than token representation of women and minorities. Penn Mutual Life Insurance of Pennsylvania, for example, and their insights became essential. I think my own special contribution came from my work in public service, where I felt my experience in government, management procedures, and personnel would be of help. I always tried to look beyond competence to assess the quality of integrity, not always an easy task. I am not a trained "numbers man" and tried to avoid the trap of being referred to as a financial expert. Nor did I want to be a "rocking chair" director, of which I saw plenty.

After I left TICOR in 1984, I accepted an "of counsel" position with the large Cleveland-based law firm Jones, Day, Reavis, and Pogue, after first saying no to being managing partner of its L.A. offices. It is one of the top law firms in the United States, with nine U.S. offices from New York to L.A. as well as offices in Europe, Hong Kong, and Japan. They asked me to "interpret" their position in the L.A. community, which I tried to do. I was not a "rainmaker"—they did not need me for that—nor did I qualify. They gave me a nice office, first in Century City and then downtown where they moved their principal office (with my strong urging). I brought with me my then ("the world's best," I would say) secretary and friend, Carolyn Kleinknecht, who stayed with me for twenty-four years. They treated us with great care, and I admired the quality and professionalism of the lawyers. After three years, my work seemed complete and I decided to leave. I gave my resignation over the phone to Richard Pogue, then the managing partner in Cleveland. This surprised him, as did my expressed feeling that they were overpaying me. They probably didn't hear that too often. Dick Pogue laughed; he thought I was joking. I was embarrassed that they paid me too well for my work.

By that time, 1987, I had immersed myself in many other things. I had effectively retired from TICOR in 1984, although it proved a long way from retirement as most Americans view it. These years of "retirement" for me have been some of my most active and invigorating and are close to my heart. They allowed me time to pursue some of my more philosophical ideas. This aspect of my life, let's call it community service, alone fills a third of my life. Assisting me in the efforts of these recent years is Virginia (Gini) Veracka, my home secretary. Invaluable, we call her the "de facto member" of our family.

FOURTEEN

THE SECOND BOTTOM LINE

A Corporate Executive's Community Duty

WHILE I HAD no idea who Ernest Loebbecke was when I first interviewed for the job at TICOR, I quickly learned of his prominence as a member of the southern California business community. He was a force. His leadership in greater Los Angeles community service is now legendary. He was one of California's most active business leaders, including a period as president of the California State Chamber of Commerce. His list of public service activities, most of which he headed, doesn't mention the thousands of people whose lives he affected in a beneficial way.

Of German ancestry, he had enormous hands, which he used skillfully in his carpentry hobby. He filled his home with the finest woodworking equipment, and he created incredible pieces. Of particular memory was his Christmas house of several floors, about five feet in length, with intricate miniature furniture and figures in the rooms. It was an art object on which he spent hundreds of hours. He sold the house for a charity, the Villa Esperanza, a home for the mentally handicapped. His only son had benefited from a stay there.

Because of Ernest Loebbecke and others, TICOR had a reputation in the community; it was synonymous with community service. I learned much about the business world from Ernie, but even more about the role of the public corporation as it affects American society. He saw more than the bottom line; he saw the responsibility that business owed to the American community as a whole. He once said, "any company, if it is to remain successful, will contribute as much to society as it receives from it."

I felt extremely lucky to find such a good job with such a great company. I could have found a job where the boss discouraged any sort of community service. Private enterprise is far different from public service. The tests of performance are different. The phrase *bottom line* is real. Did you make money or didn't you? You can never forget the bottom line. As I took over the company, Loebbecke continued to encourage me to be active in the community. I welcomed it. As I look back, I realize that my sense of accomplishment from those years comes not so much from my work as a big businessman, but more from my community service. Mixing the two—private enterprise and community service—as I did during my tenure at TICOR brought me great satisfaction.

This form of public service, as juxtaposed with my work in government service, had distinct advantages. Public service has something that you don't find in private enterprise—different criteria for evaluating job performance. My government career was shaped in the executive branch, where we worked with—even reported to—the legislative branch. Our constituency was very broad—the whole of the American public. Here, in the realm of the corporate world, community service was more independent. I could be selective in the type of service I pursued.

I spent a great deal of time with the external side of corporate life, which was worrying about community service and serving organizations like the California Chamber of Commerce and the Greater Los Angeles Chamber of Commerce. I had never been a big fan of the Chamber of Commerce, at either the national or the local level, but I ended up being quite active in the Greater Los Angeles Chamber of Commerce. I served as a director for seven years and became a senior vice president as its chairman of the Federal Affairs Committee. I saw firsthand the influence of the ultraconservative small businessman whose limited vision would demand that complex public issues be made simple. For example, one day a board member loudly objected to the acceptance of any federal money for education because then, he said, we would lose our autonomy. His statement was astonishing considering that federal monies have long supported the whole state and local educational infrastructure. I did speak up. The chamber is obviously probusiness—it should be. But there often seemed little research to support many of their positions. Many times I felt votes were taken without careful pro and con analysis. Emotion was dominant. Eventually, I was asked to get "into the chairs" to become chairman. I had to make a decision. I didn't want to be a hypocrite and take public positions with which I didn't agree. As chairman, I would have to testify and defend positions that I personally could not accept. So I refused and shortly afterward asked not to be reelected.

In 1972—while we were still new in the L.A. community—H. Russell Smith, a TICOR board member and head of Avery-Dennison Corporation, invited me to become a board member of the Los Angeles Philharmonic Association. One of the most public-spirited leaders I've ever met, he became my California mentor. The idea intrigued me; I had never explored that aspect of community service. I accepted, thinking I could learn about a public musical organization with little, if any, responsibility. A rocking-chair kind of assignment, I thought. I found the intricacies of the organization fascinating. After three years or so they asked me if I would be a vice president, just to use my name. They assured me there was no work involved. I said okay. Shortly thereafter, Thornton Bradshaw, president of ARCO (later president of RCA) and also the association president, got into a dispute with Mrs. Norman "Buffy" Chandler, then the most powerful woman in California and the creator of L.A.'s Music Center. Bradshaw resigned. I was the only vice president on board at the time, so it was pointed out that I was the only available successor.

The president of the Philharmonic is the chief executive; the position requires a great deal of time. In my case, it came in 1977, just as I had finished one year as TICOR CEO. I was still learning about title insurance, mortgage insurance, financial printing, and so on. I could not give day-to-day attention to the operation of the Philharmonic. And the Philharmonic was at a point of great need and facing a million-dollar deficit in the approaching year. The groups composing the Performing Arts Center had intense competition for money at that time, including the Center Theater Group (which had three stages), the Master Chorale, and the Philharmonic (the Los Angeles Opera came later). I quickly added some good people to the board, including some from my own corporate family. In particular, I recruited David O. Maxwell, the talented head of a new TICOR subsidiary (TICOR Mortgage Insurance), to be treasurer. I also relied heavily upon James R. Galbraith, an adroit "wordsmith" who had become TICOR's vice president of public affairs. I had recruited him from D.C., where he was executive director of the Republican Governors Conference.

All orchestras in America face the same challenge—providing a good performance for a willing audience able to buy tickets to fill the concert hall. The classical music audience, for several reasons, has become a shrinking one in many places in the United States. The problems at the Philharmonic centered on the simple knots of money and egos. For all of my time as president and then chairman, the Philharmonic had an internationally famous executive director, Ernest Fleischmann. Even today, I view him as the world's best impresario. He knows music in all its aspects, from the composer to the player to the orchestra. Extremely devoted and capable, he loved the men and women of the orchestra. He also happened to be a British chartered financial accountant, and so he managed to blend high finances and classical music. In those days—the 1970s—his irascibility sometimes hindered him. We all admired his mastery of the technical, but his contrariness was noticeable in some interpersonal relations. I called him a "genius maverick." His skills as a speaker and writer at times only complicated matters.

In the larger arena, Buffy Chandler was the visionary responsible for the creation of the extraordinary Music Center of Los Angeles. As its czar she governed all music and theater operations in Los Angeles, and everyone knew it. I found her charming, pragmatic, and tough as nails —the supreme judge of what could be done and by whom. I quickly learned why Thornton Bradshaw had resigned.

Fleischmann stood in the middle of this boiling cauldron and needed some help. Before I became president he ignored me. He had ignored Marion, even though he shared an identical background as a German Jewish refugee. He and Marion were born in Frankfurt in the same year and fled Germany in the same year, 1938. Ernest went to South Africa, whereas Marion went to Boston via Portugal. After I became president, we became close associates. I learned the complications of his intricate personality—his shyness coupled with a drive that knew little boundaries—all supported by an overall brilliance.

In my new role, I assured him that I was there to support him. But I then asked him to clear all of his letters of a certain type with me. He had a fit. He could not understand why. I explained to him that he was killing himself with his own letters.

He had no idea that the recipients were copying his letters and using them to denigrate him. Quickly, my "review" of his letters was unnecessary. We worked closely together in building support for the Philharmonic. Our good relationship became a warm one over the years. Behind his contentious personality, I found an extremely sensitive and loving man. I spent hundreds of hours with him. We trusted each other, and I like to think I helped him in his job as managing director, which he held for nearly thirty years and for which he gained worldwide respect and recognition. The Philharmonic has become a world-class orchestra, one of the top in the United States. I must recognize the leadership given it by Carlo Maria Giulini, Zubin Mehta, André Previn, and, now, the young and sensational Esa-Pekka Salonen. This success was primarily Ernest's doing. It is a public orchestra, really owned by its audience. After nine years as president, and then as chairman of the board, I was later elected a lifetime board member.

Many years later, in anticipation of his retirement, Ernest was honored at a black-tie dinner and dance (not his first by any means). Marion was commissioned to create a painting honoring him, which she did—unbeknownst to him. In her best modern style, she used a canvas shaped as a large *M,* which stood for *music.* Positioned within it she painted his initials, E. F. She used very vivid colors. The whole thing was called *Music in Ernest,* a takeoff of *The Importance of Being Ernest.* It was a huge hit. When she presented it, she pulled back the cover and she spoke to him in the Frankfurt dialect of their native German. As she presented it, she quoted from memory a poem written by one of Frankfurt's most famous poets, Friedrich Stolze. Basically, Stolze said, he could not get it through his head how anyone could not be from Frankfurt. The thrust was obvious: Frankfurt is the center of all that is good in the world. Anybody growing up in Frankfurt at that time knew that poem. Though the poem caught him by surprise, Ernest finished it in the Frankfurt dialect in a moving and very private expression between the two of them.

Even as a corporate executive, I always asked the big societal question: Where are we going? Within that context, what do we do to make our society a better place? You have to choose among the many objectives; all require that you lay the groundwork, attempt to build a consensus, and work through the proper channels. My style: work within the system, even when you try to change it.

Education is the key. Most issues I am drawn to take time, even years, to accomplish change. The best example is our work on campaign finance reform. Everyone attacks the status quo, but most are nonetheless comfortable with it. The old saw says, "The devil you know is better than the devil you don't." I find it best to accept the status quo—the pragmatic me—while trying to develop reasons to persuade people to change.

For many years I have been deeply involved with an organization now called the Center for Governmental Studies (earlier the Center for Responsive Government), an umbrella organization that covers several specific public service areas. Tracy Westen, a Renaissance man, created it in May 1983. A steering committee was formed consisting of Frank Wheat (a partner of the Gibson, Dunn, and Crutcher law firm), Stafford Grady (a well-known bank president), Donald R. Wright (former chief justice of the California Supreme Court), and myself. All of us had extensive government service backgrounds. The Weingart Foundation made a substantial start-up grant, and shortly thereafter, in 1983, Robert Stern, former general counsel to the California Fair Political Practices Commission, joined as the general counsel. Tracy Westen was the chief executive. The two men understand acutely the current trends in American society and politics and realize how those trends can stray from our nation's established principles. They planted the seeds of this organization in a commission in which I was heavily involved as cochairman, the California Commission on Campaign Financing. The commission was organized in 1984 and, at first, focused solely on campaign financing practices in California legislative races. We wanted to find the cause and possible solutions of the problem, which seem so obvious to some but not all of the voting public.

The California Commission was a bipartisan, nonprofit, private organization. We deliberately designed the commission with a broad spectrum of twenty-one Californians from the state's business, labor, agricultural, legal, political, and academic communities. Both Republicans and Democrats agreed to serve as commission members. I shared the chairmanship with two others, Frank Wheat, who was also a leader of the California bar, and Cornell C. Meier, the vigorous chairman of Kaiser Corporation. At the beginning, I announced to the commission that in the end I looked forward to our report having unanimous agreement. This, you can imagine, was greeted with disbelief. We had people of deep-seated polarized beliefs sitting across the table from each other. But they were at the same table and open to the idea of finding a solution to this problem. I expected the disbelief. And I intentionally proposed a unanimous agreement before we drew any conclusions.

We gathered data from the California campaigns of 1958 through the November 1984 general election. After an eighteen-month study, we issued a final report in October 1985 called *The New Gold Rush: Financing California's Legislative Campaigns*. We found that the spending in state legislative races had jumped 3,100 percent since 1958. The average legislative candidate, at that time, raised 92 percent of his or her money from outside the home district. Some campaigns generated funds at least ten times more than an assemblyman's annual salary. Tom Hayden in 1982 spent more running for his assembly seat—$2 million—than did all 1958 legislative candidates combined. At that time, we predicted that by 1990 the *average* assembly race would cost $1 million. In the 1980s, approximately 96 percent of all incumbents who sought reelection won their seats, generally because they could easily raise more funds than their challengers. Some senators outraised their opponents by a 229-to-1 ratio in the primary elections! The commission concluded that the precipitous rise in legislative campaign expenditures, and shifting sources of contributions, distorted the legislative process, deterred competition, and undermined public confidence in the state's legislative institutions. The present system of campaign fund-raising needed (and needs) drastic change. We all agreed that we needed reform to preserve representative government at all levels.

With the numbers in, and the damage to our system obvious, the commission's work was done. In our report we drafted a legislative bill and an alternative initiative that could carry out the recommendations. Speaker of the Assembly Willie Brown introduced our model law as his own bill, but it never came out of committee! It was clearly just a gesture. We recognized that the reform being advocated would be most difficult because the incumbent legislature would never pass this into law. So we had to turn to the state's ballot initiative system. We separately organized an initiative committee to obtain the required number of signatures to get it on the ballot. A farsighted and broad-gauged colleague of mine, Walter B. Gerken, chairman of the board of Pacific Mutual Life Insurance Company, became the spirited leader of what became known as the "Gerken Initiative."

At that time, in 1986, I was chairman of the California Business Roundtable, which had been organized in 1976 by a group of CEOs of the major California corporations. It was modeled after the National Business Roundtable, which consists of the nation's largest corporations. The three founders of the California Business Roundtable were Ben Biaggini, then Southern Pacific chief executive; the late David Packard, cofounder of Hewlett-Packard; and the late Justin Dart, then chairman of Dart Industries. I knew Biaggini through our service on the Pay Board (which preceded his company's purchase of TICOR). Packard served as deputy secretary of defense during the Nixon administration when I had the same position in the Commerce Department. I became one of the founding directors of the roundtable. It is a nonpartisan, nonpolitical organization dedicated to improving the overall economic climate in California. Because the membership was limited to no more than the state's one hundred largest corporations, such as Hewlett-Packard, PG&E, Southern Pacific, Chevron, and Levi Strauss, the media dubbed us "the Clout Club." The roundtable represented more than eight hundred thousand employees in a state that had the sixth largest economy (in 1986) in the world with an annual output of $500 billion a year.

As vice chairman and then chairman of the California Business Roundtable, my principal challenge was to lead my fellow "equals" carefully. The egos of CEOs are always very evident in a congregation of this kind, and Mary Anderson, the longtime executive director, helped me immeasurably. Roundtable members and their deputies were anything but unanimous in their ideological and political views. Unanimity per se was never the goal. Ironically, in most cases the issues themselves were the unifying force.

Though not a lobbying organization, the members encouraged the personal development of the key executives (chief executive officer or other principal officer) in each corporation to assert their positions on important economic issues. The primary purpose, thus, was to get the CEOs of the major corporations to know one another, to talk to one another, to discuss matters common to all corporations in a constructive, nonsecretive fashion, staying, of course, nonviolative of any of the antitrust laws, and to make our presence known in a responsible way. An example of the last point is the chambers of commerce—local, as well as regional and state organizations. Chambers of commerce have a useful role, but too often the responsible CEOs of major corporations have walked away from that type of organization, delegating the representation to functionaries. We wanted the personal involvement of the CEOs of the major corporations of the state. We urged these top businessmen to maintain a perspective beyond their industries, to take an interest, a personal role, in society and the economy. It isn't easy to do. I can't say we always did what we wanted to do with some of the members of the companies because some of those member CEOs were just too busy or it wasn't their thing. They didn't feel comfortable or they weren't knowledgeable. Also, not every CEO has an understanding of the need to participate in public affairs. Indeed, some strongly disagree that they have any role. I understand that point of view, but obviously think otherwise. There's a second bottom line in business, and that is the concern for the American public.

We chose issues, researched them, and discussed them. Then, we hoped, we could come to a general agreement on an action plan. We had a considerable amount of versatility and unique talent sitting around our table with which we could formulate a coordinated position on specific issues. I found myself answering a lot of questions about how the government operates. That's something I think every businessman should know, as well as he knows the inside of his own home. Though we had the highest caliber of in-house expertise when examining each issue, we did not claim to have all the answers. We selected issues wherein the roundtable effort could make a difference.

The emphasis was to focus on the identification of emerging issues and developing appropriate business positions *before* they reached the legislative process. This meant being prompt in our response to specific legislation. Our focus was also inward. We worked toward establishing internal procedures for business performance standards and sought to develop greater employee understanding of issues.

In its first ten years the roundtable built a reputation as the most potent public policy organization in California. With our low-profile manner void of personal aggrandizement, we stayed focused on issues affecting the public and society. In this way, we became a major contributor to the public policy process and one of the most productive resources for corporate involvement in California. It isn't often that businesspeople come together to focus on problems and issues usually considered the exclusive province of legislators and executive-branch policy makers, especially if these issues seem unrelated to the immediate business concerns of the roundtable membership. But the nature of the issues frequently poses a clear and present threat to California's economic development. We established a pragmatic method of creating task force projects for improvements in water supply, education, tort reform, transportation, energy and waste management, jobs and immigration, and public finance. These resulted in the development of research (which we usually contracted with outside specialists), leading to recommended positions. The objective was the integration of our dialogue with that of various components of the public sector. By the public sector I mean all aspects of it: the state legislature, the executive branch, the media, trade associations, labor unions, and ethnic and religious organizations.

When I became chairman in 1986, we had already done a good deal to improve California's business image. The roundtable recommended ways to finance improvements to the state's surface transportation system. We released a RAND Corporation study on hazardous materials and waste management in California, which was one of the roundtable's greatest concerns. Of equal importance, for all of California, is maintaining the water supply for its growing population. The water task force made a significant contribution toward passage of the Coordinated Operation Agreement (COA) between the Interior Department and the California Department of Water Resources. The passage of the COA, which protects California's state water quality standards, had statewide support from California business, water interests, environmentalists, and state and federal water contractors. The *Los Angeles Times* wrote, "COA is a milestone which recognizes the reality of limited water supplies and the need for conservation, cooperation and sound management." They called it "an historic peace treaty" between northern and southern California.

The COA work was comparable to the education effort of earlier years when the roundtable helped pass needed educational reform, which upgraded technical, math, and science programs. Simply put, members of the California Business Roundtable helped create the political climate for agreement between the governor and the legislature.

We studied California's growing Hispanic population, which was certainly evident in the beginning of the 1980s. We did not focus on whether the immigrants were legal or illegal. I felt we had to face the fact: they are here and they live here. It was (and still is) vital that California provide upward mobility for the waves of new workers immigrating to the state from Asia and Latin America. In 1985, we contracted a RAND Corporation study that detailed the impact of California's growing Latino population in the state that shed the light of new facts on old opinions regarding California's growing Hispanic population. At that time, the challenge of the future was to provide a place in California for the emerging minorities in the business life of the state. Its conclusion: education is a must—the number-one priority.

At that time, AIDS became headline news, yet people still sort of whispered about it and did not really face up to it. President Reagan was supposed to be concerned about developing a national policy, yet his administration ducked and weaved from the issue. I pushed for an AIDS task force, even though some members failed to see the business problems inherent with the disease. I brought a San Francisco doctor before the group to explain the ramifications of the disease. It didn't take long for my colleagues to realize the seriousness of AIDS and its threat to our society. Using an outside consultant, we developed a publication called *AIDS: A Reference for Managers,* and sponsored lectures on that subject as well as other health topics, including drug abuse in the workplace.

My greatest interest remained campaign finance reform. This issue is not popular with legislators, and the public does not know how to speak up. Legislators usually give lip service in support of reform, but they are not serious when push comes to shove. The cost of running a successful campaign in California has gotten out of hand. I publicly stated, "We [business executives and companies] are being besieged by requests from political people. We get as many as ten requests a day during campaign time."

The recommendations of the California Commission on Campaign Financing were passed unanimously by its twenty-one members. We had focused on educating everyone, before they voted. Frank Wheat, Cornell Meier, and I doggedly made sure that everyone was informed. We insisted that the top staff officers of the commission, Tracy Westen and Bob Stern, take their draft reports and in advance personally visit every member of the commission. This took a year and a half before we *all* came to the conclusion that *limited public financing,* the central issue—and the most controversial—was a significant solution to the campaign finance problem. Once we had agreed on that, other differences weren't so important. There were no dissenting statements. Procedurally, we strove for unanimity, a strategy copied somewhat from the national Committee for Economic Development (CED), on which I had served as a trustee for many years.

Unanimity gave strength to the recommendation. When the commission was able to unite all Democrats, Republicans, and independents, the impact was obvious. Example: Warren Christopher and Mickey Kantor (prominent Democrats) were in agreement with Bob Monaghan, the former majority leader of the state assembly (a well-known conservative Republican).

I had to be very careful at the time because of my association with the California Commission on Campaign Financing, which had researched the problem and issued the study report. As cochairman of the commission I felt I should avoid active advocacy while chairing the roundtable. This was not too difficult, inasmuch as several roundtable members were also members of the California Commission on Campaign Financing, such as Walter Gerken and Robert R. Dockson, of CalFed, Inc. (also a noted academic when at the University of Southern California). They were the "spear carriers" at the roundtable meetings. The roundtable used the commission study as a starting point for deliberations. The members voted to take a position (a two-to-one vote) to support what became known as the "Gerken Initiative" ("The Campaign Spending Limits Act of 1986") to qualify the measure for the November 1986 ballot. Some roundtable members helped individually to finance the campaign. The issue put the roundtable out in front of the public in 1986.

The initiative was based on the commission's recommendations to establish contribution limits and establish voluntary expenditure ceilings. The voluntary ceilings would be supported by limited matching public funds. There would also be voluntary taxpayer checkoffs. We knew the legislature would never touch campaign finance reform and so attempted to use the state initiative process.

Much to our disbelief, the initiative failed to qualify for the November 1986 ballot due to low signature validity rates in San Francisco and Alameda Counties. A total of 631,000 signatures were turned in, which we were told was 200,000 more than needed to qualify. Yet when we turned it in, the state agency said there were not enough signatures. We initiated a recount. Eventually, we proved the point that we had enough signatures to get it on the ballot. By then it was too late for the 1986 election! Though we had failed in our first effort, it was not over. I predicted in my roundtable chairman's annual report that "the ballot measure did not make it this year, but no doubt the need for reform is still burning—and it will be back."

My chairmanship at the roundtable ended after one year. To conclude my ten years at the California Business Roundtable as chairman of the board was rewarding, even though watching some sixty to eighty principal officers of major corporations with diverse backgrounds discuss public policy issues is always an adventure into the unknown. One of the statements of purpose of the roundtable always comes to my mind: "[To encourage] members to maintain a perspective beyond their own industries." I think we satisfied this objective during those years. The roundtable made a difference in a constructive way.

In 1986, during my roundtable chairmanship, I had been retired as TICOR CEO for more than a year but by the end of that year had helped found and become chairman and CEO of American Health Properties, Inc. This was a relatively small real estate investment trust (REIT), which became listed on the New York Stock Exchange. We started the REIT with ownership of seven of the finest hospitals operated by American Medical International. As immediate past chairman of the California Business Roundtable, I remained somewhat active, but my role became gradually one of less and less involvement. Later, the roundtable moved its headquarters to Sacramento, and it continues today, though it is not as prominent as it was in its earlier years.

My interest and role continue with the California Commission on Campaign Financing. Incidentally, I have not changed my advocacy of *limited public financing* of political campaigns. In the beginning of our study, I had been opposed to public financing of any sort. After a year and a half of study, argument, and discussion, we came, however reluctantly, to the conclusion that there was no alternative. The commission's recommendations in 1985 were direct—a combination of campaign finance reforms that included voluntary expenditure ceilings, contribution limitations, and limited public matching funds for candidates who accept expenditure ceilings. Opponents had a number of arguments against the last recommendation—limited public matching funds. The primary one is that it would support frivolous candidates. To ensure that public money would not be available to frivolous candidates, we proposed that candidates must first raise the threshold amount (specified); those who could not would be ineligible for limited matching funds. The goal is to devise a system that permits everyone to compete on a level field. This is what we had proposed. It is a long educational process to get legislators and the public to realize that there is another approach besides the one with which we have become accustomed: the squeeze play on individuals, unions, and corporations.

In 1988, we tried a second time. The California Campaign Financing Reform was put on the ballot as Proposition 68. This time it passed with 53 percent of the votes, but another initiative, designed to negate ours, Proposition 73, passed with 58 percent. We proposed that the two measures be considered together, which was the prevailing California Supreme Court law. The California Supreme Court changed this interpretation and ruled that when there are two mutually inconsistent measures, only the one with the most votes prevails.

This issue at hand had to do with the amounts of money that can be given for political campaign purposes. Proposition 73 was written by those who feel that there should be no restriction on the amount of contributions or expenditures for political purposes. Controls can be placed on contributions, but it is not possible to put controls on expenditures if a person is spending his own money. The Supreme Court held in the 1976 case of *Buckley v. Valeo*, the bible of campaign finance reform, that the spending of your own money cannot be regulated, because it is akin to free speech. Obviously, the multimillionaires or billionaires in our society are free to do what they want.

A U.S. District Court and the Ninth Circuit Court of Appeals ultimately threw out most of Proposition 73 as unconstitutional. The U.S. Supreme Court had described political money as tantamount to political speech because money allows candidates to communicate their views to the public; it equated money with political speech. Though Proposition 73 was declared unconstitutional, the ban on public financing was excepted.

We had the option of pushing for a decision on restoring the validity of our initiative, Proposition 68, which had passed, though it was negated. A number of us, including Walter Gerken, Frank Wheat, Melvin B. Lane (a publisher), Jean R. Wente (a wine maker), and myself, petitioned the California Supreme Court, asking them, now that they had thrown out Proposition 73, to reconsider Proposition 68, which also passed with a majority. Our legal theory was based on the argument that an unconstitutional measure (Proposition 73) cannot invalidate a constitutional one (Proposition 68) that also passed at the same time.

The Supreme Court of California, in late 1993, decided against us with a four-to-three decision. They reasoned that since the initiative passed in 1988, seven years had elapsed. They expressed other technical objections. The irony: Proposition 73 was designed to defeat Proposition 68 and did so, even though it itself was found invalid. Basically, it was too late. We lost it by just one vote. This was the second time that we had failed, even though this time it had enough popular support.

We immediately tried again. Again the same group of people put it on the ballot in November 1996, but this time without including limited public financing. Proposition 208, known as the Political Reform Act of 1996, passed convincingly with 61 percent of the vote. Much to our surprise, another initiative (Proposition 212), which had been created to negate ours, just as had been done successfully in 1988, did not pass. It was close. Proposition 208 details expenditure ceilings, variable contribution limits, true disclosure in campaign advertising, bans on off-year fund-raising, limits on total and aggregate nonindividual contributions, voluntary spending limits, and other reforms. Proposition 208 had been drafted to conform with our interpretation of *Buckley v. Valeo.* Proposition 208 passed and immediately went to the federal courts for review. Basically, we had to wait for the U.S. Supreme Court to make a decision on the constitutionality of *low* contribution limits to campaigns. The Court did this in 2000, which supported the approach taken in Proposition 208. In 2000, out of fear that Proposition 208 would be upheld on appeal to the California Supreme Court, the legislature put another initiative on the ballot—Proposition 34. It passed. As a result, further action on Proposition 208 had to be dropped, and so the need is still there.

In sum, our efforts resulted in two measures passing, Proposition 68 and Proposition 208. Both stimulated efforts by legislators to soften the provisions. Although these efforts succeeded, the result is that the measure of campaign reform is very limited—in my view and that of my Center for Governmental Studies colleagues.

Lesson: When political reform directly affects the legislature's own interest, legislators can
   —refuse to legislate and force you to use the expensive and time-consuming initiative process,
   —raise movements to campaign against your initiative when it reaches the ballot,
   —put a competing measure on the ballot to confuse the voters or get more votes,
   —litigate and challenge your successful initiative, and

—put a subsequent initiative or legislative measure on the ballot to supercede yours.

Unless there is a political earthquake (Watergate comes to mind), it takes years for the general public to accept ideas calling for a political change. Recommendations for reform take a long time to be understood. Obviously, the state legislatures, aided and abetted by the executive branches of the states and federal government, are the primary bodies who must understand the need for political change. In addition, there is always a small group of activists who want change—of any kind.

We started studying campaign finance reform in 1984, and it was many years before some results came to fruition. We were early; I don't think any other group persisted as much as we did in California. Our major successes have been in cities: Los Angeles, San Francisco, Oakland, and others have adopted limited public financing progress. Other states have picked it up, and there is a small trend appearing. It is, of course, a federal issue, with Congress recently enacting long-overdue legislation. Thanks to Senator John McCain, it even became a campaign issue in the 2000 presidential election. He, Senator Russell Feingold, and Representatives Martin Meehan and Christopher Shays deserve many plaudits. I am also pleased with the supportive role the Committee for Economic Development played in getting the federal legislation passed. I expect that even more change will come on the national level—sooner rather than later.

᠊ᢒ

TO GIVE YOU an idea of the things I had to deal with in regard to political preferences and egos, here is an exchange of letters between two prominent members of the California Business Roundtable. Copies were sent to me by the parties.

November 21, 1980
Dear David:
I know that you are as grateful as I am for the overwhelming sweep of the Republican Senate. Nothing so good has happened since Eisenhower.

I hope you are proud of the fact that you helped elect one of the most irresponsible Senators whose voting record matches very well with Kennedy's and most of the Senators who are extricated from the U.S. Senate. I know you did this because you like Alan Cranston. I like Alan, but I don't like one damn bit of what he stands for—and you don't either.

I am ashamed that California distinguished itself by sending another unbelieving Senator back to Washington when Ronald Reagan begged you not to do it.

Senator Cranston voted for the Labor Reform Act, giving Labor more clout in the Senate. He voted against cloture. He voted wrong all the way until the last day when he knew he couldn't win. Then he changed his vote. This is typical of Alan Cranston.

Your support of Alan Cranston put California in the class of two or three other states that sent equally irresponsible Senators back to confront President Reagan. You did this because you liked the guy—he made love to you and I understand that. But your responsibility, now having supported this guy, is to see that he supports Ronald Reagan all the way. He is a vacillator and if you put enough pressure on him he will do it.

If you think I have made any mistakes in my allegations, please point them out to me. Am often wrong, but don't enjoy it.

If you think I'm right, then please see that he performs like an American—not like a U.K. laborite.

You are my friend. I respect you and I hope you will rebut any errors I have made.

Warm regards,

Jus (Justin Dart)

December 1, 1980

Dear Jus,

I am sorry to learn through your letter of November 21st that your involvement in the recent political victory has brought on such a serious case of debilitating senility.

I hope after the flush of victory is over you will be able to restore yourself to your normal level of good common sense and judgment to the extent that you will be able to respect the opinions and actions of your good friends, even though you don't agree with them.

With all good wishes for a speedy recovery.

Sincerely,

David Packard

FIFTEEN

THE J. PAUL GETTY CENTER

J. PAUL GETTY died in 1976 an enormously wealthy man, having built his Getty Oil Company into a substantial worldwide enterprise. A couple of years before his death he had established a museum in nearby Malibu. It housed an eclectic assortment of art, including French decorative arts, classical antiquities, and European paintings. It reflected his personal interest, though the paintings were not too special. The day after Mr. Getty's death, the senior vice president and head of the trust department of the Title Insurance and Trust Company came to me. He announced that we were the executors of the largest private estate that had ever been probated in the state of California.

Mr. Getty's estate, at that time, was valued at about $700 million. The vice president had observed a trust department rule of silence. As so often happens when you deal with enormously rich people in their estate planning, it is conducted only on a need-to-know basis. In Mr. Getty's case, that excluded the chairman of the parent company, me.

In comparison to other trust companies, TICOR's trust department was relatively small, though it maintained two attractive features: founded in 1893, it was the oldest trust company in California, and it remained independent. Mr. Getty chose TICOR Trust primarily because we had no ties outside of California. Initially, he had worked with Bank of America as the executor of his trust. Bank of America, however, did business in England, where he lived, and it concerned him that after his death, the British might claim taxes on his California income and property. He wanted to have an independent trust company with no ties abroad. About six months before his death, he switched his whole estate over to TICOR Trust.

Because of the size of his estate, the probate ran into a lot of problems along with some lawsuits. I wasn't at all involved in the litigation or the settlement of the estate. That was not my job, let alone my expertise. Mr. Getty had left his entire estate to his own J. Paul Getty Trust and its J. Paul Getty Museum. Toward the conclusion of this probate, we (the executors also included two Getty sons) decided it necessary to diversify the holdings (it was all in Getty Oil stock). I became involved in the selection of the investment banking firm to handle the stock sale (called a "secondary"). We selected Morgan Stanley as the primary banker, and the sale ranked as the second largest stock secondary on record for the New York Stock Exchange (only a Ford Motor issue had been larger). It took six years and more than $26 million in legal fees to probate the will. When the J. Paul Getty Trust got its money in 1982, the value had grown to $1.2 billion. It has been very well managed and has continued to grow.

In 1981, in the days just prior to the actual turning over of the whole estate to the J. Paul Getty Trust, Harold B. Williams was appointed president and CEO. Widely recognized for his brilliance, Williams had distinguished himself in business, government, finance, and academe. As a twenty-one-year-old graduate of Harvard Law School, he used his mastery of accounting and tax law to build a meteoric career in the business world (as chairman of Norton Simon) and in his early forties became dean of UCLA's Graduate School of Management. He left the Carter administration where he had been the chairman of the Securities and Exchange Commission to join the J. Paul Getty Trust.

I had first met Harold in the early 1970s at a business conference. We, along with our spouses, hit it off quite well. We had traveled to the Republic of China together in March 1978, before the United States had recognized China. The seven couples on that trip had a wonderful two weeks seeing China under the Communist government. They treated us like the Henry Kissinger party because they wanted recognition from the U.S. government, and they thought our group could help in that effort. Most important, my friendship with Harold blossomed with our shared philosophical and political views, regardless of our party affiliation.

Shortly after the conclusion of the probate management by TICOR, which freed me of any possible conflict, Harold asked me to come on the board of the J. Paul Getty Trust Foundation, which I accepted and began in April 1982. Mr. Getty had left a lot of money and a wide-open definition of how to utilize it. In Mr. Getty's own words, we should spend the money "for the diffusion of artistic and general knowledge." The board, in its infancy, had many of the original trustees who had known Mr. Getty—people such as Stuart Peeler, a son of the founder of the law firm that Mr. Getty used; Pat Whaley (of the Peeler firm), Mr. Getty's tax lawyer; Harold Berg, chairman of the J. Paul Getty Oil Company; and Norris Bramlett, an executive secretary to Mr. Getty. Mr. Bramlett made it clear that he felt we should carry out Mr. Getty's personal wishes. I think most of us new members disagreed with that. We didn't know Mr. Getty, so we couldn't say what Mr. Getty would have thought. The new additions to the board, for the most part, came from business, professional, and academic backgrounds. Not too many of us had a professional understanding of art, but, in addition to our own professional expertise, we brought an eagerness to learn. The Getty Trust board offers no compensation, a stipulation in Mr. Getty's will. In the end, I would spend more hours on the never-ending challenges of the Getty business than I did on any of the corporate boards for which I received pay.

After intensive research, Harold and others developed an unusual plan that would, we believed, give the art world a needed boost. All the board members shared his excitement over the possibility of creating an organization that would be more than just a museum. We all felt the enormity of the available funds. We had an easy unanimity. In addition to the museum, the central public activity, we created institutes for art conservation and education, a research institute for art history and the humanities, and a grants program.

We had to find an appropriate place for the Getty, whatever it might become, to do its work. I was selected as the chairman of the building committee, which included site selection (in addition to Harold

Williams, the committee included fellow trustees Jon B. Lovelace, John T. Fey, and J. Patrick Whaley). I felt it a peculiar chore. Because of TICOR's involvement in real estate throughout the country and particularly California, I had access to every broker in the world. We could have asked for guidance from any number of companies, if we needed it. This effort did not fit into that easy category. We did not want publicity and so began a quiet, even secretive, process.

We wanted a site that met a number of tests. Of primary importance, the site needed good access and natural beauty. We also wanted something of sufficient size to house numerous programs in one place so that they could interact. We considered the existing Getty Museum in Malibu, but it was too small and had severe legal limitations. We had to serve the greater Los Angeles community—one of the largest counties in the United States, covering four thousand square miles, eighty-eight separately incorporated cities, and with some twelve million people in the area. We felt that this site not only had to service all of these communities, but be in a position to attract visitors from around the world. We could not forget Los Angeles's dependence on the car, so we felt it important to find something centrally located.

Harold and I, sometimes with two or three others, went out looking. We searched with a very substantial piece of property in mind, 100 acres, we hoped, though we considered everything over 25 acres. We didn't think downtown would be any more of an attraction than it is today. Among the most promising possibilities was the old Ambassador Hotel on Wilshire Boulevard (political quicksand) and the Veterans Affairs land in West Los Angeles. We toyed with the notion of the Veterans Affairs site because the Reagan administration considered selling its empty acreage. Unfortunately, that would have come with all kinds of legal problems with the U.S. government, if we could even find a large enough piece. We looked at the Santa Monica Airport—a decent area, good-sized, and undeveloped but with enormous legal challenges. We talked about Simi Valley, and drove up that way. But it would be hard to convince people in greater Los Angeles to drive north to Simi Valley.

Then one night in the fall of 1982, I went to a political dinner held at Twentieth Century Fox for the mayor of San Diego, Pete Wilson, during his successful U.S. Senate bid. The speaker, the recently elected president, Ronald Reagan, surprised us by not speaking at the dinner or after the dinner, but *before* the dinner. I had no interest in eating the dinner and so left. I went out to look for my car, but my driver, not thinking I would be that quick, had left.

At that moment I ran into Tom Jones and his wife, who shared my predicament. We both had a sardonic laugh about our situation, and while we waited for our cars we began to talk. I knew Tom Jones as chairman of Northrop Corporation, one of the Fortune 500 companies. He occasionally called me, as chairman of TICOR, regarding property he personally owned on a hilltop overlooking most of Los Angeles. He planned to build some thirty-five very upper-class homes overlooking the valley on all sides, but getting the building approvals from the Los Angeles city authorities had many contorted problems. Frankly, I did not follow his issues, but he would call me personally to make sure we responded to his concerns. I then would call the chairman or the president of our title company to make certain we satisfied Tom Jones's concerns. So I knew about his property, and in fact, he had called me no more than a week or two before this encounter.

As we talked a thought occurred to me. I asked him if he would be interested in selling his property on the hill. He looked at me. He was not a developer; he just owned the property. The incessant fight with the building authorities had made him tired and weary of it all. After he received building approval he would still need a developer to build the homes. His mood was right. I told him the Getty was looking. I had never considered that site, but while we talked it really seemed like the right place. I got back home and called Harold Williams. We discussed the price, and Tom Jones accepted it. We bought it within two weeks.

With that purchase we obtained the top 25-acre pad upon which the Getty Center now stands, plus an adjacent 100 acres or so. We still had other concerns. We thought that if word were to get out, something might happen to the rest of the land around there. People would want to be right near it. So very quietly, using "dummy brokers" (who were informed), we bought the pieces around it. The trickiest purchase included two developers who owned a couple of hundred acres nearby. We knew they faced the impossible chore of getting the land approved for home construction because of the soil condition and the steepness of the slope. Nonetheless, they were very smart in the business. I am convinced they knew very well who was buying, even though we tried to hide it from them.

The last piece, about 500 acres farther to the north, we bought from the University of California. They were deaccessioning it through a one-time sealed auction bid. Harold and I discussed our bid, and we wanted it badly because we didn't want to worry about that piece. We finally increased it to a point where, when we won, we outbid the runner-up by ten times. The money went to a good cause, the University of California system. They would never have built on it either. (One ticklish note: Harold, as a regent of the University of California system, abstained and took no part in the sale of the property.) We now had a total of about 750 acres.

That property passed all of our tests. It offered great natural beauty, an elevated lookout point offering a unique perspective on the Los Angeles basin, and great access from an immediate freeway to other nearby freeways connecting the city's other population centers, including the San Fernando Valley. Of course, the ability to build became our own concern, but we thought we could get the approval with conditions. We never anticipated the enormity of the task. The City of Los Angeles imposed more conditions on us, a hundred plus, than on any builder of any project in Los Angeles. Some of the conditions seemed extreme, and it took several years. The director of the Getty building program, Steve Rountree, an astute, balanced, imperturbable person, deserves the principal credit for getting it done.

At this time, the early 1980s, everyone had opinions and concerns about what the Getty would become. Institutions in southern California envied us, and Europeans feared the Getty would buy up all the art. Unfortunately, we couldn't allay their fears. We described what we hoped to do, and what we hoped to become. The rumors spread. In the art world, people talked about "the Getty factor," particularly in Great Britain. We went to London and tried to dissuade them from thinking that we would raid their collections. Ironically, we were promising not to behave as the British themselves had in acquiring so much of the world's art. Eventually, art prices escalated to such extremes that even the Getty has been forced to be selective. Most important, we wanted to erase the concept that the Getty was out to scalp the art world.

Next the building committee undertook the selection of an architect. We had begun an international search for an architect in 1983 using an outside selection group. From that, seven initial finalists were selected in February 1984, and then our building committee (none of whom had played a role in the selection of the initial seven) looked at the three finalists: James Stirling of London, Fumihiko Maki of Tokyo, and Richard Meier, an American based in New York. We visited museums that these men had designed. We went to London and then Stuttgart, Germany, to look at Jim Stirling's work. Marion loved his "purple socks" and his quixotic design with bright colors (a see-through orange elevator) in the Neue Staatsgallerie in Stuttgart. We flew to Japan and saw the incredible detail, requiring exceptionally skilled craftsmen, of Fumihiko Maki's work. In Frankfurt, we had seen Richard Meier's work on the Museum für Kunsthandwerk, though it was not finished. To me, it was clear that we should choose Richard Meier.

We came back to Los Angeles, and—in a very eventful moment—the five trustees on the building committee met to select the architect. Just before I called the meeting to order, to my surprise, two of the trustees told me that they thought Maki would be ideal. When they said that, I realized we could have a difference among strong-minded board members. We needed to arrive at a unanimous decision to give the selected architect full and immediate support.

We all had loved Mr. Maki's work, especially the detail he obtained with Japanese workmen, but I did not like his building plan. He proposed hiring young American architects and working with them for a year or two in Japan so they could learn his methods, style, and techniques. Then they would return to the United States and help him do his job here. He had never done a job in the United States, even though he had taught at Harvard. His plan seemed difficult and complicated, along with the fact that he was not an American-experienced architect.

I wondered about the will of the two Maki supporters. I knew they preferred Maki from the aesthetic point of view and wondered if they would argue their belief. Without hesitation, I acknowledged that some of them would like Maki, but my preliminary poll indicated that the majority of us wanted Richard Meier. There was a sudden shift, and five votes were recorded for Richard Meier.

When we announced Meier's commission in October 1984, it was called the "architectural commission of the century." It was estimated the project completion date would be in 1991 at a total cost of about $200 million. Things started out slowly, due to site complications, earthquake hazard, neighborhood concerns, and building permit approval. By 1991 we had seen many of Meier's designs, and the final one was under way. We had earlier realized that we had an extraordinary architect who couldn't be held back.

The enormity of putting this construction and all of its contents together—it would employ more than one thousand people—was a great effort. People always said, "Oh, you have all that money, you don't have any problems." We had a thousand problems, beginning with the attitude that we could do anything. We had a period of wide-open creativity in those early years. We added ideas without cost concerns at times. But the price kept going up, and the time to build it grew longer. From time to time, we would announce cost estimates lower than I thought true, not that it really mattered for a private project. For a while it was three hundred, then four hundred million dollars. As time went on, it grew to five hundred million. As the years passed, the costs constantly overran projections. This infuriated several of the trustees, who felt that they were not hearing the full story. The costs went up in respect to the little work we saw accomplished. The rest of us were not too concerned. My own view is that in all building projects more is spent than planned. And the Getty could afford to build the best—a statement often bandied about, but that was true.

As we came toward the end of the project, Meier really pushed people's patience. Some trustees even mentioned termination. His attitude often seemed impossible, which should not be regarded as anything unusual for an architect. He is also a genius, and few architects fit in that category. A major difficulty was Meier's frequent refusal to listen to anybody else. He wanted to do it all. He could design anything, from a bottle to a building to cutlery. His control over design included the chairs you sit in (nice, too). This building complex became a memorial to himself. I think it's incredible and he did a marvelous job, but the last few years were very tense. He had very little interaction with the board of trustees, not giving the "right" people the proper amount of attention. And even though we threatened termination, and it scared him, he probably correctly figured that he would not be dumped because it would reflect on the trustees if, as was the case, the project was 70 to 80 percent complete. The construction—a fourteen-year drama—cost about one billion dollars.

Harold Williams retired after seeing the Getty Center to its splendid—yes notable—completion in December 1997. It consists of a twenty-four-acre six-building arts-and-humanities community. I find it impossible to describe. Everyone always thinks of it as a museum, but it consists of so much more than that. The Getty is an international cultural and philanthropic organization, which serves both general audiences and specialized professionals. It is now under the creative leadership of noted educator Dr. Barry Munitz. The overall aim is the presentation, enjoyment, study, and conservation of the visual arts in order to increase the public's knowledge and sensitivity, expand its awareness and creativity, and sharpen its understanding and caring—all with the conviction that cultural enlightenment and community involvement in the arts can help lead to a more civil society. Today, the J. Paul Getty Trust is a growing seven billion dollar nonprofit institution. While this amount of money gave it a boost in becoming a world center of arts scholarship, the center has done a great job of being active in the greater Los Angeles community with extensive arts education programs.

This whole process of creating and building the J. Paul Getty Center has played a central role in the evolution of Los Angeles. The Getty, as a part of the city's cultural coming of age, has become a benchmark. During the same period of time, we saw the opening of the Museum of Contemporary Art, the Skirball Cultural Center, and the growth of the Los Angeles County Museum of Art. The Norton Simon Museum, a gem, opened (a redo) in Pasadena. And the spectacular Walt Disney Concert Hall (by noted architect Frank Gehry) opened in October 2003. The acoustics in the Walt Disney Hall are exhilarating!

Marion and I have also shared in the emergence of the Skirball Cultural Center, the nearby neighbor of the Getty Center. Marion's name is attached to one of its libraries. Together, the Getty Center and the Skirball are abuzz with creative family programs: lectures, theater, music, dance, and film. All this is in addition to exciting and famed paintings being offered at the Getty Art Museum. The Skirball's orientation is on American Jewish life, but its broad programming appeals to all. The cultural pieces are falling into place to make greater Los Angeles an envied part of the world.

My business career allowed for public services activity. I worked as cochair of a state board initiative drive to aid state parks, beaches, and wildlife. It passed. Governor Ronald Reagan was a strong supporter.

In 1978, I watched two legends say good-bye to each other. Mrs. Norman "Buffy" Chandler, founder of the L.A. Music Center, bids farewell to Carlo Maria Giulini, conductor of the Los Angeles Philharmonic, as he was returning to Italy.

As building committee chairman I worked with fellow Getty trustee John T. Whitehead in the building of the $1 billion J. Paul Getty Center. The center is now a world-class art and education institute with a noted museum. With his back to the camera is Richard Meier, the Getty architect, speaking to Jon Lovelace, chairman of the Getty Board.

The spectacular view of the J. Paul Getty Center.

Three World War II combat veterans with another common cause—to perpetuate
the legacy of Dwight D. Eisenhower through the Eisenhower Memorial Commission.
Left to right: Senator Dan Inouye (D, Hawaii), me, and Senator Ted Stevens (R, Alaska),
at the Getty Center in Los Angeles.

253

Marion at her art show in Berlin, 1993. A time of reflection for a German Jewish refugee.

Marion and I in front of her *Coming to America*, which was commissioned by the Skirball Cultural Center in Los Angeles. Even after macular degeneration damaged her vision, she continues painting in a new style. The Skirball acquired ten of these recent works and presented them in a special exhibit in 2003.

Marion was commissioned to create a painting honoring Ernest Fleischmann, the executive director of the Los Angeles Philharmonic Association. She called it *Music in Ernest.* Here they are reciting a familiar regional poem in their native Frankfurt German, which she, unbeknownst to him beforehand, began and he finished. The audience was bemused.

Marion and I traveled to Nepal in November 1985. We are wearing sherpa "Tribute" shawls presented to us by our head sherpa guide, after an eight-day hike with our children Vincent, Fred, and Maria.

Marion received the Cross of the Order of Merit of the Federal Republic of Germany on February 14, 2001. From the left are grandson David Siciliano, daughter Maria, Consul General Wolfgang Rudolph, Marion, and myself.

An unplanned but welcome brief visit with Gordon B. Hinckley, president of the Church of Jesus Christ of Latter-day Saints, in 1999.

Former president George H. W. Bush received the annual Eisenhower Leadership Prize in 1996. As chairman of the Eisenhower Institute, I presented the Air Group 51 emblem to Mr. Bush.

In 1997, Nobel laureate Elie Wiesel received the Eisenhower Leadership Prize. General Colin L. Powell, who had received it in 1993, was a speaker.

The immediate family. *Left to right:* John and Wendy Siciliano; Fred Siciliano; Maria Siciliano; Loretta Siciliano and her husband, Scott Silverman; Susan and Vincent Siciliano.

Marion was chair of the TreePeople in its early days. The group is now nationally recognized for advocating the urban forest. Here, with Maria, she visits with actor and environmental activist Gregory Peck.

My 80th birthday on March 4, 2002, with Marion and seven grandchildren!
First row: Alex Siciliano, Marion, David Siciliano, Stephen Siciliano, and Stuart Siciliano.
Back row: Michael Siciliano, me, Jacob and Rachel Silverman.

SIXTEEN

AN AMERICA THAT WORKS

FOR AMERICA, immigration is, has been, and always will
be a double-edged sword.

Immigration has shaped our identity, and it remains the lifeblood
of our country. America is one of the few successful countries built on
people of all different kinds of color, race, and religion. Our diversity is
one of our great assets. Yet, at times, we have rejected immigrants. I
know the experiences of my parents and my grandparents. In their
effort to become citizens they experienced difficult pressures, opposition, and great prejudices. Even today this issue stays in the headlines:
we have an economic and cultural amalgamation of foreign immigration that brings benefits and concerns to American society.

"I don't like the description of America as 'the melting pot.'
America has not melted and molded all the peoples and cultures which
have come to it into any homogenous, dull gray mediocre standard
type." I wrote that in a speech as a thirty-two-year-old assistant secretary of labor and delivered it to the Columbus Day Committee of
Philadelphia on October 12, 1954. (Columbus Day was always a busy
time for me.) It still represents my position today—nearly fifty years
later. In my speech I continued:

I prefer to say that the American society is like concrete, composed of distinct and distinguishable ingredients, each contributing its own peculiar virtues and strengths and bonded together in a common cause. Thus, our culture is variegated. Our speech is diverse. Our art is manifold in its forms.

Just as our country cherishes the variety of its culture and admires the uncommon, just as it has room for its people to express their own opinion and personalities, so its Government, if it is to reflect the people, must be a liberal and flexible instrument for the expression of the people's will and satisfaction of human needs.

To this day, I am very quick to defend immigration. My instinct is to say I am on the side of the immigrant. The role the immigrant plays in our nation has always been at the center of change. I have often called it a yeasty influence, the vitality of our competitive workforce and our nation's growth.

Even though our country is made up of immigrants and our economic success relies on immigrants, our reactions to this process are not always well thought out. Immigration interested me as a child because my parents were immigrants. Growing up in Salt Lake made it more of a concern. I wasn't in a Little Italy; we stood out. That was not necessarily good or bad. Ironically, many Mormons were immigrants or first-generation Americans, but overwhelmingly at that time they were from northern Europe and were drawn together by their religion.

I saw how these attitudes affected people over and over again as assistant secretary of labor in charge of the Mexican Farm Labor Program, known as the Bracero Program. We brought in about four hundred thousand Mexicans a year to work on our farms in more than twenty states. It helped our own farmers, the economy, and the Mexican people and nation. The Bracero Program staff was charged with maintaining the best possible conditions for this. No one thought in the mid-1950s to open up immigration, particularly for the Mexicans. The Labor Department had developed extensive regulations for the treatment of these workers, emphasizing decent living conditions. Unfortunately, too often managers of the farm associations had one attitude: the Mexicans don't need beds; they don't have them in Mexico. I was told this personally. I learned a bitter lesson: our own American citizenry—these were not uneducated people—reacted this way. It has been hard to forget.

My father and mother participated in the large rush of immigrants from 1880 to 1912. The Immigration Act drastically reduced immigration between 1921 and 1965. In the 1970s, immigration again rose at unprecedented rates. Though California saw a good number of interstate immigrants, this new rush was largely from foreign lands. During that decade, 1.8 million immigrants entered the state, more than in all prior decades together. That number nearly doubled during the 1980s (3.5 million), and the high rates continued in the 1990s. In the 1980s, tensions grew with the new wave of immigrants. Some people feared the changes, what they called "cultural fragmentation." Some people resented bilingual education, and this spawned an effort to make English the nation's "official language."

Today, one in four of California's population is an immigrant. They and their children generate approximately two-thirds of the state's population growth. The profile of these people has continued to become more diverse ethnically, as well as economically. Today, about 40 percent of California's foreign-born residents are from Mexico or Central America, and another 33 percent are from Asia.

In the mid-1980s, when I was vice chairman of the California Business Roundtable, we discussed Mexican immigration in California. We all knew that the Mexican immigrants worked primarily, at least initially, on the farms, and that they brought their families. We wondered what their impact was on American society when they moved here with their families. How did it affect workers? How did the immigrants progress economically? And, perhaps the most divisive issue, what were the costs of the social services, especially education, that the immigrants used? Were they paying for these services? The California Roundtable contracted with RAND Corporation, a nonpartisan group that analyzes public policy, to study the impact of California's growing Latino population in the state.

That's when I met Kevin McCarthy, who had been with RAND Corporation for many years. McCarthy coauthored the report on immigration with his associate, Robert Valdez, in 1985. It shockingly contradicted the common myth, because it said the net benefit of immigration—whether legal or illegal—far exceeds the negatives. It showed that the benefits of low-wage labor to the California economy outweighed the costs. But it also said the number-one concern should be education of immigrants' children—those foreign born as well as those born here in the United States. The school systems were not really prepared to handle the increases caused by the children. The report did say that the state's costs of educating the children would realize a return on the investment, but only over the long run. After McCarthy presented the report to the roundtable, we asked him to convey the same message to employer groups about the state. It received quite a lot of attention because it often seemed contrary to growing concerns and phobias.

Shortly after the RAND study, the Committee for Economic Development (CED) conducted a study that tied together two of my greatest interests—the workforce and immigration. Throughout my career I had pondered about the workforce—trying to reshape the concepts, the ideas, and the makeup of the actual workforce itself—so I immersed myself readily. This study looked at America's workforce and its demographic changes. We were all aware of the changes in our workforce—more women and greater ethnic diversity—yet, at the same time, job skills had just begun a rapid evolution.

We published our findings, almost two years in the making, in the 1990 CED report *An America That Works: The Life-Cycle Approach to a Competitive Work Force.* This widely read report proposed a different view of the population, a "life-cycle approach to a competitive work force." We used the burgeoning study of demography to look at the direction of America's population growth and found that though the future was very dynamic, an enormous derailing was possible. We could see a static birthrate causing a population reduction as well as a different composition by the end of the twenty-first century—startling to be sure and certainly not believed by the majority of Americans today. The facts showed that our country would be heavily weighted with older people, while the younger groups would be less in number than in the past and of a nontraditional makeup. These are significant changes, and our government and business policies are not prepared to accommodate them. As we stated in the report, "these trends, if left unattended, could precipitate a succession of increasingly painful economic and social crises because the U.S. work force would lack the size and skills needed to sustain economic growth." In essence, as our population shifts we will experience the necessary cultural adaptations. We realized that we had "a window of opportunity to adjust and possibly to turn some of these changes into advantages."

I have called it an "epochal" study. The CED often produces such reports when it focuses on a crucial issue. The CED is a progressive business organization and differs from many other business organizations, most of which lack diversity in their makeup and policies and are often stuck with the straight status quo. The CED does have somewhat of an elitist concept in the sense that it is made up of about 250 executives of the country's leading corporations and presidents of major universities. Corporate chief executive officers are needed because, it is hoped, they have reached a level where they can speak freely, using their own experiences. The CED's intention is to be nonpartisan and nonpolitical and at the same time do some truly constructive research on public issues of the day, particularly in the field of business and economics.

When it was formed in 1942, the CED primarily assessed our post–World War II transition from a military-based economy to a peacetime economy. It has continued to expand its interests to reflect those issues of society. The CED generates the studies through surveys of the trustees, and they tend to prefer the issues with deep impact on our society, such as public education, foreign trade policy, budget deficit, children in need, and operation of the government at all levels—federal, state, and local. And the list goes on. Each report is preceded by extensive structural discussions. The research is undertaken by a subcommittee, assisted by advisers chosen for their competence in the field under study. Two years on one report is quite common. From their research they formulate policy recommendations with the comment, reservation, or dissent by individual trustees. One of the other aspects I like about the CED is its long-term view of human resources development in America. It is big business with humanity as a guide.

The CED has earned a great deal of respect for its credible reports. Mixing academic theory with the reality of the business world causes controversy, but economics students and players study the reports. The CED is simply, in my mind, the number-one business organization in regard to its impact on Congress. Its reports are listened to more carefully, more respectfully, in my judgment, than any other such organization. You can't compare it to the U.S. Chamber of Commerce or the National Association of Manufacturers because the CED is not a lobbying organization. The CED is not an advocacy organization. Committees of Congress often do ask the CED for verbal presentations, because the reports have achieved such a scholarly reputation. Trustees testify as to what the report calls for, but they are not lobbyists.

My own involvement with the CED began when I worked in President Eisenhower's White House. Dr. Robert Steadman, employed as a consultant by the CED, came to me concerning a study on how to improve management in the federal government. It interested me because manpower and its management were my responsibilities. When I finished my work at the White House and went to work as a lawyer, I kept up contact with him and the CED, though I remained ineligible to be a trustee because a corporation did not employ me. Years later, in the late 1960s, when I was in San Francisco with the Pacific Maritime Association, I had a chance to work with the CED on that same issue—management in the federal service. I had been involved with a small group in establishing an independent research organization focused on government problems. We had received a grant of about six hundred thousand dollars from a major foundation. After we realized the futility of starting a new organization, I visited an old friend from the White House days, the distinguished, recently retired secretary of the Department of Health, Education, and Welfare, Marion Folsom, an Eastman Kodak executive, a CED founder trustee, and a legend because he helped establish the Social Security system. I went to see him at the Brookings Institute, where he was also a trustee, and asked, in effect, if the CED would like to have these funds to study government and public service. He immediately said he thought the CED could do it. They created a group called the Committee for the Improvement of Management in Government, which functioned beautifully for a number of years. Unfortunately, I didn't fit their trustee criteria (lacking a profit-making corporate affiliation). They offered to make me a nontrustee member, and I joined the Committee on Research and Policy. At last, when I became president of TICOR in 1971, they invited me to become a trustee. As with the California Business Roundtable, the CED trustees are urged to be very active, and I was while with TICOR. Over the years, I have been involved in many of their projects, as a member of a study committee, a vice chairman, a cochairman, or as the chairman of several study projects. I also served as vice chairman of the CED itself.

The CED is not one of those glittery organizations that people want to join because of the association and the glamour that are attached to it. You don't work for the CED for personal recognition; you look to it for personal satisfaction. If a CED member is active and interested—maybe sixty or one hundred are active—the CED offers an opportunity for self-growth. The organization develops, unknowingly perhaps, a person's own intellectual prowess or abilities. As a result, many CED trustees end up returning year after year because they find an opportunity to learn and at the same time to transmit their own knowledge to others. Education is constant—it never stops, regardless of age—and this is really what the CED does: it educates its own members. I was often surprised. I would find myself going in a different direction than I thought my principles would allow me to go, but only because I had learned more about the subject. I have experienced that more than once.

Another thing that I've learned from working with the CED is that education widens the scope of what you can do. You can't be black-or-white on issues. When you work on major problems affecting the society of this country, there are no simple answers. Society just doesn't work that way. Simple answers are not in the public sphere just as they are not in your home life (I won't get into the home life).

The actual work on *An America That Works* began in 1988. A "design committee" was formed to do a basic two-year evaluation and develop the thesis and course of action. In 1987, I cochaired this committee, the CED Committee on Demographic Trends, with Clifford R. Wharton Jr., then chairman and CEO of TIAA-CREF (later deputy secretary of state). We determined that demographic changes warranted a full study. In conducting the subsequent full study, *An America That Works*, my cochair on the Subcommittee on Demographics and Jobs was Frank P. Doyle, then a senior vice president of General Electric, a recognized expert in labor and personnel and overall head of human resources for General Electric. Doyle later became chairman of the CED.

As mentioned, *An America That Works* looked at the future workforce, its challenges, and how to negotiate those challenges. We found that the "projected demographic trends confronting the United States are likely to require major adjustments in both public and private policies." Because of our increasing concern about the scope and potential force of these changes, we commissioned exploratory studies of their implications for policy. Basically, we asked what the current population trends indicate about the nation's future. How will they affect U.S. economic strength and productivity? We took the facts and interpreted their full causes and implications. It was the first major business study to look at America's upcoming demographic changes.

A primary author of the report, Scott Fosler, at that time the vice president and director of government studies for the CED (later president of the National Academy of Public Administration), put it very well: "Demographic forces are significant not so much in their own right, but rather in the way they interact with other forces—economic, social, political, technological, and environmental." The study does not simply project a series of demographic trends, nor does it focus on demographic factors alone. Rather, its intent is to use demography as a way of better understanding the interaction among numerous forces, and the relationship among the various policies with which they are associated.

We used the demographics in three ways: first, for analysis of basic information and diagnosis; second, for synthesis so we could understand the relationship among interdependent forces; and third, for predicting and anticipating future developments. That left us with a picture of how different our policies might be and what political choices future leaders will be forced to make. It was a departure from a purely economic viewpoint.

The demographic trends we identified had various ways of playing out in the future, from favorable to neutral to not so favorable. Certainly, you have to view the demographic analyses with "respectful skepticism," as suggested by coauthor William Alonso, the Richard Saltonstall Professor of Population Policy at Harvard University. But clearly, their net direction and momentum added up to major challenges both at home and abroad. They suggested a future that looked very different from our present makeup, and with that would come a whole set of new challenges for our society.

What we found astounded us. Our basic finding was that *America had entered an era of an aging population and a shrinking workforce.* In this era we would see a lower birthrate, a rising average age, increased immigration, and growing ethnic and cultural diversity. The nascent study of demographics was like a crystal ball; within certain parameters and acknowledging the variables, we could see into the future. That really got the attention of the media. The "message" got through! Everybody literally got the idea from this study. It is important to say, though, that ours was not only a demographic study; it was a policy proposal (really a whole new mind-set) based on our interpretation of the demographic forecast.

Inside the crystal ball we saw a dynamic nation departing, in some cases quite radically, from the traditional America. The American population would change as the baby boomers, the 77 million people born between 1946 and 1964, worked their way toward retirement. Behind this group is a significantly smaller group. When the baby boomers reach their peak demand of services, we will have fewer people to fill the jobs.

But this problem will continue to grow in scope because the key variable—the U.S. birthrate—continues to remain much lower than in years past. To maintain a population, the replacement fertility rate must be 2.1 children per child-bearing woman (which means three babies per woman!). In 1989–1990, the U.S. fertility rate was calculated at 1.8 children per woman, though the govermental statisticians later found it to be a little over the replacement threshold of 2.1. In other words, our population is barely replacing itself, and it is also an aging population. Sometime after 2030, it will begin a numerical slide (unless attitudes change). These are known facts: demographics are often viewed as destiny. As more people age, they are not being replaced in the same numbers.

While America is just barely reproducing itself, the makeup of this population is totally different today. The Anglo-Saxon population is way under the replacement fertility rate of 2.1 children per woman. Interestingly enough, the African American population isn't much different. The Hispanic American and the Asian American populations have fertility rates exceeding 2.1. As a result, the labor force will be more diverse and, therefore, nontraditional. The younger generation does not fit the mold of the traditional manager. As we noted in the report, "our existing institutions tend to be most experienced in assimilating white males into the work force."

The crux of America's future prosperity, we realized, lay in the hands of a population that our present-day institutions would not recognize. And with fewer workers, tomorrow's workers will need to be very productive. While that is plain to see, the dangers lie hidden in the fact that policy decisions, both in business and in government, show little regard to such changes.

The first test of our predictions has already come to fruition. With the aging population, employers are facing a labor shortage for entry-level jobs. Not only do we have to find a solution to that problem, but we also need to train those young entrants in the higher skills needed to work in an era of new technology and information communication.

This requires an overall higher level of basic competence. That first rung on the ladder is going to be higher than it ever was before.

The other obvious change is the way in which Americans work. Everyone is familiar with how radically our workplace has changed. We forecasted that the rate of change would only accelerate. To repeat: The future worker will need basic skills in reading comprehension and mathematics. Social and interpersonal abilities are always necessary. Yet in 1989, we could already see a gap between what we need and what we have in these areas. With business-as-usual, the gap will only widen.

The most important changes rest on the shoulders of our citizens. As workers, we will have to adapt to the rapidly changing technologies and commit ourselves to a life of constant learning. Because of society's increased needs, retirement won't be the same. Careers will continue, in a part-time fashion, past the age of sixty-five. Congress recognized this with legislation (in 2000) that no longer reduces social security payments for those who choose to work after the typical retirement age to age seventy. That is, there is no longer an income test for those who decide to work between sixty-five and seventy. And full social security payments will begin at age sixty-seven.

When we traced the various threads of the demographic web into the future, we found the trends, if left unattended, could bring on "a succession of increasingly painful economic and social crises because the U.S. work force would lack the size and skills needed to sustain economic growth." *If the economy suffered, our quality of life would suffer. We identified a window of opportunity, between 1989 and 2030, in which we had to adjust to the changes and possibly turn some of these changes into advantages.* Demography certainly plays a powerful role in shaping the social context, but it does not preordain the future. A lot depends on how we prepare for these unfolding developments. If the problems were dealt with as a crisis, it would be eighteen years too late to initiate the only appropriate acts. This problem has the unique character of saying it can't wait for the crisis in order to cause the action.

This is why the CED report created the all-encompassing policy proposal known as the *life-cycle approach*. Lifelong education is at the heart of the idea. To gain a competitive advantage, our society needs to emphasize learning, flexibility, and productive participation in work and society *throughout a person's entire life.* Every step along the way in a person's life is critical to a competitive and healthy society. Children have to reach school age healthy and ready to learn, young people need to be prepared for a rewarding career and community participation, adults need to be self-sufficient, and older citizens must remain active and independent. The report advocates the design of policies and programs that would help Americans develop and utilize fully the skills and talents that will keep our country strong and productive.

Our life-cycle approach to human resources emphasized that investing in people during the earlier stages of life will pay dividends at later stages. Just the same, by creating policies to help older workers readjust to the changing circumstances, we can help younger workers as well. *If older people remain active and independent, not only do they lead productive lives, but they also don't draw on the system.* That relieves the younger generations of the pressure of costly dependency. One of the striking findings of our study, and a good argument for a comprehensive treatment to the problem, is that good policies in any one stage of the life cycle promise to be enhanced by the effectiveness of good policies in the other phases. These issues are all intertwined, like the threads of a spider web. The ultimate ideal is to bring America into a more cohesive, unified population. Our strategy, basically, was to bridge the social differences through economic solutions.

In order to avert labor shortages we will need to increase the proportion of our potential labor force that is actually employed and enhance the productivity of all workers. We need to improve the productivity of the U.S.-born population. We can enlarge the workforce by creating means for every potential worker to find a way into the workforce.

This—the need to expand our American-born workforce—brings up the subject I was most interested in: our immigration policies. I had always followed demographics, but this study really cemented my interest. By allowing more immigrants to enter the country, we could increase our workforce. Of course, it is not that easy.

A look at the global demographics shows that industrial countries pretty much have variations on aging populations, and it is the less-developed countries that have population explosions. *All* the industrialized European nations (except Ireland) are beginning a dramatic population slide. For very different reasons, Japan and Russia are in the same situation, maybe even worse. Italy, perhaps the most alarming situation, has an extremely low fertility rate (1.3) that will soon drive their population down by one thousand people per day. These European nations face the threat of a collapsing labor market that will threaten their production and competitiveness on an international level. The consequences, in a worst-case scenario, would be that they lose their know-how, that is, a brain drain, leaving the remaining young people without the ability to achieve education and success. They are also looking at the political dynamics of an aging population. The centers of population will shift sharply, changing the traditional balance of political power as more voters become senior citizens.

At the crux of the immigration issue lie the cultural barriers that produce these changes. In Italy, women are burdened with a disproportionate share of responsibilities, and, as a result, they choose not to have children. Japan is a good example of cultural barriers to immigration itself. Japan has no immigration policy; they keep the doors closed. The second largest population consists of some half-million Koreans; otherwise, everyone is Japanese. As their population ages, they will have difficulties negotiating a way to supplement their labor force. The *New York Times* in a major article by Howard W. French reports on Japan's population: "Shrinking faster than any other nation, [its] population is projected to decline by 17 percent during the next half century. By 2050 . . . it will dwindle to 105 million from 127 million now." The headlines continue to profile the different developed countries as each of them struggle with this issue.

The most divisive issue for other industrialized countries is America's trump card. America's heritage is tied to immigration. With today's global demographics, that will be our greatest asset. We have a racial, ethnic, and cultural diversity here that keeps us quite vital. I have great confidence in our differing types of people because that is our strength and the reason for our vitality.

One reason I'm never afraid of immigration is because we have this tolerant geography. We don't have such enormous cultural barriers toward immigration. Despite our weaknesses and problems in the past, we aren't in such deep cultural binds as other industrialized nations. Though this can be difficult for us, we are adaptable. That is our competitive strength in adapting to the global economy.

The international demographic trends show that the workforces of Africa, Asia, and Latin America will grow by about 1 billion people by 2010. Mexico alone added about 1 million people a year to its workforce during the 1990s. When those economies don't create jobs for their young workers, the young people look elsewhere. It creates serious pressure for emigration, especially to the United States. The source of immigrants is out there. For the foreseeable future, 80 percent of the labor force growth will not be stereotypical—females, minorities, and immigrants of ethnic groups different from the historic norm (from Asia, Africa, and Central America).

Even though our country relies on immigration, it is not without its problems. The tricky part of today's immigration is that the new source of diversity is nontraditional. If we don't take into consideration the past (and not so distant) reactions toward nontraditional immigration, we risk running aground on the same issues. There are so many intermingling forces, though mostly economic and cultural. People build up resentment toward "those people." I use that, by the way, as an epithet. Or "they" are the ones. The Jews were a favorite target. A century ago, you heard "wop" or "guinea" for the Italian groups. Or the word "Greek" was often used as an epithet: "Well, what do you expect? He's a Greek." Today, people use "illegals" in the same fashion as the opprobrious term "wop" (for Italians without papers). The connotation of "illegals" is unnecessarily punitive when you consider that there is much precedent for this kind of immigrant in the United States. Consequently, I prefer the term "undocumented."

The attitudes toward immigrants are entirely based on economics. When the jobs are there—in restaurants, hospitals, construction, offices, hotels, and homes—we welcome them. Obviously, Mexico has a manpower surplus, as do its Central American neighbors. So long as they can find jobs here, they will come. On the other side, during California's deep and long recession of the early 1990s, we experienced a backlash against immigrants, symbolized by the passage of Proposition 187. In this case, George Santayana's prophetic phrase is especially poignant: "Those who don't know their history are bound to repeat it." In *An America That Works* we addressed this, and, by treating the future workforce comprehensively in the life cycle, we hoped that we could prepare policies for the future immigrants that would break that cycle of resentment during downturns.

In regard to the issue of undocumented workers, I support efforts to control it (but it will be impossible to eliminate). That's why I liked the Bracero Program, because it used regulation. An attempt was made—successfully—to create a small guest-worker program for

Mexican farmworkers in the late 1980s, particularly benefiting California. Because it was a feeble program, farm organizations nationwide generally ignored it. The undocumented workers in the United States today (as I write this) number some 8 to 9 million. Initially employed wholly in agriculture, the undocumented workers are now scattered throughout the United States and the whole economy. They are noticeable in construction and the food and service industries of all types, including medical services. As education becomes more developed—and it is happening—the skills of the undocumented are being used in every type of occupation.

On the other hand, once a person is here, what do you do? Expel them? If there are no entanglements, yes. But my concern is particularly with women, especially those who have children. An episodic story: Marion and I have had several experiences with undocumented immigrants. We had a part-time housekeeper for fourteen years. She came to this country with her husband and their first-born son. Later, she had two children born in the United States. After she had her third child, she had her tubes tied—a significant trend among immigrant women. They quickly adapt, according to local hospital records. In 1986, under the Amnesty Act, Marion spent many hours helping our housekeeper prove her family's residency while in the United States. As a result, all three received their legal status. They are now U.S. citizens. They are a marvelous family, and we have a close relationship with them. Her oldest son is finishing college, and the other two are outstanding as they develop. I admit being influenced by this family's story and their desire to assimilate.

As long as our birthrate is low, we will always be dependent on immigration. Even counting *undocumented* immigrants in the 2000 Census figures, our population is barely replacing itself. Population growth is, of course, increasing numerically, which only confuses the *long-range* analysis. There is a need for more careful and explicit consideration of the labor market effects of immigration. With this in mind, our CED report called for a reexamination of immigration policies and placing greater emphasis on economic considerations. We recommended a small increase in the overall immigration quotas but with an adjustment to the mix reflecting the new economic and demographic realities, particularly the need for an educated workforce.

When we incorporated immigration in the CED study on

America's changing workforce, we wanted to make it balanced. We were keenly aware that, currently, a family reunification is the dominant criterion for legal permanent entry into the United States. Nonetheless, we proposed a small shift from the family reunification concept to immigrants with skills in labor-short vocations. Immigration is a positive contributor to economic growth, and the report recommended that the ratio of permanent immigrants permitted entry under labor market classifications should move gradually from the then one-to-ten ratio to at least four to ten by 1998, with another increase in 2000 (Congress, using our report, upped it from one to two). Educated immigrants assimilate into society faster and contribute more quickly to a productive workforce.

In the mid-1990s, Kevin McCarthy of the RAND Corporation and another associate, Georges Vernez, asked me if I would chair an advisory committee for a major immigration study (their earlier work on this subject was used by the CED for the *An America That Works* study). Though similar to their previous study of 1985 for the California Business Roundtable, this one had a broader scope. Published in 1997, RAND's report warned that the costs of immigration to California were growing. The new immigrants "are less educated, are younger, and have more children than immigrants elsewhere. They also are more likely to be refugees and undocumented." For all these reasons, they found that immigration affected California more substantially than any other state in the nation. This seemed an obvious conclusion, but the supporting findings were significant.

The RAND report found we were not reaching the new immigrants. While many new immigrants came as unskilled workers, the lower-level jobs they came for were filled, and the California economy was not producing any more. The poorly educated immigrants are very limited in what jobs they can take, and if those jobs don't exist, they make little or no progress. That adds greater costs to the state and agitates resentments.

Both *An America That Works* and the RAND studies urged that the immigration policy be changed to emphasize skilled labor. McCarthy and Vernez wrote in 1997:

To a much greater extent than in the past, the rate at which immigrants and their children succeed economically and socially depends directly on their education. Highly educated immigrants—about half of the state's total—reach economic parity with native-born residents within their lifetimes. The other half—those with extremely low levels of education who are primarily from Mexico and Central America—command low earnings and make little economic progress in their lifetimes. This raises serious concerns about whether and, if so, when their children will reach parity with other groups.

They urged that California find some way to provide upward mobility for the waves of immigrants as they join our workforce. McCarthy again said, properly, what all this means is that our number-one challenge is education for this immigrant group and their children. In 2000, Hispanic kids had upwards of a 40 percent dropout rate in high school.

RAND's McCarthy and Vernez took the CED's recommendation a step further by suggesting that our "current policies be modified to allow easier and more frequent changes to immigration quotas and entry criteria, to maintain moderate overall immigration levels over the long term, and to place greater emphasis on the educational levels of new immigrants." They argued for two modest changes. The number of legal immigrants admitted to the United States annually should be set somewhere between eight hundred thousand (the 1997 number) and three hundred thousand (the number admitted in the 1960s). In addition, a better balance should be found between low-skilled immigrants admitted for family reasons and high-skilled immigrants admitted for economic reasons.

In *An America That Works*, which came out in 1990 and is still valid today, we said we had a window of opportunity in which to adjust and manage these changes. "If we don't adapt to the changes that lie ahead, if we don't educate and empower our citizenry, businesses will be handicapped, human resources will be wasted, and America will suffer lower living standards with far too many of its people shut out from the opportunities our economy and society will have to offer, such as a rewarding career."

We thought the window of opportunity would close in forty years. Nobody paid attention to it in 1990. Today, you regularly see articles in the newspapers, and occasional references on television (not as much as there should be), about what is happening demographically to this country and to this world. People now are finally, a little late but not too late, getting the message that our society is changing because of two things: birthrate (on the decline in industrialized countries) and movement of these peoples (the heavy migrations). We are beginning to realize that society is changing not only in ethnicity but also in age composition. All of this is having a serious impact. I do think we are acting within that window of opportunity, slowly but surely. It isn't a planned activity. The business community doesn't know how to respond to this kind of thing, and the politicians wait to be told.

When I was a child in Salt Lake City, I had no role model, except A. P. Giannini, the founder of Bank of America. Otherwise, very few people of Italian extraction were important people—in business, academe, or government. There were a few in entertainment. Today, of course, you see Italian names in every walk of life. This turnaround has taken two or three generations. The same can be true of the Hispanics. They have a few role models now, and they eventually will have many more. It may take them three generations, but it will happen. Previously, ethnic groups had a Little Italy or a Little Poland, a relatively small area from which they very quickly disseminated. The substantial Little Italys in Chicago, New York, or San Francisco, though still called that, in no way resemble the concentration they once had.

I always maintain that the mother of the family is the key for rapid American assimilation. Some Italians did it in one generation. If they were young enough when they emigrated here, they would speak English. My own mother and father happened to be in that category. Thus, we did not speak Italian at home because our mother spoke English. Yet many of our contemporaries had mothers who arrived later in their lives, with little or no education. These young Italian American friends (most American born) were bilingual, but Americanization came slower for the families. (Incidentally, I'm sorry that I understand only Calabrese, a very difficult dialect.) Our experience with Hispanic employees, here in California, convinces us this group wants their children as well as themselves to be Americans, as quickly as possible.

Obviously, the important issue concerns what the undocumented do *after* their arrival here. Here, the evidence is clear. Overwhelmingly, given the opportunity, the immigrants, legal and undocumented, have become productive and responsible members of American society.

Following ample precedent, in my judgment, the great majority are and will in a twenty-five- to thirty-year period become indistinguishable from their American neighbors.

I do recognize that the millions of Hispanics who have moved to California, primarily from Mexico, are going to take a little longer to adjust. Because of their density in some areas, that may take longer than previous immigrant groups. But I agree with the RAND Corporation study—it's going to happen. The RAND findings are still true: education is the number-one challenge that we face with the Hispanics in California.

The evolution of assimilation is happening as Hispanics become involved in political offices. We don't yet have a Hispanic mayor of Los Angeles, but we will have one soon. It almost happened in the 2001 mayoralty election in Los Angeles. The Hispanic vote has become very important. Today, it is electing non-Hispanics who are responsive to the Hispanic people. Tomorrow, it will be the election of Hispanics themselves. Also, more funds are being dedicated to raise the standards of education for the minorities.

I hear some say so little has changed. Some say immigration still has the same problems it had a century ago. I don't think so. The issues are more complicated because we have more ethnic and cultural diversity, yet modern technology and communications have brought enormous progress and, I hope, tolerance among all our citizens as education takes hold.

SEVENTEEN

IN SEARCH OF GOOD GOVERNMENT

As A BUSINESSMAN, I was confused by President Carter's administration because it lacked direction. He meant well and tried very hard, but I did not feel that he brought stability or enlightened leadership to the presidency or the country that was suffering so greatly from the Watergate scandal. Economic conditions ignited public unrest. The nation idled in gas lines during the 1970s energy crunches, the cold war edged through a series of negotiations on nuclear-proliferation pacts, and the national economy suffered great turmoil. In California, we experienced a mixed bag: the economy boomed yet interest rates jetted sky high, at times cresting 20 percent. We had entered a vicious cycle. Labor disputes in the public service sector increasingly led to strikes and disruptions of public services. The taxpayers figured it out quickly—while they paid more for government services, they enjoyed them less. Politicians seized on this phrase; public employees bore the brunt of the criticism, which led, in turn, to a sagging morale in the public workforce.

The gap between understanding government and communicating with it has always been present for the businessman, and now it became a fact for the ordinary citizen. The people had little idea of their government's activities. They reacted first in frustration and then outrage.

Since the late 1970s the economy has boomed, but the sour attitudes toward government have lingered, even grown. I agree with my friend Derek Bok, the chairman of Common Cause (and former Harvard president), who said in 1999, "over 80 percent of Americans say that government is controlled by special interests and 75 percent say that elected officials don't really care what people think. Most people actually feel that Washington is the greatest threat that the country faces." Some found it is easy and even fun to bash the government. They threw out common phrases—"eliminate waste, fraud, and abuse" and "government should be run like a private business." Tragically, I think, the word *bureaucrat* has become too often an epithet. Some view government as the oppressor of individual freedoms. The experience I gained in public service provided great opportunity for me. Public service was my raison d'être, and it opened the doors. Sometimes, it offered me a unique view of society's problems and a chance to help correct those problems. For me, government structure and operation became an obsession.

Freedom has become a popular buzzword, but without definition. Eric Foner, in his book *The Story of American Freedom*, documents the transformation of our country's definition of freedom from the Founding Fathers to today. During the 1980s he notes it meant "little more than 'being left alone by others' and not being coerced into adhering to 'other people's values, ideas, or style of life.' Such a definition of freedom made it almost impossible to think in terms of a shared vision of the good life, or what social or political structures were essential to a good society."

This attitude, of course, is vulnerable to manipulation. During his campaign for president in 1980, Ronald Reagan ran on the platform that in Washington lay the root of all our problems. Suddenly, he struck a spark and it took off.

At that time, I didn't think Reagan had a chance of getting the Republican nomination, much less the presidency. I had thought the same of Nixon in 1968. So much for reading the tea leaves! Nonetheless, I thought it tragic that Reagan should win with that virulent antigovernment message. I still consider it unfortunate that some candidates declare government as our problem. It is easy to attack amorphous enemies that no one can see, such as the public service. As Foner points out, Reagan "declared freedom from 'government interference' the key to American greatness."

Reagan had picked up on the public's discontent, which reached a breaking point in 1978 in the form of a popular tax revolt in California. Rising property values and property taxes, which were controlled by the local governments, exacerbated the public's animosity toward the government. Howard Jarvis, a California realtor, led the populist revolt through a state ballot initiative. His Proposition 13 amended the state constitution and reduced property taxes by more than half and limited their rise in the future. Specifically: the property tax (for homes and/or businesses) can be no more than 1 percent of the actual sales price of the property, and any increases can be no more than 2 percent per year. It passed with an overwhelming 65 percent of the vote on June 2, 1978. The mood went national, and California's Proposition 13 swept the United States. Within fifteen years, twenty-two other states had passed similar initiatives.

I had misjudged the issue. I could understand the sentiment of the people; in fact, I shared it as a businessman because TICOR had been exposed to it for a much longer period of time than homeowners. The public demanded a property tax reduction, reduced expenditures, and government reforms. I did not think Proposition 13 offered the appropriate solution and opposed it because of the long view. I stood as one of only a few corporate leaders in the state who opposed it. I agreed with the idea of protecting the homeowner from skyrocketing tax increases on their primary residence, but they wrote Proposition 13 to stand forever.

Proposition 13 put California's local governments in a bind as it reduced their budgets by 77 percent! In just one year, those local governments were forced to make drastic cuts and adjustments of programs and services. Local governments were told to look elsewhere for funds to maintain essential programs and services at a responsible level. And it could not be done. Prop 13 was designed to cripple the taxing authority of city and county governments. It succeeded. It took away the right of cities and counties to raise funds for their own organizations, their own support services, education, libraries, and fire and police departments. It resulted in serious damage to the local infrastructure in the state of California. It also created—and this is the biggest hurdle for any future tax change—the requirement of a supermajority—two-thirds of the vote; this is a thorough rejection of the historic majority-rule concept.

Immediately after the passage of Proposition 13, then governor Jerry Brown established the Commission on Government Reform in

June 1978. He asked me to serve on the commission along with eleven others (initially called the "12 Apostles" until he appointed Helen Copley, publisher of the *San Diego Press,* and upset the nomenclature). He asked the broadly based bipartisan commission to study the long-term economic impacts that Proposition 13 would have on state and local government finances and services and asked that we recommend permanent reforms in the tax, revenue, and spending systems of both state and local governments.

California had fostered and encouraged an enormously large and complex system of local governments full of diversity and disparities, which rendered simplistic and blanket solutions impossible. Six months later, we issued our report and recommendations, but people still felt quite heady over their alleged empowerment. No one paid attention to our report. William M. Roth, one of the commissioners, commented on "the mystic aura of untouchability that hung over this particular political message" and how it hindered our effort. "Any suggestion that certain aspects of Prop 13 could be improved . . . was derided as an insult to the perfection of the amendment. Rational discussion was inhibited by political awe."

The poignant power in Proposition 13 itself brought out the ideological differences in our commission. The conservative members felt that the voters had sent a simple message. Caspar Weinberger (a fellow commissioner) explained the voters' belief that they "wanted to reduce government spending and make it more difficult to increase it in the future; that they were well aware that some of the things government is now doing for or to them would be stopped; and that we should not try to thwart this desire by thinking up plans to repeal, reverse, or seriously weaken the thrust of Proposition 13." He went on to express a sentiment that Reagan utilized in the national election: "We believe that the vote was a protest against government's increasing intrusiveness, over-regulation, and interference in the daily lives of the people." President Reagan later appointed Caspar Weinberger as secretary of defense. I have enjoyed "Cap" as a friend and intelligent partner during many heavy discussions throughout the years, though his views hardened and, at least to me, he left his ability to compromise behind on this subject.

In the end, Proposition 13 has been a near disaster. Frank Lalli, managing editor of *Money* magazine, wrote in an August 1994 editorial that Proposition 13 "has backfired. What began as a victory against big government has perversely become a vehicle for strengthening state officials and weakening local economies." Ironically, the taxpayers lost a tax break on the state level. The state, which at the time had a $4.2 billion surplus, dispersed that money to local governments in order to avert a fiscal crisis. And the property owners lost their property tax deduction, raising their tax liability on state income. In simple terms, the taxes were diverted to the state coffers. This, along with other imbalances, led to *the significant shift in power and control from local governments to the state.* While they lost it in local communities, counties, and cities, they succeeded in transferring most of the taxing power to the state legislature of California. The imbalance of power for raising taxes, according to Lalli, resulted in a "tyrannical minority roll[ing] over the apathetic majority by blocking one tax increase after another, even for infrastructure improvements and police reinforcements." The result was that Proposition 13 "snapped the link between the citizens and their local governments." Over the long haul, Proposition 13 has led to a bigger, more complex state government and weaker, less responsive local government. It did the opposite of what it promised: instead of giving people more immediate control, it took government further away from the people. No one has really even yet weighed the long-term consequences. Lalli simply concluded that Proposition 13 was "a lesson in how not to revolt against taxes." It has become sacrosanct, one of the things you can't change. You certainly can't repeal it. Most of all, it seems to me that Proposition 13 has nurtured a latent antitax, antigovernment feeling in our citizenry, the antithetical foundation of good government.

I must comment on the enormous effect that Prop 13 has had on education. As mentioned, local schools must now depend on the California State Legislature for financial support. Since the 1990s, California has ranked in the nation's bottom half in spending on a per-student basis.

Today, the questions remain the same: How do you change the government? How do you revolt against taxes? If it is clear that cutting taxes doesn't improve government, how do we improve it? The Center for Governmental Studies, which I still chair, long ago made a fundamental decision. The repeal of Prop 13 is impossible, and even mild amendments would cause turmoil. Nonetheless, we did issue a study suggesting a more balanced, professional approach to the use of the initiative process. This in 1989. Nothing has been accomplished.

I feel the path to an efficient government and reestablishing the public trust is through controlled costs and a higher quality of service, which we can produce through effective management. I had a unique perspective on the issue because some years earlier I had chaired a special committee for the improvement of management of the public service established by the Committee for Economic Development. We produced a study on local and state governments titled *Improving Management of the Public Work Force—The Challenge to State and Local Government,* and our findings convinced us of the importance of refocusing attention on the principal purpose of public service—providing effective, efficient, economical, and fair government.

In that CED study, we identified the heart of the problem as the growth of local government. In the years 1957 to 1977, the federal government increased its employees by 22.7 percent, the private sector employment increased by 47.7 percent, but most significantly, state and local government employment had soared by 131.5 percent. That made it apparent that employee deficiencies or inabilities did not necessarily cause poor and excessively costly public services. The greatest problem lay in the rapid employment increases operating under archaic and conflicting management systems—along with "collective bargaining in a political environment"—that had made state and local governments expensive and unproductive. The growth in employment led to unimaginable growth in the scope and complexity of the dealings among governments at all levels and between citizens and their governments.

Ironically, at the same time the Proposition 13 tax revolt took the government one way, the CED recommended an upgrade of the public workforce at all levels—federal, state, and local. The problem, in my opinion, centered on a lack of common purpose, excessive political competition among numerous interest groups, and a related failure of top officials to provide effective management. While I did not ignore the importance of other aspects of the problem, I believed we needed better management of people.

Thus, in response to the challenge of curbing costs without sacrificing important public services, we have two obstacles: one, the public management's political environment and, two, the hodgepodge of personnel systems that reduced efficiency (called "systemic chaos"). In the CED report, we suggested revitalizing the merit principle at all levels of government, which selected, assigned, promoted, and compensated employees on the basis of ability and performance. In another very important issue, we saw a need to restore the authority of managers to manage. *The public doesn't realize how difficult it can be to manage without the authority and the resources to accomplish the objectives for which they are responsible.*

For example, while serving as a subcabinet official in the Department of Labor, I asked the best man I could identify in the Bureau of Apprenticeship to head up a major project, which would enhance his career status as an assistant director. I anticipated no difficulty. Suddenly, the official began to weep. Astonished, I asked what the trouble was.

"Don't you realize that we never transfer in this bureau?" he asked. "It's a sign of demotion."

No amount of reassurance could change the man's mind. He refused to move and we had to hire an outsider. Such "cultural" adaptations along with the accumulated maze of personnel restrictions prevent government managers from doing their jobs. The termination of federal employees is one of the most difficult chores around. The dramatic post–World War II growth in government resulted in an inbred, multilayered type of bureaucracy that made it difficult, if not impossible, to fire somebody from federal service. Job permanence is no longer as sacrosanct; however, at that time the record was very bad.

Congress has long worked on improvements in the personnel system at the federal level. Some changes came to fruition in the Civil Service Reform Act of 1978. As a past personnel manager and CED member, I happily testified before the Senate Government Operations Committee in favor of President Carter's proposed reorganization of the civil service. That legislation (which had its origin in earlier administrations, including the aborted creation—which I witnessed—of the Office of Personnel Administration in the Eisenhower period) gave more direct authority to managers for the hiring and firing of employees. It adopted some of what was being advocated by the CED reports and realigned the system that had become insensible. The new law has helped enormously.

Unfortunately, the debate over Proposition 13 goes in a different direction. It crystallizes the growing concern over the performance and cost of the public workforce. The critical evaluation of public employees' performance, productivity, and pay bothered me. Over a twenty-year span, and four presidential appointments, I had worked for nearly a dozen years in the federal government. I had worked with these people and had seen their devotion. I could rarely accept the "guilty" judgments so often made of the public servants, by press or the politicians. The vast majority—more than 99.5 percent—of the people in public service are not elected. These are the "public servants." They are not politicians, nor do they work to advance their own political leanings. Of course, the political appointees quickly realize they are dependent on the very people some may have earlier criticized. During my service as a presidential political appointee, I often found myself between politicians and the public servants. I could if so inclined attack the public service, but once I saw the caliber of these people—with their high motivation and efficiency—I easily became a strong supporter of the public service. To me, the public servants I worked with, particularly the Washington group where I spent most of my years, were among the most competent and most highly ethical people that I have seen. Often, I wish that our business community would emulate some of the idealism found in our finer public servants.

In the larger discussion, we have much more at stake than saving a few tax dollars or building conceptually ideal management structures. *The real stakes are people's lives, because people need government services to survive.* And our form of government ultimately depends upon public confidence and support. Improving the performance of government requires that elected officials, managers, and employees at all levels of government develop mutual respect, recognize their common goals, and acknowledge their joint responsibility and the public trust in which they all are held. I can see that if the government does not take constructive action, the public will continue to become more frustrated and disgusted. When the public strikes out, they can cripple government through fiscal limitations or elect incompetent demagogues who promise easy and instant cures. These issues, if neglected too long, could result in a national crisis.

Besides these controlled costs and a higher quality of service through effective management, the president plays an enormous role in managing an efficient government and reinstating the public trust. I have been a longtime trustee of the National Academy of Public Administration (NAPA), a private organization based in Washington, D.C., made up mainly of people distinguished for their service as public service managers. NAPA was launched as a nonprofit, nonpartisan organization in 1967 (chartered by Congress in 1984) by three distinguished public servants: James Webb, John Macy, and Elmer Staats. Webb was close to President Truman and a NASA administrator. Macy had a distinguished career in several different administrations, including Eisenhower's, where I first met him. He served as chairman of the U.S. Civil Service Commission, which by its nature was nonpolitical. And Staats was unbelievably nonpolitical; he served in Republican and Democratic administrations right up to his fourteen-year appointment as comptroller general of the United States, a tremendously important but relatively nonpublicized investigative accounting agency that reports to Congress. These were unusual men: balanced, even, and brilliant in their evaluation of government.

NAPA is made up primarily of these sorts of people who have had federal government experience (though more recently they are bringing in people with state- and local-level experience). These people may have been appointed by Republican or Democrat presidents, but having worked with many of them, I found they were rarely ideologically fixed. If you want to find objectivity, it's this group. Their expertise is their active, experiential point of view. They are consumed by what makes government work, and doing it. They identify emerging issues of governance and provide assistance to federal, state, and local governments on how to improve their performance. They focus on structure and administration rather than policy per se. In 1999, they did fifty projects for ninety-eight federal agencies, state and local governments, international organizations, private foundations, and other funders.

At NAPA in the mid-1970s we discussed this interesting phenomenon, wherein people were "picturing the federal government as an alien and menacing presence rather than an embodiment of the popular will," as Eric Foner puts it so well. It was similar to what the new form of government faced in the 1780s—our capacity to govern ourselves. Where does the power rightly belong: in a centralized federal government or dispersed among the states? The public's distrust of the government had led to this debate. At the heart of government's inability to function is the presidency, the fulcrum of modern American government. At NAPA we decided: we can begin to strengthen the forces of cohesion and integration in our political system by strengthening the capacity of the presidency for leadership.

In the summer of 1978, Donald C. Stone and Sydney Stein Jr. (now two legends in the annals of the public service) proposed to NAPA that we evaluate the forty-year history of the institutional presidency. We created a panel of twenty-four members emphasizing the diversity in experience and political affiliation as well as a knowledge of governmental management and crucial national issues. The panel was not restricted to academy members or career types. We included former members of Congress, the cabinet, and White House staffs. We drew from both parties and from leaders in business, academe, the military, and labor. All were distinguished and possessed talents, expertise, and interests that would strengthen the work of the panel. We spent fourteen months taking a deep, tough look at how the presidency works, and how it doesn't work. Incidentally, one member of that panel is now back in active public service as this is being written: Don Rumsfeld (secretary of defense for George W. Bush).

The panel had cochairs, myself and Don K. Price. Don was a very close friend and colleague. We first met and worked together when I was special assistant to President Eisenhower, from 1957 to 1959. Don also served as a consultant on public administration and structure to the Eisenhower, Kennedy, Johnson, and Nixon administrations. He went on to become dean of the John F. Kennedy School of Government from 1958 to 1977. His obituary in the *New York Times* said it well: "Shrewd, patient, and self-effacing, Price lived by the maxim that a man can accomplish a great deal if he will let other people take the credit." Price knew that from his knowledge of the presidency.

President Franklin D. Roosevelt initiated the first study in 1936, through the Committee on Administrative Management. Known as the Brownlow Committee (Louis Brownlow was its chairman, with Luther Gulick and Charles Merriam as members), they concluded, "The President needs help." The Brownlow Committee recommended the establishment of an Executive Office of the President, with the Bureau of the Budget as the keystone agency. Thus was born the "institutional presidency." It also coined the phrase that stands as the first rule in appointment of White House staff assistants to the president: they must have "a passion for anonymity." Price also served on one of the two Hoover Commissions on the Organization of the Executive Branch of Government (in 1947–1948) under President Truman. Their task was to overhaul the national security component of government. Ever since then, there have been many proposals to reform the presidential office.

Each president has tinkered at the edges, perhaps adding an agency or a cabinet department, but much of the structure has remained the same. That structure, itself, was seriously outdated. In 1978, the principles laid down by the Brownlow Committee, the Hoover Commissions, and the other special panels of the 1960s and 1970s did not equal the challenges of governance in the 1980s.

While the previous commissions were under orders from presidents to look at the internal structure of the presidency, the NAPA panel was the first set up under private auspices. This gave us more freedom to define the purpose of presidential management in terms of broader values than bureaucratic efficiency, and then to criticize freely not only the way in which the presidency was organized but also its relationship with Congress. We knew that we couldn't assess a president's individual capabilities, but we could examine the tools and resources that should be available to every president to help him do his job. We were looking for a way to clarify the president's role in managing the federal government. A more effective presidency would strengthen the rest of our democracy. If we strengthened the presidency as an instrument, it would lead to more effective self-government.

The panel's consensus became *A Presidency for the 1980's,* a fifty-six-page booklet issued by NAPA that evaluated the broad responsibilities of the president, analyzed his constitutional role, and made sixteen comprehensive recommendations on how he might organize his White House staff and that of the Executive Office to deal more effectively with day-to-day management of the federal government and for instituting a systematic and realistic approach to his burdensome responsibilities as chief executive of the federal government.

We finished the report in time for the 1980 election of Ronald Reagan. The *L.A. Herald Examiner* commented, "Mr. Reagan has bemoaned with good reason the regulatory bureaucracy of the U.S. government. When he raises his lance against that dragon, he will find himself confronting a classic example of the limited ability of a modern President to change the things he finds wrong."

The *San Francisco Chronicle* summed up the report: "What makes this report useful to an incoming President is its attempt to tell him to work more collaboratively with Congress, to seek and take unbiased, nonpartisan advice, to screen and organize the matters he takes under consideration, to keep his immediate staff small, and to keep his hands off a lot of the levers of action by limiting his operational responsibilities." They also noted how the report "seem[ed] to have been drawn up with an eye to accommodating the preferred Reagan style of governing."

I summarized our report in a letter to President-elect Reagan, which was printed in the *Los Angeles Times* on Wednesday, January 14, 1981. I titled it "Whipping the Oval Office into New Shape." I pointed out that our basic conclusion was only one word longer than the 1936 Brownlow Committee's statement, "The President needs help." Forty-five years later, we had concluded, "The President *really* needs help."

Reagan brought to the presidency what the public loves, a spectacular kind of vision. It did, however, have its failings. With some extraordinary exceptions, I think the people who surrounded him were, too often, political advisers who had only modest abilities as professional managers. Similarly, Kennedy was the first one to bring in political types who were reminiscent of the nineteenth-century White House days. Both Reagan and Kennedy had men who thought they could do it quickly, and who paid very little attention to anything but political concerns. In order to get that kind of agenda across, the president and his staff end up being personally involved in too many management decisions.

I saw it firsthand when Kennedy came in. White House assistants asserted their power. Dick McGuire, a genial, intelligent Bostonian who had been treasurer of the Democratic National Committee, came over to see me at the law firm. He wanted to know all about my job as special assistant to the president for personnel management because they didn't know if they were going to continue it. That job had been created by executive order of President Eisenhower. McGuire saw its value and recommended that it be continued. Kennedy, nonetheless, rescinded the order and so killed it. One night I went to a dinner with these new men from the White House. I was the only outsider except for the dinner chairman, who was the legendary Truman adviser Clark Clifford. I was invited because of my past association with the White House. Sitting next to me was a counsel to Kennedy who asked me which job I liked best—assistant secretary of labor or being in the White House.

With hindsight (I replied), I enjoyed my assistant secretary's job more than being in the White House, though the White House had more prestige. I was not a staff man. I was responsible for the management of people and programs.

He couldn't see that, because, as he said, "I can do all that from the White House."

This attitude was only added to later when Johnson, who was a pre-eminent political animal, and his people were there. Johnson did get things done, and I personally agreed with much of that, but the White House took on a different kind of structure. Cabinet agencies became less important. Then, each succeeding administration, Republican or Democrat, it seemed to me, only added to the crumbling status of the cabinet secretary. Nixon definitely violated that, and his people even more. Nixon said he would return authority and responsibility to the cabinet agencies, but he did not do it. Almost immediately, a couple of his associates exercised—or attempted to exercise—overt control from the White House. That is one of the reasons I left his administration when I did. I felt the absence of understanding of the role of cabinet secretaries and the mission of the various agencies.

One of the principal assistants to President Nixon carried out this same technique by attempting to deal directly with lower-level career people, resulting in intimidation. He did not care about the objectivity and analysis offered by other knowledgeable colleagues. He ignored the management processes. I confronted this assistant on the telephone, insisting that he get his reports from the Commerce Department agencies through the secretary or my office as the deputy. When the White House aide calls a GS-15 in the recesses of the Commerce Department, the employee jumps through the roof. He or she drops everything. Often, the White House staff person was not only new but also totally unqualified regarding the matter. But this seemed to be what Nixon wanted. Succeeding presidents have permitted this control effort by the White House staffers to grow and grow.

I thought nostalgically of those days in President Eisenhower's White House with its tight-knit control—you knew who to go to. You weren't allowed to call people, three or four or five levels down; you dealt only with the peer person, that is, the secretary or the under secretary. President Eisenhower allowed the cabinet officers and their principal deputies to manage those major government agencies. President Eisenhower set the standard concerning the operation of the White House.

Eisenhower had a deeply schooled belief in organization. He lived his whole life with military structure, and he established his White

House on that type of hierarchy. You knew your rank in that pecking order, but it lacked any militaristic feeling. The Eisenhower White House was surprisingly informal—constant small group discussions and good humor. We all knew our jobs, which included where to go if you had questions. In my case, a lengthy presidential executive order explicitly spelled it out. Our job descriptions permitted creativity, but they had a circumference. We knew the political forces well, but we also knew that we could ignore them if we felt that the cause was strong enough. No one would come in and undo it. The senior political appointees handled political questions. In my judgment, this was unique in a modern presidential administration. And Eisenhower was the last president to permit this.

With the passage of time, my view has been confirmed by historians. The writer Joe Klein, in the *New Yorker* in October 2000, has summed it up succinctly: "In the modern presidency, the real power resides in the White House staff; all but a few Cabinet members are peripheral." The result of the central control is that none of the civil servants feel they are being trusted. We know clearly through the Nixon tapes that he did not trust them. Shortly after I began as under secretary of commerce, I received a call to attend a top-secret conference in the Bureau of the Budget. The group, a task force of about five people chaired by Assistant Attorney General William H. Rehnquist (later chief justice), was called to develop a top-secret paper that was to radically change the job security of the existing civil service system. From my experience as special assistant to President Eisenhower for personnel management, I had intimate understanding of the civil service infrastructure, thus my involvement in this task force. Frankly, the thrust of what they said at this meeting frightened me. They asked us to leave all our papers on the table. I didn't like the tone and expressed my concerns. They told us that the president personally wanted something to be done. I went to two, maybe three, meetings and continued to express my disapproval of the concept. I definitely did not share Mr. Nixon's views toward the federal civil service. They never asked me to attend further meetings. I am thankful nothing ever came of the project—nor have I ever read anything about it.

This control effort made me very unhappy. You can't run the U.S. government with a few hundred employees in the White House. This macro-versus-micro argument has been a fundamental criticism for years. Presidential policy management has given way to micromanagement—Who can use the tennis courts today? That's what we were saying in our NAPA report: we have a structure here; observe the structure. You should respect the authority of the cabinet officer and the political appointees who have been brought in. The president should delegate, as much as possible. The operational responsibilities should be pushed away from the Executive Office of the President and given to line agencies, where the detailed knowledge exists, but always with full accountability to the president. This inefficiency feeds into the negative attitude of the public toward the government. That 1980 NAPA report is of topical value today.

Thus, in order to control (read "coordinate") these policies, there have developed the present-day White House and Executive Office staffs—the so-called institutional presidency. The one thing that has made the presidency so different from when I worked there is the creation of the internal subparts dealing with the world. The Brownlow Committee, which basically created the institutional presidency in the early 1930s, suggested six administrative assistants and the transfer of the Bureau of the Budget from the Treasury Department to the Executive Office. This happened under FDR. When I was there, Eisenhower had two offices with staffs (not counting the press secretary)—my office (which had four professionals and five secretarial positions) and the national security officer (with a much larger staff). At that time, it was unique to have a staff. Since then, the White House staff has mushroomed. It now has more than 450 employees. The growth has been so haphazard and varied that it is difficult at any given time to keep an exact record of its component elements.

That number doesn't actually represent the full staff. Clinton pledged he would cut the Executive Office staff by 25 percent. He claimed to have done it, but many of the people in the White House are on "detail," meaning they are on "loan" from another government agency. When I was under secretary of commerce, we had several of our people who went over to the White House. One man classified by my office as a special assistant left for the White House, never to return. He was paid by the Commerce Department, but he worked in the White House. Those people usually don't show up in the White House count.

Our intent in the NAPA report did not really concern numbers, whether it was too many or too few; we really wanted to address the function of the presidency. Thus began the initial staff growth, as a basis of function. Eisenhower influenced this to some extent when he created, by executive order in 1953, the Schedule C category of appointment— defined as noncareer and political, even though operational. At the time, it really shook up the establishment. When I came in as assistant secretary of labor, my able secretary, Blanche "Bunny" Lavery, was a Schedule C appointee because she had a "confidential" relationship to a Schedule C person. I could have removed her because of this. It allowed political appointees to bring in their own secretaries. Before long, a court ordered that incumbents in Schedule C positions would, if replaced, be given an equivalent position (not an easy thing to do for a GS-18, an incumbent head of an agency). Of course, I didn't remove her; she was an outstanding career person, with many years of service, serving eventually as secretary to a Supreme Court justice.

President Kennedy felt even more strongly that he wanted to have people of his own political and philosophical persuasion. He wanted them to be uniquely his. He extended the political appointee approach into the Department of State by, for example, going beyond the long-established practice of appointing only a small number of "political" ambassadors vis-à-vis foreign service career ambassadors.

Understandably, all the presidents feel that they have to get closer to the world's problems. So they assign staff to work close to them on those problems. What started out as a special assistant grew into the White House national security adviser's office, which was a combination of the Defense Department and the State Department. The presidents following Eisenhower saw a need to develop White House staff on domestic as well as foreign economic matters and so set up internal staffs to do just that. This bothered Secretary Stans and me in the Commerce Department, because we could see it developing under Nixon. John Ehrlichman became the overall head of domestic policy matters with a huge staff. From our point of view, we were the Commerce Department. We were supposed to do that. We had programs that affected the same domestic and international economic matters.

Basically, this led to a duplication of the work in departments and agencies that possess operating responsibilities. We had no reliable means for integrating the specialized perspectives of these staffs. These special-interest appointments have some short-term political advantage, but it ultimately hampers the president in bringing a government-wide, national perspective to problems. We proposed in our 1980 NAPA report that the institutionalized presidency be reduced to encompass only those functions that are vital to the president in the performance of his government-wide duties, not to mirror various special interests in our society.

The combined experience of our panel knew that *a large staff impedes* rather than enhances a president's ability to function effectively. Our report suggested that "[a]n unrelenting effort should continue to transfer any functions that are not essential to fulfill presidential responsibilities on a government-wide basis." We suggested reorganizing and streamlining the offices. We proposed a design of four senior assistants to the president: three to head the policy-coordinating staffs for domestic, international, and economic affairs, and one to head the secretariat. These assistants, plus the director of the Office of Management and Budget, would be responsible for what we have called the core processes of policy coordination: policy advice, information flow, and management. These policy workhorses would, in essence, operate as the eyes, ears, and hands of the president. These people would not engage in substantive decision making, but would be entirely process oriented and administrative in nature and neutral with regard to particular policies.

One thing is clear about the mélange of units and staffs. Though they exist for a variety of reasons, their principal purpose is their higher status that comes from closer association with the presidency.

The staff's growth was already well under way by the time Eisenhower arrived. For example, in FDR's administration, there were 73 Senate-confirmed presidential appointees. In 1960, Eisenhower's administration had around 200, and he added to its growth. This trend accelerated under Reagan, and it exploded under the senior George Bush. Under Eisenhower, I was one of 8 special assistants to the president, at that time a very high-ranking position. Today, more than 80 have the words *to the president* added to their titles. Looks impressive, I know, on the White House stationery. What once was called a "staff assistant" has moved up in a process known as "title creep."

That growth within the office of the president has also been copied by the various departments, and not always because of growth in function. In the Labor Department we had an under secretary and three assistant secretaries, plus a fourth who was an administrative assistant secretary, a career person. Today, Labor has 10 assistant secretaries, and it has 3 or 4 others with under secretary rank. Years later, in 1969, when I became under secretary of commerce, I was the only one and was the deputy secretary and general manager of the department. Today, the Department of Commerce has a deputy secretary, 5 under secretaries, and 10 assistant secretaries. Most important, the functions basically have changed little since I left in 1971. The Commerce Department may have added programs, but it also lost some (for instance, maritime). The title upgrades clearly are being done in order to make political appointment easier with more prestigious titles. Deputy assistant secretaries become assistant secretaries, and assistant secretaries become under secretaries. This is known as "job creep." This escalated in the Reagan administration, when political appointees multiplied far more rapidly than the expansion of governmental programs. During the period of rapid expansion in governmental responsibilities, from 1933 to 1965, the number of cabinet and subcabinet appointees grew from 73 to 152. Between 1965 and 1989, while federal civilian employment held steady, the number of political appointees nearly quadrupled to 573. It took Kennedy 2.4 months to get all of his new principal appointments approved. It took Clinton 8.5 months.

Today, each new presidential administration is able to fill more than 3,000 federal government jobs. They sweep out everybody in the top four echelons—the secretary, deputy secretary, under secretaries, and the assistant secretaries. Most of the deputy assistant secretaries are also replaced. One of my closest friends and one of the nation's most dedicated public servants (the only individual in American history to lead four cabinet departments along with a number of other senior posts under six presidents), the late Elliot Richardson, in his provocative book *Reflections of a Radical Moderate,* points out that half of those 3,000 jobs are the most interesting, rewarding, and challenging positions available in the federal government. Lately, the political appointees have dipped into the fourth-echelon positions, which were previously reserved for career people. While the title of deputy assistant secretary may not sound too impressive, from that position a person can have a wider impact on the national interest than all but a few senior corporate positions.

This shrinkage of opportunities at the top affects the morale of the senior civil service. They work for twenty or thirty years and aspire to get into those high-level positions, only to see them given away to minimally qualified outsiders as political favors. In earlier smaller administrations, the president was able to get direct advice from the career civil servants, people who knew the operations of government. They are not there for policy decisions or political advice. When senior civil servants are involved in high-level policy discussions, they are glad to put forward their ideas, but they do not see themselves as performing a policy-making role. Nonetheless, as Elliot Richardson writes, "the ballooning of political appointments has magnified the suspicion that career people are not to be trusted to give full and loyal support to their political superiors." They lose out on the opportunity to work the more demanding, rewarding jobs. That alone diminishes the attractiveness of government service.

I remember when we promoted Millard Cass in the Department of Labor from a special assistant to the secretary to deputy under secretary of labor. That was the highest that any career person had ever attained in the Department of Labor. The *Washington Post* ran an editorial complimenting this action, saying this should be the goal of all careerists, to move up into those top positions in the agencies. Without such possibility, we are losing our career civil service.

Completely overlooked in this, the Senior Executive Service (created—finally—in 1978) is composed of the government's top careerists. They are valuable because they have interagency mobility. The Brownlow Committee recommended that the president's office be staffed heavily by career personnel. Since it has gone the other way, the president is deprived of people who are skilled in staff roles, experienced in government management, and suited to lend continuity and consistency. It's easy to see how differently the president might work with Congress. The president should appoint the senior White House assistant, and below this top level there should be a combination of noncareer appointees and civil servants. Career civil servants can and do function effectively in highly sensitive policy roles. The White House chief clerk, William Hopkins, was a legend already when I entered service in the White House in 1957. He was the silent, indispensable man to whom all went for guidance and, yes, advice. Note the inconspicuous nature of his title. Of course, political appointees often have a technical competence that transcends their political-party credentials.

This work is not just a mechanical process. Those who do it must have a passion not simply for anonymity, but also for making the machinery of government work. Rather than handing down presidential decisions that fulfill some personal policy agenda, their mission is to help the president frame and implement his national agenda in conjunction with the many other participants in our complex government system. The senior civil service can do this well.

All of these recommendations with the help of some "government planning" would alleviate much of the crisis management we experience. A president must look beyond the next headline and his own short-term political needs. The Executive Office of the President needs an institutionalized arrangement for longer-term policy research and analysis. The establishment of a long-range planning mechanism would force government officials to consider more carefully the effects of their decisions and their programs. As I heard President Eisenhower put it, "Plans are unimportant; it's the planning that counts" (citing Prussian general Carl von Clausewitz).

We knew the NAPA report's comprehensive treatment was not an easy formula to remedy the problems. More important than any one recommendation was the interrelationship among them all. As the *L.A. Herald Examiner* noted of our effort, "Though in some cases their idealism exaggerates what should be expected of human nature, they offer a foundation on which a strong leader with infinite patience could erect an executive framework within which Presidents might function as true executives."

What we were trying to do was to create a momentum in the right direction, with arrangements that can work equally well under a variety of circumstances and in whatever legal manner a president may choose to perform the duties of his office. Without some sort of reform, we all suffer the consequences. It's just messy public administration.

We finished the report and delivered it to President-elect Ronald Reagan the day after his election in November 1980. We also sent it to key congressional leaders and other government officials. The report became a "best-seller"—requiring a second printing. I was told that President Reagan personally reviewed it. Edwin Meese, his counselor (and later attorney general), spent more than four hours in a careful review with some of my colleagues. Don Price and I received very nice letters of appreciation (each different) from President Reagan (I noticed later that my letter was signed on the day he was shot). In his letter to me, Reagan said "we have attempted to implement some of the suggestions, and have given all of them serious considerations."

Years later, the academy did an update, *Executive Presidency: Federal Management for the 1990's,* which involved some of the same people from the earlier study. The two reports, which could easily be read together, are filled with the savvy kind of judgments made by people who have been in the public service for many years. It is a good historical read for its analysis, but it should be read for what is being proposed in terms of the management in the operation of the office of the president. What we wrote in 1980 is as valid today as it was then.

This interaction between the public and the government, its faltering trust and spiraling morale, has become known as the "quiet crisis" in the government. The result is that many of our best senior executives have left government. At the same time, not enough of our talented young people are interested in joining. This depletion of talent in the public service hinders our government. Elliot Richardson has said it succinctly: "It ultimately damages the democratic process itself." We need to find a way to attract, motivate, train, and retain highly qualified public servants. Our political system is continuously confronted by excessive demands from the public. This is in spite of the political clamor for "less government" or the "problems in Washington." New problems—those only the government can deal with—arise and multiply. We need to integrate leaders at all levels of government. The search for good government starts with good leaders. The question is how do you get good people, and there are a lot of them, into positions of responsibility in the public service? How do we improve the leadership?

We addressed these issues on the National Commission on the Public Service in the years 1988 to 1990. This independent nonpartisan commission was created to acquaint the public as much as possible with the need to rebuild the public service. Known as the Volcker Commission after its chairman Paul A. Volcker, the former leader of the Federal Reserve System, it was made up of a distinguished group of people: Derek Bok, President Gerald Ford, General Andrew J. Goodpaster, Vernon E. Jordan Jr., Yvonne B. Burke, Walter F. Mondale, Edmund Muskie, Father Ted Hesburgh, Donald Kennedy, Donald Rumsfeld, Elliot Richardson, Elmer Staats, John W. Gardner, Donna Shalala, and Anne Armstrong, among others. One of the most prestigious groups with which I have ever served, the thirty-six commissioners included men and women with broad experience in government and private life. We had a broad spectrum of political views, and we differed on many questions of public policy. Collectively, however, we unanimously shared the conviction that rebuilding an effective, principled, and energetic public service must rank high on the nation's agenda.

We held public hearings in Washington, D.C., Los Angeles, New York City, Atlanta, Boston, Ann Arbor, and Austin. We relied on research by government agencies, such as the Government Accounting Office and Office of Personnel Management, as well as by individual scholars and practitioners across the nation. And we benefited from input by other organizations, such as the National Academy for Public Administration, and hundreds of concerned citizens, college students, and public servants who contacted the commission on their own initiative.

Five task forces were created: Pay and Compensation, Education and Training, Public Perceptions of the Public Service, Relations between Political Appointees and Career Executives (a very ticklish one that Elliot Richardson chaired in his elegant style), and Recruitment and Retention. I chaired the last one, though Patricia W. Ingraham, my project director, deserves the principal credit for putting together our section of the report. She was, and is, a Distinguished Professor of Public Administration at Syracuse University, and her book, *The Foundation of Merit—Public Service in American Democracy,* should be standard reading for good government advocates.

In April 1989, we presented our finished report, *Leadership for America: Rebuilding the Public Service,* to President Bush. Paul Volcker, Derek Bok, Elliot Richardson, and I took turns presenting the various aspects of the report to him in the Cabinet Room.

President Bush was very accommodating. Then again, he had already come out in favor of the public service. He had done something unusual immediately after taking office. At a special convocation of senior civil servants in the State Department auditorium he told them how important they were. That was very well received. Bush knew the civil service intimately. He worked with the career group in the CIA and as ambassador to China. He had a much deeper understanding about what the public service is all about, and a much more favorable attitude than his predecessor. I think he held that meeting deliberately to overcome what President Reagan had done. From our point of view, we thought it heralded a new turn. At least it was the right move for an incoming president. In his April 5 letter to me after the meeting, President Bush was specific: "I have benefited greatly over the years from the work of career civil servants. Having the support of high-quality and dedicated professionals is indisputable." More important, he went on to add, "We must attract a new generation of able young people into the ranks of our Federal Government." This is still true—even more so—today.

Our report was, in effect, an outsider's effort to wake up the American society as to what the public service is all about and to try to improve it. We went very much against the grain of the national trend as expressed in the media. Both parties worked to downsize the government and come to grips with the deficit of the federal budget. As we saw it, the need for a strong public service was growing, not lessening. The American government has so many responsibilities—from protecting our basic freedoms to providing a common defense. We *expect* so many things of our government. It's common sense to find a way to improve the public service.

We shaped our report around three themes: leadership, talent, and performance. Like the earlier NAPA report, it was comprehensive and therefore interrelated. We thought of the proposal as a framework in which the president and Congress could pursue basic goals. *For starters, the president and Congress must make exemplary public service a national priority.* They have the power to do so much in creating the environment for effective leadership and public support. Educational institutions can contribute to this effort. On the inside of government, we must do more to simplify and control the complexity of modern government. With respect to the American people, while they demand first-class performance and the highest ethical standards, they must be willing to pay their public servants what is necessary to attract and retain needed talent.

We retouched on themes in the NAPA report, asking the president and Congress to strengthen executive leadership by clearing away obstacles to the ability of the president to attract talented appointees from all parts of society, make more room at senior levels of departments and agencies for career executives, provide a framework within which those federal departments and agencies can exercise greater flexibility in managing programs and personnel, and encourage a stronger partnership between presidential appointees and career executives.

In the task force on recruitment and retention, we found a very different atmosphere. When I finished law school, all veterans, with very little exception, thought public service was a natural progression for law graduates. From there the next step could be private practice or the corporate world. Many went to work in Washington, D.C., which is the reason I went to Georgetown Law School. Public service gave us an understanding of the public policy and processes.

Today, people bypass that first choice. Lucrative offers by law firms and businesses are difficult for the young person to ignore. The economic scene has changed. Simultaneously, public service has fallen into disrepute; it is down at the bottom of the list of student priorities. They may recognize the necessity for it but don't, it seems, want to pursue it. There are at least two reasons for this. First, societal pressures have changed sharply. I was a product of the Depression days—not a participant, but a young and growing observer. At the culmination of the Depression we entered World War II, which united our country for a national common purpose. That effort conditioned millions of young Americans to think of their government as a friend you wanted to support in all the ways you could. Obviously, this attitudinal change affects how and where the country goes.

The second reason is the loss of trust in government. Lack of respect for politics taints the image of the public service. This drives away much of our best talent. Surveys of top graduates show that they did not perceive public service as an occupation in which talented people could get ahead. A whopping 86 percent thought that a federal job would not allow them to use their abilities to the fullest. Interestingly, the respondents attached high importance to making money. We suggested that this could mean that some of their distaste for public service may be a reluctance to accept its financial limitations. That goes back to the public paying for their services. The surveys also showed us that the challenges of public service were not being conveyed to these graduates.

The whole career mission, from my point of view, is very important because the attitude of today's business leader has become very different from the 1950s, '60s, and even '70s. Too many of today's business leaders have false knowledge, or no knowledge, of how the government is operating or is supposed to operate. Both aspects are important. So many easily adopt a cynical or an overly critical attitude toward the government. Business has always focused on the bottom line, but what about *corporate public responsibility?* This term astonishes some business leaders and disgusts others.

Careers have become highly mobile, with retraining a significant part of an executive's career. The need for continuous training has carried over into public service. We need to show young people that public service offers a challenging opportunity, adds excitement to a career, and confers a deep commitment that may not be found in other jobs. Success in public service is not easy to recognize. It is a moving target, and evaluation methods are constantly changing. Helping mankind sounds noble, I know, and is a psychic satisfaction—and it does have its "highs."

In President Eisenhower's second term, Congress passed the Government Employees Training Act of 1958. It started, modestly at first, with the in-house and outside training opportunities that are now found throughout the federal government, including the Federal Executive Institute. And I helped get it started! This is the kind of job satisfaction that is so difficult to describe.

The more a person learns about public service, the more one can see the challenges and offerings. But there's more to public service than an intellectual challenge. What these people do at any given level matters more and has more social impact than what businesspeople at a comparable level do. What businesspeople do is good for the management and the stockholders, and sometimes, if they're lucky, for all the customers as well. A public servant's day-to-day role can affect the well-being, the survival even, of millions of people. In that is a job satisfaction that private enterprise rarely achieves.

What is out of sync here is that people are unaware of just who the public servant really is, and the rewards that come with doing public service. The tarnished image needs revamping. Public service hasn't changed. A career with the government is as valid today as it was ten, twenty, or fifty years ago. One of the differences is that fifty years ago when I got out of the army, there was a buoyancy added to it—we had licked the Nazis and the world was our handbasket. No one could stop us.

Today, we are in the midst of a sea change. Pearl Harbor in 1941 and September 11, 2001, are identical in one respect: an intense national unity was created instantly. Our citizens are seeking ways to satisfy their idealism and belief in our country. For those able and young enough in spirit, public service is a choice. Some may follow the military, but others can find satisfaction in pursuing the some two thousand different careers available in government service.

Our schools—at all levels—are prepared to train and assist our young people. Retraining is more and more becoming the direction of older citizens. This splendid resurgence of national pride changes the pessimistic warnings of some political observers in recent years.

More than patriotism is involved. Our people want to help others. No longer do I hear questions raised about the qualifications of those in our government. For example, we take for granted the competence of those flying in the skies—military or in space—and we look to the Weather Service or the Atlanta Center for Disease Control for guidance.

We should still remember to start with the kids in school—all grades. They need to understand what is happening in our contemporary society. Young people are the least-active group of all. "It is not that they are selfish or only interested in their careers as is often alleged," said Derek Bok. "Actually they volunteer more than their parents did. They simply lost faith in politics and government and don't see them as useful ways to address the problems of society." College students are willing to volunteer their time but until 9/11 appeared not to trust their government. Former treasury secretary Robert Rubin, an outstanding business leader before he became an outstanding public official, summed it up in a wise statement to graduates of the Harvard Business School: "In some fair measure our country's future will depend on enlisting its most gifted and best trained in the great issues of the nation."

Some years ago, in 1979, I had a fortuitous encounter that allowed me one way to address this challenge. Because of possible conflict, I had to resign from a company's board of directors. As I left, Bill Fishman, the chairman of the company, then known as ARA Services, Inc., and called to say that the company would like to make a contribution in my honor to a university of my choice. I accepted the offer, and ARA gave a modest fifteen thousand dollars to the Robert H. Hinckley Institute of Politics at the University of Utah to be used for public policy internships. The internships are designed for one purpose: early exposure for students as to what the government is all about. The majority go to Washington, D.C., for a brief look at a government agency or Capitol Hill. Most interns are where they can observe Congress in action (rule making) or government agencies in the execution of laws. By their letters to me I know they are challenged and excited by what they find. Some write that they have "come alive"; they are realizing how important government is and how much Washington has become the world center. One refrain is constant: they will not forget it—no matter what career they pursue. Some muse that ten or twenty years from now they may decide to try public service in an elective sense. Political appointments take on new meaning or career civil service beckons.

I have financially supported this program since that beginning year. The program has made a difference for dozens of young men and women over the past thirty-four years.

My participation in the University of Utah Hinckley Institute intern program was only the beginning. Marion and I have long sought to help others to study or participate in the ways in which ideas flow freely. Ideas often become reality, for the public good or even otherwise. With this in mind, in 1997, we created at the University of Utah the Rocco C. and Marion S. Siciliano Forum: Considerations on the Status of the American Society. Its purpose is to enhance the thoughtful deliberation of public issues. Public presentations deal with the country's most pressing, least tractable issues.

Harold M. Williams, the president of the J. Paul Getty Trust, was the auspicious inaugural speaker, on the need for change in public education. U.S. Senator Robert F. Bennett, the son of my mentor, the late senator Wallace F. Bennett, gave the stimulating dedicatory address. Subsequent speaker topics have included demographic change and immigration challenges, two of my favorite subjects.

In October 1998, John D. Evans, a cofounder of CSPAN, gave a memorable presentation on the revolution in global communication systems. In November 2002, Karl Rove, senior adviser and assistant to President George W. Bush, participated in a full day of appearances at the forum, which included question-and-answer sessions. In his principal address, and in a spirited and scholarly fashion, he described "the changeless characteristics" of presidential greatness. He easily satisfied my concern that the forum make every effort to avoid hyperbole and political partisanship.

The University of Utah College of Social and Behavioral Science is the home of the Siciliano Forum, and its birth was brought about under the wise leadership of Dr. Donna Gelfand, then dean of the school. The present dean, Dr. J. Steven Ott, has continued with extraordinary effort to make the forum a major part of the intellectual life of the university campus.

It is evident to Marion and me that our children—now longtime adults—have accepted and become a part of the informed citizenry. I am reminded of the quotation of Cicero (which I have made less sexist): "We plant trees to benefit another generation."

To explain further, Loretta, now a tax lawyer, supplemented her Stanford education with summer experience on a Senate committee on Capitol Hill. More important, these same qualities of public service have been evidenced in her life in Los Angeles, where she chaired the social action committee of her synagogue. She also provides pro bono legal services for indigents appearing before the U.S. Tax Court in Los Angeles, as well as for poor people dealing with the Internal Revenue Service. Scott Silverman, her lawyer husband, achieved a notable victory in a pro bono case.

Vincent, now a bank president, has demonstrated leadership in the San Diego community where he has lived for twenty years, including active roles on the boards of the Chamber of Commerce, San Diego Symphony, and International Trade Commission. Before his banking career began, he had used his environmental engineering degrees from Stanford and UC Berkeley working for the California Coastal Commission. Thereafter, his early banking career included more than seven years for Bank of America in Asia, where he learned Mandarin Chinese (in order also to keep up with his wife, Susan Campbell, a Chinese scholar!).

Fred, a licensed acupuncturist and a doctor of Oriental medicine, is active in California state certification of those seeking to enter his field. Earlier, he worked for the National Oceanic and Atmospheric Administration in its tuna and dolphin research program.

John, a money manager, worked extensively on Capitol Hill through high school, college, and business school (Pomona and Stanford) and continues that commitment in Los Angeles. He has led the Los Angeles chapter of the National Conference for Community and Justice, as well as serving for ten years as a member of the board of the California Community Foundation—the second oldest community foundation in the United States. He is on a major local hospital board and a member of the board of visitors of the Peter F. Drucker Graduate School of

Management in Claremont. His wife, Wendy Westlake, takes a leadership role on the school boards of their three sons.

Maria is a Wellesley College and Kennedy School of Government (Harvard) graduate with a sense of passion for people and issues. Having worked at USC's Annenberg School of Communication as well as the School of Public Administration, she is now seeking to become involved with those learning English as a second language. She had several years as an organization management administrator at the University of Washington College of Engineering.

I'm proud that my children have seen government in action and continue to want to be part of the action—but it is not surprising, having grown up in a home with incessant contact with the American political scene. They learned the importance of being a citizen who votes. Interestingly, their political views differ widely—not really what I expected. They have their own independent minds as they approach political issues. Most important, they evaluate. The next generation, our grandkids, will have their chances. Our oldest grandchild, and only granddaughter, Rachel Silverman, is finishing at University of California Medical School (Irvine) and has already spent several months in a birth clinic in the Dominican Republic (while at Brown University). Her brother, Jacob, a junior at Emory, continues his many years of Russian study (including visits) to a point where he has been asked if he is a native speaker. Of our six grandsons, the oldest, Michael Siciliano (a University of Southern California senior), has already had a six-week Washington internship and now writes a political column for the USC daily. His cousin Stuart was high school student-body president, which helped him get a president's scholarship to Southern Methodist University. And so it goes with the others, Alex, Stephen, and David, showing lively interest in public affairs as they finish high school and enter college—no doubt under the influence of their parents! I am very optimistic. They are becoming engaged participants in the mobile society of America today.

Marion has, in her usual quiet but persistent fashion, done much for the public good. A high point has been her chairmanship of TreePeople. The tree-planting organization in Los Angeles was created by Andy Lipkis when he was fifteen years old. One of its initial goals was the planting of one million trees in time for the 1984 Los Angeles Olympics. A creative visionary, Andy and his TreePeople have been honored by all, including U.S. presidents and international groups. In its early years, Marion helped it become the effective and respected organization that it is today.

Education is a constant process; there is no blackout in life. And for those who want to serve mankind and to help their fellow citizens, public service should be considered right alongside other public professions such as doctors or lawyers. Our nation needs good citizens, obviously beginning with the very young, to commit, to maintain, and to adjust to the present and future needs. The challenges will never cease. And participating individuals make the difference.

EPILOGUE

A FEW DAYS BEFORE he died at the age of ninety-two, my father-in-law, Fred Oppen, told me on the phone that he "would have liked" (speaking in the past tense) "a few more years"—"there is so much happening out there." He knew that his life was ending before any of his family did. He died in April 1981. His health appeared good, and he had an indomitable spirit. Born Friedrich Oppenheimer in Germany, he was the wisest man I have ever known. A German veteran of World War I, he served for five years as an artillery officer. An Iron Cross winner, he had been a brilliant law graduate from Berlin University before beginning his law career in Frankfurt. There was little he had not observed or experienced during the greater part of the twentieth century. He reflected on some of those lifestyle changes and events on his ninetieth birthday, much to the warm delight of members of his family. He recalled some events from his long life: the replacement of the horse and buggy with the horseless carriage and the advent of the combat airplane and the army tank in World War I. After the ashes of World War I began to recede came the disastrous German inflation of the 1920s and the ascendancy of Adolph Hitler, who initiated World War II—a true world war, he said. He commented on the incredible and energetic rise of the post–world war economies of the 1950s through the 1970s, including those of the former American enemies. Russia's *Sputnik* was followed by the U.S. walk on the moon. He even spoke of the rise of a new "revolution," that of the computer industries. Some of these latter-day recollections had touched me personally, even though my thoughts of the 1930s Depression were only those of an adolescent, conscious of the abundance of food at home while very aware of the needs of my neighbors. My father-in-law recalled the disaster of Pearl Harbor and saw the end of the Vietnam War, and I have thought of him throughout the tumultuous decades since then. Throughout his life, he gently reminded us, he had remained an optimist. "Be optimistic," he said. This was the only advice he gave to those listening. His strong personal religious faith was never mentioned that evening. He did not have to; we all knew he was living it. I think often of Fred Oppen as I pass my eightieth! Fortunately, as I write this, I am blessed with good health—and the challenges of the future are still there.

On August 30, 2000, President Bill Clinton appointed me as a public member of the newly created Dwight D. Eisenhower Memorial Commission. Our bipartisan mission is simply stated in the statute: "An appropriate permanent memorial to Dwight D. Eisenhower should be created to perpetuate his memory and his contributions to the United States." The Eisenhower Commission owes its establishment to Senators Ted Stevens of Alaska and Daniel Inouye of Hawaii, bosom buddies of different political hues. I was privileged to be elected chairman at their instigation at the first commission meeting in April 2001. I share with the two senators personal recollections of a great man and great president. It is a privilege to honor the man whom I consider the most outstanding public servant of our nation during the twentieth century.

On the eve of my seventy-fifth birthday, I lay awake in bed thinking. I got up and wrote my thoughts down on a cardboard insert of a dress shirt. I have carried the verse with me since then, and occasionally I reread it as the future comes close.

Age has little to do
with it
The mind governs the
pace of life
Curiosity pushes and
pulls
And satisfaction is a
fleeting thing
Mankind is here to
wonder
And God watches.

INDEX

demographics. *See America That Works*
Department of Agriculture, 127
Department of Commerce, 136, 183–95, 296
Department of Defense, 136
Department of Labor, 108–109, 115–19, 120–30, *140*, 285, 295–96
DePumpo, Philip, 97
Dern, George, 15, 178
Deseret News, 35
Dirksen, Everett, 109
Dockson, Robert R., 235
Dodson, James, *140*
Doyle, Frank P., 267
Dubinsky, David, 112
Dulles, Allen W., 134
Durkin, Martin P., 108, 110, 114

Ebony magazine, 158
Economic Development Administration, 187, 189
economic policy, of Nixon administration, 197–209. *See also* taxation
Economic Stabilization Act (1970), 198
education: and California Business Roundtable, 233; constant process of, 308; early life of Marion Stiebel Siciliano, 102; ethnicity and early years in Salt Lake City, 11–12; high school years in Salt Lake City, 39–44; and home environment, 9–10; and immigrant population in California, 234, 263–64, 278; and law school in Washington D. C., 97–100; of mother, 31, 38–39; and Proposition 13 in California, 283
Ehrlichman, John, 187, 192, 294
Eisenhower, Dwight D., 108, 120, 131–38, *140*, *141*, *142*, 153–74, 291–92, 293, 294, 295, 298. *See also* Eisenhower Memorial Commission
Eisenhower, John, 90

Eisenhower, Milton, 173
Eisenhower: The Dangerous Years (Colburn), 154–55
Eisenhower Memorial Commission, 253, 310
employment, during high school years, 38. *See also* corporate executives; labor and labor movement; legal career; public service
Employment and Training Administration, 124
Engar, Keith, 9
Environmental Protection Agency (EPA), 191
ethnicity: and civil rights movement, 158–59; and corporations in postwar period, 114; and diversity of workforce, 272; and Eisenhower administration, 129–30; and law school, 99; and Nixon administration, 192; and social structure of Salt Lake City in 1930s, 7, 10. *See also* Hispanic-Americans; Italian-Americans
Europe: demographics and workforce of, 271–72; military service during postwar period, 89–96. *See also* Austria; Germany; Italy
Evans, John D., 305
Executive Office, staff of, 293–301
Executive Presidency: Federal Management for the 1990's (NAPA), 299

famiglia, la, 21
family: and education, 9–10; father's life and Italian-American immigrant experience, 13–28; immigration and reunification concept, 275; role of mother in, 31–32, 277
Farmer, James, 185
Federal Pay Board, 197–209
Federal Personnel Manual (Civil Service Commission), 137

Federal Security Act, 115
Feingold, Russell, 239
Fey, John T., 244
finances, and role of mother in family, 32–33
Fishman, Bill, 304
Fitzsimmons, Frank, 205
Flanigan, Peter, 150, 191–92
Fleischmann, Ernest, 227–28, 255
Flemming, Arthur S., 169–70, 173
Fogarty, John E., 124
folklore, and southern Italy in 1945, 94
Folsom, Marion, 266
Foner, Eric, 280, 287
Ford, Gerald, 299
Fort Benning, Georgia, and military training, 69–73
Fort Sill, Oklahoma, and military training, 69
Forty Years a Guinea Pig (Morrow, 1980), 159, 168, 172–73
Fosler, Scott, 267–68
Foundation of Merit—Public Service in American Democracy, The (Ingraham), 300
Fox, Don, 55, 64, 72, 75, 84, 86–88
fraternities, and University of Utah, 59–60, 62, 67
French, Howard W., 272
friendships, and boyhood in Utah, 36–37
Frost, Robert, 153, 176

Galbraith, James R., 226–27
Garda, Lake (Italy), 83
Gardner, John W., 299
Gehry, Frank, 249
Gelfand, Donna, 305
Geneen, Howard, 220, 221
Georgetown Law Journal, 98
Georgetown University Law School, 97–100
George Washington University, 98

Gerken, Walter B., 230, 235, 237
Germany: awarding of Cross of the Order of Merit to Marion Stiebel Siciliano, 256; Stiebel family's escape from prior to World War II, 101. *See also* World War II
Getty, J. Paul, 241, 242
Giannini, A. P., 29, 277
Gibson, Andrew, 189–90
Giulini, Carlo Maria, 228, 252
Gladieux, Bernard L., 146
Goldwater, Barry, 109
Goodpaster, Andrew J., 299
Goodwin, Robert C., 115
Gothic Line (Italy), 75
government, search for good, 279–308. *See also* Congress; Department of Commerce; Department of Labor; Eisenhower, Dwight D.; Nixon, Richard; politics; Senate
Government Accounting Office, 300
Government Employees Training Act of 1958, 303
Government Standard, 138
Grady, Stafford, 229
Granger, Lester, 142, 161, 163, 164
Granieri, Sam, 3, 4
Great Britain, and art acquisitions of Getty Center, 246
Great Depression, 3, 5, 9, 33, 309–10
Greater Los Angeles Chamber of Commerce, 225–26
Green, William, 112
Green River (Utah), 196–97
Greenstein, Fred L., 132
Griffith, Calvin, 142
Gulick, Luther, 288

Hagerty, Jim, 160–61
Haight-Ashbury (San Francisco), 181
Haldeman, H. R. "Bob," 181, 187, 192, 193–94, 209

Man without a Country, The (Hale), 4–5
March on Washington (1963), 166
Marcus, Louis, 178
Maritime Administration, 189–90
Maritime Advisory Board, 190
marriage: of author, 102–104, 118; of
    parents, 31
Mashburn, Lloyd, 110
Mastroianni, Rosaria (great aunt), 30
Maxwell, David O., 226
McCain, John, 239
McCarthy, Joe, 154
McCarthy, Kevin, 263–64, 275–76
McDermott, Albert, 125
McDougall, D. C., 27–28
McGovern, George, 208
McGuire, Dick, 177, 290
McMahon, William C., 85–86, 91, 92, 95
Meany, George, 112, 122, 181, 202,
    204–205
Meehan, Martin, 239
Meese, Edwin, 298
Mehta, Zubin, 228
Meier, Cornell C., 229, 234
Meier, Richard, 247–49, 252
Merriam, Charles, 288
Merton, Thomas, 118
Mexico: and Bracero Program, 115–16,
    125–28, 262, 273–74; and demo-
    graphic trends in workforce, 272, 273;
    and immigration to California, 263.
    See also Hispanic-Americans
Mezzogiorno region, of Italy, 20–22, 30
military: and African-Americans, 99;
    and desegregation, 156; and manage-
    ment style of Eisenhower adminis-
    tration, 291–92; service in Italy and
    Europe during World War II, 74–88;
    service in postwar period, 89–96;
    training during World War II, 63–73.
    See also Army Reserve; Reserve
    Officers' Training Corps

Milliken, Eugene D., 115
mining industry, 34–35, 199–200
Minority Enterprise Small Business
    Investment Corporations (MES-
    BICS), 189
Mitchell, Barbara, 209
Mitchell, James P., 116, 120–22, 124–25,
    129, 136–37, *140*
Mitchell, John, 194, 209
Monaghan, Bob, 235
Mondale, Walter F., 299
Money magazine, 282–83
Montana, 23–24
Montgomery, Alabama, and civil rights
    movement, 155, 157
Moore, Richard, 192
morale: and military, 66; and Nixon
    administration, 193–94
Morgan Stanley, 242
Mormons. *See* Church of Jesus Christ
    of Latter-day Saints
Morrow, E. Frederic, *142, 147,* 158–62,
    165–66, 168, 170, 172–73
Morrow, Winston, 220
mortgage insurance, 215, 221
Moss, Ted, 183
Munitz, Barry, 249
Munoz Marin, Luis, 153
Murdock, Abe, 103, 107
Murray, Philip, 112
Museum of Contemporary Art (Los
    Angeles), 249
Museum für Kunsthandwerk, 247
Muskie, Edmund, 299

National Academy of Public
    Administration (NAPA), 286–89, 300
National Advisory Council, of
    University of Utah, 178
National Business Roundtable, 231
National Commission on the Public
    Service, 299–302

National Council of Negro Women, 161
National Industrial Pollution Control
    Council, 187
National Labor Relations Board
    (NLRB), 107, 112, 177, 194
National Oceanic and Atmospheric
    Administration (NOAA), 188
National Origins Act of 1924, 35
National Press Club, 165
nativism, 24–25, 26, 35, 47
Neue Staatsgallerie (Stuttgart), 247
New Economic Plan, 197, 199
*New Gold Rush: Financing California's
    Legislative Campaigns, The* (1985),
    230
Newhouse, Samuel, 6
Newsweek magazine, 202
New York City, and Little Italy, 23
New Yorker magazine, 292
New York Stock Exchange, 216, 236, 242
New York Times, 134, 168, 203–204, 207,
    272, 288
Nixon, Richard, 134, *149*, *150*, 181, 182,
    183–95, 197–209, 214, 291, 292
Northern Pacific Railroad, 23–24
Northrop Corporation, 245

Occupational Safety and Health
    Administration (OSHA), 191
Office of Foreign Direct Investments,
    and U.S. Travel Service, 187
Office of Independent Counsel, 207
Office of Management and Budget, 182
Office of Manpower Administration,
    96–97
Office of Minority Business Enterprise
    (OMBE), 188
Office of Personnel Management
    (OPM), 173–74, 300
Officer Candidate School (OCS), 69–73
Office of Special Projects, 158
O'Melveny, Henry, 214

O'Melveny and Myers (law firm), 214
Operation Wetback, 126
Oppen, Fred (Friedrich Oppenheimer),
    58, 100, 309–10
orchestra. *See* Los Angeles
    Philharmonic Association
Ortona, Egidio, *152*
Ott, J. Steven, 306

Pacific Enterprises, 222
Pacific Maritime Association (PMA),
    179, 180, 189, 204
Packard, David, 231, 240
Parks, Rosa, 155
*Parting the Waters: American in the
    King Years, 1954 to 1963* (Branch,
    1988), 167–70
Paso Robles, California, 64, *65*–66
Pastore, John, 116–17, 183
patriotism, 4–5, 304
Pay Board, 191
Peck, Gregory, *259*
Peeler, Stuart, 243
Penn Mutual Life Insurance, 223
personality: of Eisenhower, 133; of
    Nixon, 191–92
Persons, Wilton, *140*, *172*
Peterson, Joe, 28
photograph collection, of California
    Historical Society, 217–18
Pi Kappa Alpha fraternity, 59–60
Plessy v. Ferguson (1896), 155
Pocatello, Idaho, 24–28
Pogue, Dick, 223
Political Reform Act of 1996
    (California), 238
politics: and Bracero program, 115–16,
    125–28, 262, 273–74; and campaign
    finance reform, 229–30, 234–35,
    236–39; and civil rights, 158–59; and
    college years at University of Utah,
    60; and Eisenhower administration,

255; as Jewish refugee from Germany, 101, 227; and McCarthyism, 154; and Martha Mitchell, 209; meeting and courtship, 100–104; and move back to Washington D. C. in 1969, 184; and move to Los Angeles, 216; and public service, 259, 307–308; and river running, 152, 196; and Skirball Cultural Center, 249; and undocumented immigrants, 274

Siciliano, Mary Arnone (mother), 16, 29–39, 45–46, 47, 49, 50, 56, 96, 103

Siciliano, Michael (grandson), 260, 307

Siciliano, Rocco C., 48–56, 139–42, 144–52, 251–58, 259: college years at University of Utah, 59–63; early childhood in San Francisco and Salt Lake City, 3–12; father's life and Italian-American experience, 13–28, 45; and legal studies at Georgetown University Law School, 97–100; military service in Europe during World War II, 74–88; military training during World War II, 63–73; mother's life and Italian-American experience, 29–39, 45–46. See also community service; corporate executive; legal career; public service

Siciliano, Salvatore (grandfather), 24

Siciliano, Sam (brother), 3, 15, 31, 40, 41, 48, 49, 51, 56, 96

Siciliano, Stephen (grandson), 260, 307

Siciliano, Stuart (grandson), 260

Siciliano, Susan Campbell (daughter-in-law), 184, 258, 306

Siciliano, Vincent (son), 118, 141, 144, 151, 184–85, 258, 306

Siciliano, Wendy (daughter-in-law), 258

Sigma Chi fraternity, 60, 62

Silverman, Jacob (grandson), 260

Silverman, Rachel (granddaughter), 260, 307

Silverman, Scott (son-in-law), 258, 306

Skidmore, Mary, 60

Skirball Cultural Center (Los Angeles), 249–50, 254

Slight, F. Ray, 55, 72

Smith, Alexander, 109

Smith, C. R., 149

Smith, H. Russell, 226

Smith, Joseph, 6

Snook, John, 27–28

Snow, Kathryn, 9

society, of southern Italy in late 19th century, 20–21. See also class; culture

South, American: racism and ethnicity in, 114; segregation and violence against African-Americans in, 155

Southern California Gas Company, 222

Southern Pacific Corporation, 219, 220

Soviet Union, and space program, 134. See also cold war; Russia

Spanish civil war, 40–41

special assistant to president, and Eisenhower administration, 131–38, 153–74

Special Commendation Award (Secretary of the Army), 182

Sputnik, 134, 309

Staats, Elmer, 287, 299

Standing Fast (Wilkins), 168–69

Stanford University, 44–45, 185

Stans, Maurice, 137, 149, 173, 181, 182–83, 186–87, 187–88, 189, 190, 191, 192–93, 208, 294

Steadman, Robert, 266

steel industry, 198

Stein, Herb, 203, 205, 208

Stein, Sydney, Jr., 287–88

stereotypes, of Italian-Americans, 35

Stern, Robert, 229, 234

Stevens, Ted, 253, 310

Stiebel, Herbert, 101

Stiebel, Marion. See Siciliano, Marion Stiebel